Y0-BYA-108

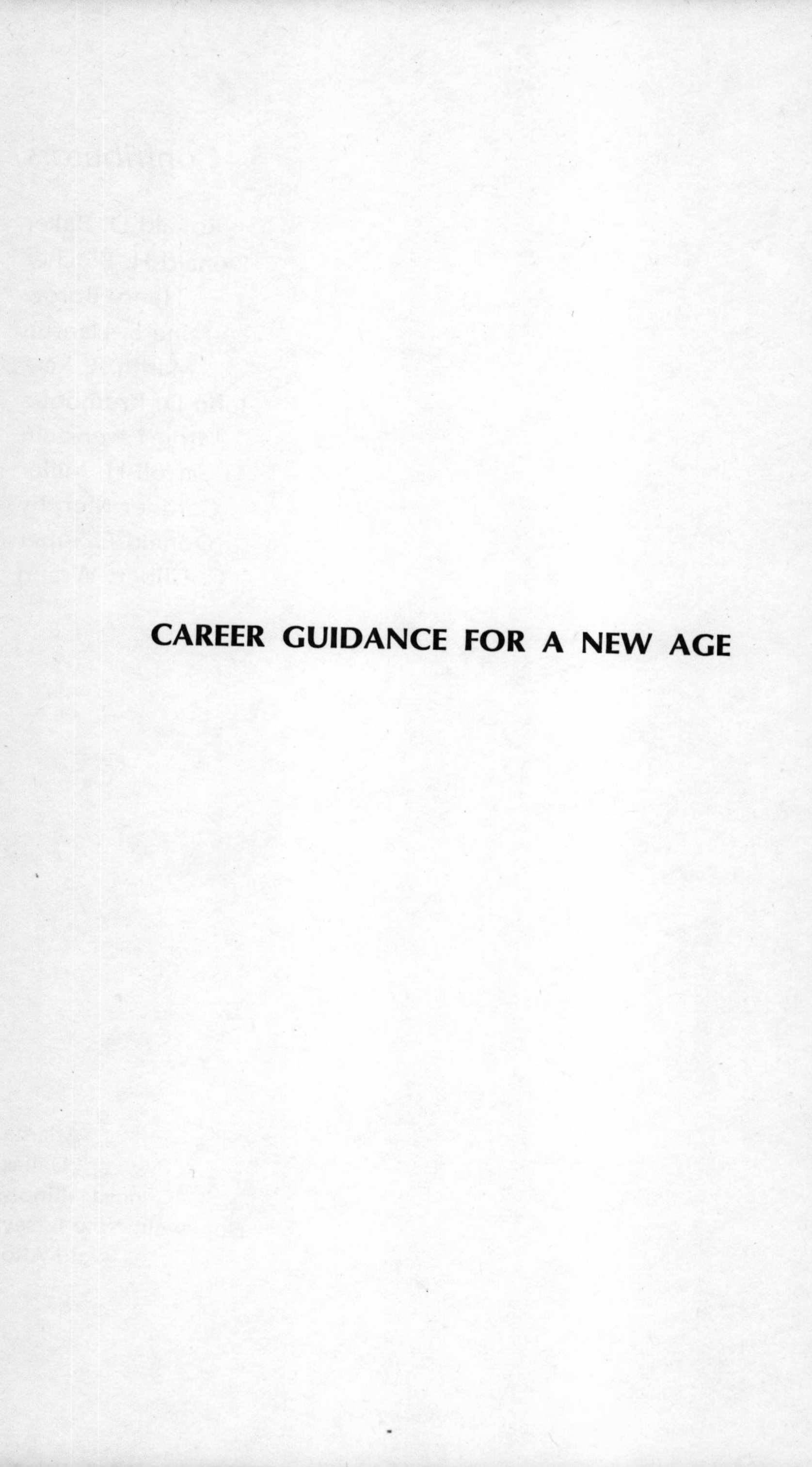

CAREER GUIDANCE FOR A NEW AGE

Contributors

Ronald D. Baker
Donald H. Blocher
Henry Borow
Lorraine S. Hansen
Martin R. Katz
John D. Krumboltz
Aaron Levenstein
Carroll H. Miller
Gardner Murphy
Donald E. Super
C. Gilbert Wrenn

Atlanta
Dallas
Geneva, Illinois
Hopewell, New Jersey
Palo Alto

Edited by
Henry Borow
University of Minnesota

Career Guidance for a New Age

Houghton Mifflin Company Boston

Sources of figures:

Hardwick, A. L. Career education—a model for implementation. *Business Education Forum,* May 1971, 3–5.

Senesh, L. Fulfillment of human aspirations: The strength of a social system. Paper presented at Workshop on Career Development and the Elementary Curriculum, University of Minnesota, Minneapolis, June 30, 1971.

Hale, J. A. *Review and Synthesis of Research on Management Systems for Vocational and Technical Education.* Columbus, Ohio: Center for Vocational and Technical Education, The Ohio State University, 1971.

Cooley, W. W. and Lohnes, P. R. *Predicting development of young adults.* Palo Alto: Project TALENT Office, American Institutes of Research and University of Pittsburgh, 1968.

Printed in the U.S.A.

Library of Congress Catalog Card Number: 72–7924

ISBN: 0–395–14362–4

contents

foreword

Career Guidance for a New Age is another effort by the National Vocational Guidance Association to continue its leadership role among counselors and personnel workers who are contributing to the vocational maturity of active and potential workers. It represents a contemporary companion piece to NVGA's 1964 commemorative volume, *Man in a World at Work,* by exploring the dramatic relationship which exists today between individual career needs and the demands of the economic, social, and political environments. The pace of change in these environmental realms has accelerated rapidly over the last decade. By contrast, the individual's needs for satisfaction remain relatively constant, a circumstance which compounds the individual's problems of vocational adjustment and adaptation to his work and his work environment. Physical and psychological barriers further limit individual choices and widen the differences between worker qualifications and motives and job requirements.

Demands on the counselor expand in proportion to the increasing complexity of the adjustment process for the individual. The many specific and often conflicting demands on the counselor endanger his basic holistic professional role. The range of counselor problems, from furnishing information about job-related topics to dealing with relevant counselee attitudes and feelings about both job and nonjob issues, presents a challenge to the best practitioner. It is not enough that the individual is helped to adjust to the requirements of the labor force. The counselor's role is rather to facilitate the growth and development of the person consistent with the multiple criteria of individual maturity. The mature individual makes better decisions, is more keenly aware of alternatives and of the consequences of his decisions; and he makes a better employee than the immature individual.

A review of significant periods in the vocational guidance movement during the six decades of NVGA's history (1913–1973) reveals a consistent concern for the welfare of the individual worker. The professionalization of vocational guidance was contemporaneous with social welfare legislation and the rise of the organized labor movement. Frank Parsons had written *Choosing a Vocation* in 1908. NVGA and the Department of Labor were both founded in 1913. The Association has been most active and influential during critical periods of social and economic stress: the depression years of the thirties; again, immediately after World War II when fears of massive unemployment and another depression prevailed; during the 1950s with the reordering of educational and employment priorities engendered by international space competition; and, more recently, as a joint consequence of rapid population growth and dramatic technological advances which have brought about an increase in job-ready workers without a commensurate growth of job opportunities.

The multifaceted process of vocational development requires the contributions of many professional disciplines. NVGA's diverse membership, which distributes itself over several disciplines and many work settings, permits it to assume a unique integrating role. *Man in a World at Work* and *Career Guidance for a New Age* evolved from extensive inquiries into the Association's functional and professional identity. Nourishing that developing identity have been the dedicated efforts of NVGA's national officers and Board of Directors, of its State Divisions, and of the researchers, counselor educators, and counseling and personnel practitioners who form its ranks. All these, and now the notable contributions of the distinguished authors of *Career Guidance for a New Age,* give the Association new directions and deepen the commitment to those we serve.

HAROLD J. REED
United States Department of Labor

preface

It was not so long ago—one recalls it was in the mid-1950s—that we were disquietly contemplating the advent of a new world of automation with little or no work to occupy man. Major national concern dwelt far less upon ecology, pollution, and the ravaging of natural resources, far more upon the social consequences of an onrushing technology which had, it was claimed, led us to the threshold of an "age of affluence." Somehow, we seemed less disturbed then by the plight of the economically disadvantaged who were victimized by maldistribution of goods and services than by well-publicized warnings that our new capacity to generate consumer goods faster than they could possibly be consumed would surely lead to wholesale unemployment and force us to shape a national policy on mass leisure. The time was soon upon us, we were told, when the nation's work would be managed by a small, highly trained, mainly elite occupational corps and when most Americans would be paid *not* to work. The Twentieth Century Fund's study of *America's Needs and Resources* traced the decline in the length of the average work week since the middle of the nineteenth century and projected an estimated work week for the year 2000 of 15 hours!

Man's fascination with prophecy is not always matched by his talent for accuracy. Work is not becoming obsolete and, as a personal value for most Americans, it is not going out of style. That the nature, extent, and centrality of work as human experience may have changed, sometimes in keeping with shrewd predictions, seems incontestible, however. Thus, although the effects of change fall differentially upon various segments of the labor force, weekly work-hour totals have, as anticipated, declined since World War II. For increasing numbers of workers, the vision of a 4-day work week is becoming a reality. Young people today typically spend more years in formal schooling, enter the full-time work force at a later age than did their parents, and face the strong prospect of earlier retirement. Traditional meanings of work are under attack, particularly in the counter culture. To labor as a matter of duty or civic obligation, or as a means toward self-fulfillment, is openly challenged by those who see work as a depersonalizing condition of an economic system they reject. They seek escape from careerism, delay in assuming the occupational role, or the creation of alternative work objectives linked to altruism and the desire to effect societal change.

Yet, real and significant as are these trends, they hardly provide us with a balanced perspective of work as a contemporary social institution. However fanciful and inventive one's image of the future may be, it is difficult to envisage a world in which man's occupational status is trivial and peripheral. Substantial numbers of workers involved in the production of material goods have been replaced by others who render a variety of services, but society's broad-scale need for work remains. Although vocational motives are obviously less deeply rooted in biological survival or physical security needs or in a sense of religious duty, occupation nonetheless continues to supply a rich assortment of life meanings and life styles. One must agree with the observation that, in the remote possibility that a futuristic economy permitted work to go out of existence, psychological man would be compelled to re-invent it. That the national posture has been one of commitment to the importance of vocation is witnessed in many ways—in federal manpower legislation, in job training and employment projects for economically bypassed populations, in the growth of counselor preparation programs, in enactments in support of improved occupational education like the Vocational Education Act of 1963 and the Vocational Amendments of 1968, in the rapid rise of the occupationally oriented community colleges and the post-secondary vocational-technical schools, and, most recently, in the career education thrust initiated by the United States Office of Education.

The National Vocational Guidance Association, as a close

observer of the trends noted here, has constantly sought to reinterpret the meaning of work adjustment in contemporary terms and to reassess its own mission accordingly in serving the cause of career guidance. An official definition of vocational guidance was first adopted by the Association in 1920 and revamped several times thereafter. It is in NVGA's most recent concerted efforts at redefinition, launched in the mid-1960s, that the origins of *Career Guidance for a New Age* are to be found. At the urging of past president Harold J. Reed, the Association established Project Reconceptualization and entrusted it to a task force headed by Dr. Reed. A working paper by Mary Wannamaker tracing the history of the concept of guidance and a series of position papers on changing concepts of work and career guidance were commissioned. Over a period of approximately three years, Project Reconceptualization and the resultant first-draft papers provided the framework for interchange between NVGA and its state and local affiliates and served as the theme of open sessions at the annual conventions of the American Personnel and Guidance Association.

NVGA's intentions and expectations for *Career Guidance for a New Age* closely parallel those established for the Association's golden anniversary volume, *Man in a World at Work,* published by Houghton Mifflin nearly a decade ago. That earlier book, which has been widely used in counselor education courses, offered a comprehensive state-of-the-art account of career guidance and proposed an enlarged mission for both prospective and practicing counselors. Like its predecessor, *Career Guidance for a New Age* has been planned with a view to its contribution to the formal training of counseling and guidance personnel and, in particular, to the strengthening of the career development and career education components of counselor education programs.

The chapters by Carroll Miller, Donald Blocher, and Martin Katz are extensively revised versions of Project Reconceptualization papers. Those by Gardner Murphy and Aaron Levenstein, which I believe to be minor classics on the potentialities and historical interpretations of human work, are revisions of papers presented at the NVGA Airlie House Invitational Conference on Implementing Career Development Theory and Research Through the Curriculum. I am much indebted to Kenneth Ashcraft, conference administrator, and Wesley Tennyson, conference director, for making these papers available for publication here, and to Dr. Tennyson in particular for his meticulous hand in guiding these papers through the post-conference editing stages. The remaining chapters in *Career Guidance for a New Age* were expressly invited in recognition of recent significant developments in the field and to provide a balanced and comprehensive view of the current status of vocational guidance.

The editor acknowledges with deep gratitude the wise and experienced counsel of C. Gilbert Wrenn and the valued contribution of Herbert Burks of Michigan State University in the style editing and checking of factual details for several of the chapters. Finally, genuine thanks are due the officers and trustees of NVGA for extending to the editor strong and generous support throughout the duration of this publication project.

HENRY BOROW

CAREER GUIDANCE FOR A NEW AGE

1

historical and recent perspectives on work and vocational guidance

CARROLL H. MILLER
Emeritus, Northern Illinois University

For the counselor to know his heritage, to appreciate the shifting social and economic tides which produced prototypic vocational guidance around the turn of the twentieth century, is to understand better the conditions which challenge him now as he attempts to assist his clients in the search for a comfortable and realistic career identity. Most of the issues and dilemmas which vocational guidance confronts today had precursors in the formative years of the guidance profession. Historians of the movement, such as John Brewer, E. G. Williamson, and Richard Stephens, have furnished revealing insights into the national forces which produced vocational counseling and allowed it to flourish. In Chapter 1, Carroll Miller draws upon the scholarship of these authorities and others, extends and reinterprets significant historical vectors in the light of recent developments, and identifies both the long-persisting and the newly emerging conditions of man, the worker, which constitute the unfinished business of career guidance.

The pioneering work of Frank Parsons, Miller reminds us, did more than provide a systematic rationale for assisting people with problems of vocational choice, the so-called method of "true reasoning." Parsons was an ardently progressive social reformer whose philosophy of Mutualism flatly repudiated the notion that man's occupational destiny ought to be rooted in the precepts of social Darwinism. He believed in the improvability of man through supportive intervention, and he saw guidance as a major instrument by which that might be accomplished. But Parsons' primal version of vocational counseling, or at least the interpretation placed upon it by his followers, was lacking in several respects. It overplayed the importance of self-analysis as a means to helping the individual know his vocational potentialities, oversimplified the dissemination of occupational information as a way of shaping vocational decisions, subordinated the influence of personal values in choice making, and lent at least tacit support to the single-job-for-life hypothesis. And yet, remarkably, there were in the pronouncements of Parsons and other early leaders prophetic images of a career guidance that closely match some of the dimensions of our present-day conceptions.

Midstream developments in the history of vocational guidance included attention to personality dynamics in occupational choice and adjustment, emphasis upon developmental aspects of vocational behavior, and reexamination of work meanings in a society in which some of the traditional values associated with work were being significantly eroded. Miller relates these emerging trends to far-reaching economic and industrial changes in the American scene which have both broadened the spectrum of occupational opportunities and altered the nature of typical work careers. He specifies three coordinates of worker mobility—geographic, job, and status—and raises important implications for career guidance practice. Miller also raises some hard questions. Acknowledging that large numbers of Americans trapped in low-status occupations cannot realistically hope for fulfillment of the American dream through upward job mobility, what view of career guidance must we now adopt?

H. B.

Seldom if ever can any complex development in modern society be traced to a single source or chain of events. Certainly this is true of vocational guidance. Reed (1944) observed that apparently spontaneous happenings in the beginning of the movement were really symbols of change taking place in the established cultural pattern. A recent study by Stephens (1970) furnishes an account rich in detail of the early backgrounds and developments. Stephens writes,

> The thesis to be supported is that the guidance movement in American education was but one manifestation of the broader

> movement of progressive reform which occurred in this country in the late nineteenth and early twentieth centuries. Further, the central values of social and economic efficiency that characterized the broader reform movement were manifested in the schools in the form of vocational education and guidance, conceived of as a unitary reform with complementary functions [p. 5].

And in a statement given as one part of a summary interpretation Stephens says,

> The Progressive era was characterized by the desire of the middle class to reform the adverse social conditions that grew out of the industrial movement. These conditions were the unanticipated effects of industrial growth. They included: the emergence of cities with slums and immigrant-filled ghettos, the decline of puritan morality, the eclipse of the individual by organizations, corrupt political bossism, and the demise of the apprenticeship method of learning a vocation [pp. 148–149].

Stephens objects to the too easy acceptance of the interpretation made by Brewer (1942) that "vocational education did not furnish the impetus necessary for the birth of vocational guidance [p. 71]." Perhaps, Stephens suggests, two discrepant positions have emerged on the historic relation of vocational education and vocational guidance because of differing definitions used by Brewer and later writers such as Krug (1964) and Rudy (1965). Brewer defined vocational guidance in very broad terms, while Rudy and Krug seem to refer more narrowly to occupational training and placement. It is true (Stephens, 1970) that during the early years vocational education and guidance were "conceived as a unitary reform with complementary functions [p. 5]." However, through the years definitions have changed considerably, resulting in one of the persistent problems of interpretation. Vocational guidance has roots that go back to before the turn of the century, but the movement failed to achieve wide influence until well after the years upon which the Stephens study is focused. The development of vocational guidance with an emphasis upon counseling is found in accounts such as that by Williamson (1965).

The Early Years

As suggested by Reed (1944), the practice of vocational guidance began in a number of scattered localities. Beginnings were not limited to any one locality nor to any one person—not even to the man who is generally credited with initiating systematic guidance practice in the United States, Frank Parsons. Nevertheless, one of the earliest statements, and probably the most influential, about the nature of the enterprise was made by Parsons (1909) in his classic book, *Choosing a Vocation.* Parsons was an active participant in the reform movement of the time, but his views may well have reflected some of his own experiences and varied activities. He was graduated from Cornell as an engineer, but before he actually began employment the railroad which had employed him failed in the panic of 1873. At one time or another he was a laborer, a high school teacher, a lawyer, and a college professor. He even ran for mayor of Boston and lost by less than 1 percent of the votes. He was the author of thirteen books, six of which dealt with social and economic reform. Gradually he evolved a philosophy he called Mutualism (Mann, 1950), which offered a plan for a commonwealth in which he strongly opposed social Darwinism (the idea that the social as well as the organic world was subject to inexorable laws of the struggle for existence and the survival of the fittest). The spirit of his devotion to social and economic reform is well described by Davis (1958).

> The driving spirit behind his philosophy was his belief in the infinite goodness of man, coupled with his capacity to win the war of good over evil, of law over anarchy, of cooperation over competition, of reason over blind domination, and of the individual over forces which compelled him to become more beast like and a brother to the ox [p. 118].

But Parsons brought to vocational guidance more than a zeal for reform. In his *Choosing a Vocation* (1909), published a year after his death, he outlined his conception of vocational guidance in the following way:

> In a wise choice there are three broad factors: (1) a clear understanding of yourself, your aptitudes, abilities, interests, ambitions, resources, limitations, and their causes; (2) a knowledge of the requirements and conditions of success, advantages and the disadvantages, compensation, opportunities, and prospects in different lines of work; (3) true reasoning on the relations of these two groups of facts [p. 5].

At the risk of oversimplifying Parsons' ideas, his three aspects of vocational guidance might be loosely translated into somewhat more modern terminology as appraisal of the individual, furnishing of occupational information, and provision of counseling.

It seems that Parsons stood astride two somewhat divergent streams of development or at least two differing emphases. One stream of development expanded upon his first principle through an elaboration of psychological techniques for the appraisal of the individual, often leaning heavily upon psychometric methods by which abilities, interests, and various other characteristics of the individual were judged. Williamson (1965, p. 78) notes that Parsons recognized the need for such techniques; but the psychology of his day had relatively little to offer. In the absence of objective methods for assessment of the individual, Parsons appeared to rely heavily on the model of the case study, perhaps adapted from the social work of the day with which he was familiar.

The second stream of development resulted from the confluence of Parsons' second and third principles, the giving of occupational information and counseling or "true reasoning." But the emphasis was strongly upon the dissemination of occupational information, and counseling became a rather directive, advice-giving undertaking. There was little room in this pattern of thinking for such ideas as meeting needs or values of the individual, or helping the individual achieve self-realization through occupation by discovering an occupation congruent with his self-concept. There seemed to be an implicit faith that, given accurate and ample occupational information, the individual could somehow utilize the results of his personal analysis and with a little advice and assistance reach a proper choice of vocation.

These two early lines of varying emphases were more nearly parallel than sequential. There was no abrupt transition. Before *Choosing a Vocation* was published, industrial psychology was under way with the work of Munsterberg in identifying through tests the abilities of men for various jobs. Again an observation by Williamson (1965) is pertinent. "One may observe that Munsterberg and later industrial psychologists understood Parsons' reasoning and strategy better than did vocational educators and some psychologists who were content with job observations and second-hand descriptions as well as with self-analysis [p. 98]." The psychometric influence continued strong outside of schools for a number of years. In the advising of military veterans following World War II, for example, Bingham's (1937) *Aptitudes and Aptitude Testing* was commonly found in the offices of vocational counselors. The companion to psychometric study of the individual was a functional analysis of jobs, reflected in the earlier work of such influential men as Frederick Winslow Taylor, Walter Dill Scott, and Morris Viteles, as described by Williamson (1965). In the schools, psychometric interest was much more frequently centered upon the measurement of intelligence and scholastic achievement than upon the aptitudes needed for jobs.

Along with these early developments in industrial psychology, there appeared in the schools what might be considered a manifestation of the second stream of development, with heavy emphasis on occupational information and little concern with psychological study of the individual. Often attempts were made to incorporate such information into the curriculum. Courses in occupations appeared frequently. Yet counseling was not rejected. Davis (1915) noted that "Each institution needs a counselor who can guide the student wisely and sympathetically amidst the confusion of special courses and the influences of the specialists [p. 421]." Three years later, a Committee on Vocational Guidance of the Commission on the Reorganization of Secondary Education of the National Education Association (NEA, 1918), with Frank Mitchell Leavitt as chairman, proposed what was to become essentially the definition of vocational guidance of the NVGA: "Vocational guidance should be a continuous process designed to help the individual choose, to plan his preparation for, to enter upon, and to make progress in an occupation [p. 9]." The Committee report went on to label as false the "idea that in some mysterious way we can look into the future, determine what each child should be, and prepare him specifically for that ultimate end [p. 10]." Rather, the Committee proposed that:

> Vocational guidance, properly conceived, organizes school work so that the pupil may be helped to discover his own capacities, aptitudes, and interests, may learn about the character and conditions of occupational life, and may himself arrive at an intelligent vocational decision [p. 9].

Almost from the first, then, the germ of a concept of developmental guidance was present. It was not yet developmental counseling, since the approach was through the curriculum. However, the role of the counselor was recognized, in the Committee's statement of its ideal of that functionary, as "something of a psychologist, but he will also be a sociologist, an economist, and most of all an educator in the best modern sense of the word [p. 27]." Translated into modern parlance, this description of the ideal counselor might be taken as an indication of the interdisciplinary basis for counselor preparation.

The Committee went on to propose a "reasonable and comprehensive vocational guidance program [p. 10]." The program included a survey of the world's work, studying and testing of the pupil's possibilities, and guidance in choice and rechoice. This statement must not be taken as indicating a firm commitment to psychological appraisal in those early years, but at least testing was not ruled out. The Committee also struck an early note of social intervention, advocating as part of the plan "Progressive modification of economic conditions." Or perhaps this was just an echo of the reform ideas of Parsons.

In general, it is probably fair to say that in the years from Parsons to about the time of World War II guidance in the schools emphasized giving information about occupations and integrating such information into the curriculum. Brewer (1932) thought that the best approach was through the curriculum by affording children "the opportunity to learn living in the laboratory of life [p. 3]." A few years later Jones and Hand (1938) advocated that, ideally, "Guidance and instruction would be functioning as inseparable parts of a unitary educative process [p. 26]." Psychological analysis of the individual, except for limited use of testing, was seldom an important part of guidance programs in secondary schools. Counseling was discussed, but often regarded as a responsibility of the teacher and typically conceived in the spirit of advice giving. This was the day of the teacher counselor.

Vocational guidance in relation to vocational education deserves special comment. Vocational education, especially as realized through reimbursed programs, was devoted to equipping students with salable skills with which to enter the labor market, and the associated vocational guidance tended to emphasize a "tryout-through-training" approach. It is natural, therefore, that much stress was placed upon occupational information. It is understandable, also, that relatively little emphasis was given to psychological appraisal of the individual; for one thing, vocational educators had not typically been trained in psychology. But it is rather surprising that the developing industrial psychology did not make more of an impact on vocational education since industrial psychology seemed to offer considerable hope for assistance in placement. Counseling was recognized and gained strong support from the George-Deen Act of 1938 which permitted the use of federal funds for the training and support of vocational counselors. The relationship of vocational education, with its rather closely restricted clientele, to general education was a topic of continuing discussion. In 1944, the Vocational Education Division of the United States Office of Education (1950) undertook a study of "Vocational Education in the Years Ahead." Several conferences were held, leading to a statement of "Life Adjustment Education," defined as "that which better equips all American youth to live democratically with satisfaction to themselves and profit to society as homemakers, workers, and citizens [p. 1]."

Prior to these developments in vocational education several relevant events had occurred. In 1939 came the first edition of the *Dictionary of Occupational Titles*, which furnished a new way of ordering information about occupations. Meanwhile, research was continuing on the *General Aptitude Test Battery*, which was released for experimental use in 1945. The *Battery* was at first intended as an aid to placement of inexperienced workers and later was made available to the schools for guidance purposes. As the GATB was extended into guidance use, it represented an elaboration of the trait-and-factor approach to appraisal.

In general, no new concept of vocational guidance emerged from vocational education. Rather, a highly objective kind of vocational information was emphasized, appraisal of the individual remained a limited enterprise, counseling was still strongly directive and advice giving, and research continued to center about occupational surveys and follow-up studies.

Thus, the two strands of development brought together by Parsons continued as dominant influences until about the time of World War II. Then new voices began to be heard. In his 1950 presidential address to NVGA, Hoppock (1950) recounted the story of vocational guidance and commented:

> Massive as this program has been and still is, the foundations upon which it rests are beginning to crumble. Starting quietly with the publication of *Counseling and Psychotherapy* during the war, what we have variously known as non-directive or client-centered now challenges the basic assumptions underlying the whole concept of testing and diagnosis as the indispensable preliminary to clinical counseling [p. 498].

Later Developments

Three major lines of thinking relevant to the conceptualization of vocational guidance came into focus. One was an increasing recognition of the basic importance of personality dynamics in vocational choice and adjustment, coupled with a rising interest in psychotherapy. The second innovation was an emergence of the developmental view of the individual. The third line of thought centered about a reconsideration of the meaning of work. A review of the "Milestones" in the history of vocational guidance identified by Borow (1964b) suggests that the first two of these developments came into prominence largely during and after World War II but that there were earlier antecedents. In 1896 Lightner Witmer opened the first psychological clinic with emphasis upon the learning difficulties of schoolchildren, and Morris Viteles, one of Witmer's students, began a vocational guidance clinic. It is difficult to believe that any clinical procedure, even in those days, would not have taken cognizance of personal factors, but details are vague on this point. William Raney Harper, whose work is also listed as a milestone by Borow, is credited by Williamson (1965) with having actually predicted "that special school officers, trained in counseling, would be employed half a century in the future [p. 82]." The child study movement helped to focus attention on personality dynamics and therapeutic treatment, but this recognition of the importance of personality dynamics and psychotherapy had little direct impact on concepts of vocational guidance, at least in early years. The third influence, reconsideration of the meaning of work, was post-World War II in the sense of making a broad impact on thinking; it is still very much an open area.

It is interesting to note that the first of these new challenges to vocational guidance on the basis of personality dynamics and psychotherapy came not from the practices of secondary school guidance nor from vocational education but from efforts to provide improved assistance to returning veterans. McCully (1957) has noted that the 1945 version of the Veterans' Administration *Manual of Advisement and Guidance*, although reflecting traditional concepts, also included for the first time systematic treatment of rehabilitation counseling of the disabled and recognized the importance of affective factors in describing and authorizing "personal adjustment counseling." By 1951 the need for reevaluation was evident, and a committee was appointed (McCully, 1957) consisting of Edmund G. Williamson (chairman), Daniel D. Feder, and Donald E. Super. From the committee's considerations, "It seemed apparent that vocational advisement, like the vocational guidance movement, had lacked a firm orientation in personality theory [p. 25]." Two changes emerged: the name of the Service was changed from "Advisement and

Guidance" to the "Counseling Service"; and a new position to be called "Counseling Psychologist," was approved in 1952 by the Civil Service Commission. Also within the context of counseling veterans came some of the early client-centered writings, including *Counseling and Psychotherapy* (Rogers, 1942) and *Counseling with Returned Servicemen* (Rogers & Wallen, 1945), as well as a number of related articles.

Several more or less unrelated events illustrate the growing acceptance of a more psychological approach to vocational guidance—"psychological" in the sense of greater recognition of personality dynamics and affective factors. When the American Psychological Association was reorganized in 1947, Division 17 became a vehicle for the psychological emphasis in counseling. Two years later, the Policy Committee of the National Vocational Guidance Association (NVGA, 1949) recommended "counseling on problems of personal-social development" as one of the objectives for vocational guidance. In 1954 the *Journal of Counseling Psychology* was established. Although not limited to vocational guidance, the journal provided a means of expression for those who engaged in this enterprise. Further emphasis on psychology was provided by the report of the Commission on Guidance in American Schools, (Wrenn, 1962) under the aegis of the American Personnel and Guidance Association. While this project was concerned with broad issues in counseling, the recommendation for counselor education certainly carried a message for the vocational aspects of counseling, and with an added interdisciplinary flavor. The project report recommended that a minimal program of graduate study should include two major cores—one in psychology and one in "the study of societal forces, and culture changes [p. 167]."

Meanwhile, changes were also appearing within the area of occupational information itself. In 1956 the United States Employment Service published the results of an extensive study of estimated worker trait requirements, including training time, aptitudes, temperaments, physical capacities, as well as working conditions (United States Department of Labor, 1956). Only parts of this research were utilized in the latest revision of the *Dictionary of Occupational Titles* (United States Department of

Labor, 1965), but at least the worker achieved greater status as an individual human being in the 1965 edition compared to the worker described in the original 1939 *Dictionary.* Perhaps the clearest call for a more meaningful and humane kind of occupational information for counseling purposes came from Samler (1961) in the criticism of traditional materials. He pointed out that the bulk of available occupational information seemed devoted to "Economic Man," with very little attention given to the needs of "Psychological Man."

A second major change in the conceptualization of vocational guidance came in the shift to a concept of vocational development and away from the more static notion of matching men and jobs. Super, Crites, Hummel, Moser, Overstreet, and Warnath (1957, p. 8) note two European writers as important sources of the concept of developmental stages, Buehler (1933) and Lazarsfeld (1931). In this country the idea was used by Ginzberg, Ginsburg, Axelrad, & Herma (1951) in *Occupational Choice.* Clearly, there is much common ground between the stages-of-development idea and the strategy of developmental tasks as used by Havighurst (1953). In the Career Pattern Study much use was made of the concepts of life stages and of career patterns, the latter being drawn from the work of the sociologists Miller and Form (1951). More recently, Super (1967) contrasts occupations and careers, and he defines a career as "the sequence of occupations, jobs, and positions throughout a person's working life [p. 3]," noting further that this concept of career may be expanded at either end by adding prevocational or postretirement years. Super continues that "the psychology of occupations has been essentially a static *differential* psychology," while "the psychology of careers is essentially a dynamic developmental psychology [p. 4]." The concept of career patterns appears to offer a means of encompassing the unstable sequence of semiskilled employment (serial careers) which is not easily dealt with as an occupation. Super (1967) is thus able to call for "An all-class theory of vocational guidance, as contrasted with a middle-class theory [p. 24]" which will take into account socioeconomic status and its normal concomitants; a continuing vocational guidance from elementary school years through later school years and into employment [p. 26]; and a revamping of vocational education to meet modern realities [p. 27].

Both of the new emphases thus far sketched have brought with them a new vocabulary almost completely foreign to guidance of the first decade. Terms such as self-concept, ideal self, personal needs, vocational models, values, status, job satisfaction, discontinuities, therapy, culture, subculture, and existentialism have turned up in the literature, so that it is evident to even the casual observer that the climate of thinking about vocational guidance has changed in a major if not a radical way. Some of these terms suggest a trend toward subjective considerations almost unknown (or at least unverbalized) in the early years.

A third shift in the conceptualization of vocational guidance might be labeled a reconsideration of the meaning of work. It is difficult to relate this shift to any specific historical event; it was and is more in the realm of ideas than of activities or programs. But the change is nonetheless real. Of course, it is not really new—certainly not strictly a post-World War II product. Wrenn (1964) points out that the meaning of work in the early years of this country came from two sources—one religious and the other social—and that these meanings derived from the social class and religious systems of Western Europe. Thus, on the social side, work reflected a class distinction of feudal times between common man who worked and the noble whose status rested on family and land. On the religious side, manual work was dignified when performed by members of religious orders and in this country was later supported by Calvinism. Katz (see Chapter 3, this volume) notes the trend toward secularization and develops the implications that the changing meanings of work have for vocational guidance.

We are still plagued with problems of definition not only of *work* but also of such terms as vocation, career, leisure, occupation, job, and position. The last three have acquired fairly well-standardized definitions in a technical sense. Thus, *occupation* refers to a group of similar jobs in various establishments; a *job* refers to a group of similar positions in a single plant, business, or establishment, an educational institution, or other organization; and *position* is a group of tasks performed by one person (Shartle, 1952). But there is considerably less consensus regarding the other terms noted. Wrenn (1964) reports, for example, that he found 46 noun and verb definitions for the word work in the *American College Dictionary.* The problem of the meanings of vocation, career, and leisure is discussed at some length by Katz (see Chapter 3, this volume). Sheer terminology becomes important in any attempt to reconceptualize the kind of assistance which we have been referring to as vocational guidance.

The problems encountered in trying to define such terms as work, vocation, career, and leisure reflect basic changes in our socioeconomic patterns. More attention will be given to these later, but at this point let us suggest the following tentative propositions.

a. Work is a major source of identity for the individual, especially those of the middle class or those who accept middle-class values.

b. With a few exceptions, such as certain dedicative religious pursuits, vocation has become largely a secularized activity rather than a "calling."

c. A career, in the sense of a stable pursuit of a single occupation throughout the work life of the individual, is becoming increasingly unattainable in our industrialized society for a large portion of the work force, and something like "serial careers" is an inevitably emerging reality.

d. With the passing of craftsmanship and changes resulting from more advanced technology, an increased percentage of the working population is no longer able to follow occupations which offer a source of the kind of identity historically available in work. Notable exceptions can be found in certain professional and managerial occupations, in the arts, in a few crafts, and possibly in some semiprofessional and technical occupations.

e. The portion of the day which must be devoted to the business of earning a living is decreasing and will probably decrease further. The quest for a meaningful use of leisure is already strongly felt and will become more intense.

f. It is an open question as to whether or not the increased pursuit of leisure activities made possible by the decreased time needed for earning a living can supply the individual with the needed source of identity and meaning for living.

It is tempting at this point to launch into an exploration of the meaning of work, for surely this is an underlying issue. But it would very soon become disturbingly clear that not only the meaning of work as such would have to be dealt with but also work in relation to total living. There are other parts of this big picture which must be examined first, such as changes in the family, in the role of women, in opportunities for minority groups, and the whole quandary of changing values. These will be discussed in the following chapter by Blocher.

In passing, however, it may offer some small comfort to note that this concern about work and living permeates our culture in a surprisingly widespread way. No one group has a monopoly on this concern; not social reformers alone, nor intellectuals looking for a timely topic for a new book. The concern is shared also by businessmen, labor unions, college students with or without long hair, economists, sociologists, psychologists, and practitioners of vocational guidance. One example: an issue of *Kaiser Aluminum News* was devoted to "The Theory of the Leisure Masses," in which the meaning of work in an affluent society was examined (Fabun, 1966).

Economic and Industrial Changes

In the past few decades changes have been so rapid that the counselor can no longer depend upon his own work experience in trying to assist youth in finding their places in the world of work. And, as is often noted, many of these changes have been drastic and have far-reaching effects. The following brief description makes no pretense of offering either a complete analysis of the present situation, or of forecasting the world of work of the future. Rather, the intention is to illustrate some of the changes which carry implications for vocational guidance.

The Shift from Farm to Nonfarm Production

This change has become so familiar that its importance may easily be overlooked, but Wolfbein (1964b) has suggested that it may well rank first in importance among industrial changes of the past half-century. He goes on to point out that:

> One out of every three workers in the United States was employed on the farm at the turn of the century; today the figure is less than one in ten. The shift has been persistent, and even accelerating in recent years. As late as 1940, for example, 20 per cent of all workers still had jobs on the farm. This proportion has been cut by more than half [p. 159].

The Shift from Production of Goods to Production of Services

The rapid growth of industrial technology has changed the nation's occupational structure, particularly the distribution of goods-producing and service-producing work. Goods-producing industries may be classified as manufacture, agriculture, mining, and construction. Service industries include transportation, trade, finance, insurance, real estate, government, and personal services. Since World War I, increases in the number of workers in the goods-producing industries have been consistently smaller than increases in the number of workers engaged in providing services. In 1945 Americans employed in the production of goods still outnumbered service workers, but by the early 1950s the reverse was true (Wolfbein, 1964b). By 1980 it is anticipated that the service-producing sector of the economy will employ about 60 million workers, about twice as many as the goods-producing industries (United States Department of Labor, 1970, 1972b).

Employment's slow growth in the goods-producing industries does not indicate a correspondingly slow expansion in the production and distribution of goods. On the contrary, the rate of manufacture has steadily risen at such a pace that between 1900 and the early 1960s the per capita gross national product in the United States tripled. We had become a nation capable of creating and consuming goods at an unprecedentedly high rate, despite the allocation of larger and larger portions of the work force to service enterprises. The explanation lies chiefly in a burgeoning technology which has continued to boost individual worker productivity. While this economic reality has generated both temporary and long-term unemployment problems in many industries, it has developed numerous service fields which have transformed the nation's occupational structure, opened new work training opportunities, changed consumer habits, and altered personal and family life styles. Examples of expanding service-producing industries are electronic data processing, travel and recreation, and the paraprofessional health care fields.

Technological Changes

In a very general sense, technological changes represent a continuation of the Industrial Revolution. Some of the currently visible changes such as containerization in shipping, the shift to synthetic fibers in textiles, and prefabrication in construction are only recent examples. But one kind of technological change revolving about automation and the use of computers has attracted special attention since about the mid–1950s, both in general discussions of employment and in vocational guidance as such. New and distinctive elements are involved. In trying to specify these distinctive elements, difficulties of definition are encountered. Schultz and Baldwin (1964) have pointed out that most forms of technological change (such as the introduction of coal-cutting machinery) have been specific to a particular industry, whereas automation represents a generalized form of technological change applicable to a wide range of manual and white-collar operations. Automation (as the term is often used) is a family of several technological developments, of which three of the most fundamental seem to be: (*a*) the linking together of separate manufacturing operations into lines of continuous production ("Detroit automation"); (*b*) the use of "feedback" control devices or servomechanisms which permit individual operations to be performed without human control; and (*c*) the use of general and computing machines capable of recording and storing information ("computer technology"). However, somewhat more precise distinctions have developed. Wiener (1954) invented the word cybernetics, derived from a Greek word meaning "steersman," and used the word to refer to the processes of control in man and machines. Michael (1962) introduced the term cybernation and used it as a matter of convenience to refer at the same time to both automation (the use of devices for automatically performing sensing and motor tasks) and the use of computers. These usages adopted by Wiener and Michael seem to have become rather standard. In his testimony before the Subcommittee on Employment and Manpower, for example, Striner (1963) used "automation" in the sense of "Detroit automation," while he referred to cybernetics as "the application of electronic devices to provide the means of extending our mental abilities [pp. 273–274]" and cybernation as the joining together (in the Michael sense) of physical "doing" equipment with "thinking" equipment capable of controlling decisions—"computer technology." This same pattern of meanings seems to be the one employed the following year in *Manpower Report of the President* (United States Department of Labor, 1964).

The question of prime importance for vocational guidance is the extent to which and the manner in which technological changes such as cybernation are affecting and will continue to affect job opportunities. Unfortunately, there does not seem to be a general answer—at least, not any generally accepted predictive answer. We are immediately caught up in the continuing controversy as to whether or not, in the long run, technological change—and automation in particular—creates more new jobs than it renders obsolete. That the introduction of cybernation along with other new management techniques does indeed cause a reduction of jobs in some areas, at least for the short run, can scarcely be denied. In the same period the automobile industry, while increasing production, eliminated 170,000 jobs (United States Department of Labor, 1963). There may also be an upgrading of job requirements, with an increase of more jobs for the well trained and a reduction in jobs for the less skilled or unskilled (United States Department of Labor, 1964):

> Changing skill requirements result from technological advances which render many skills obsolete and diminish the need for unskilled and low-skilled workers while many of the newly created high skilled jobs go begging for lack of qualified workers [p. 25].

Almost any degree of optimism or pessimism can be found regarding probable effects of automation upon employment. At one end of this continuum is the statement of Wiener (United States Senate, 1958) that "Automation will create an unemployment situation which will make the thirty's seem like a pleasant joke, because the automatic machine is the precise equivalent of slave labor [p. 558]." And Venn (1964) warned that

> The full impact of the new technology has been slow to register on the American consciousness. To date, the instances of "technological unemployment" are like the cap of an iceberg. . . . Indeed, the nation has been assured for years that for every job destroyed by automation two new ones are created, and this notion has been slow to die. . . . Thus, many educators and other public leaders have not discerned that the forces of technology are *immediate* in importance and *national* in scope, and that they carry serious consequences for the economic and social life of the entire country [p. 5].

At the opposite pole are those (Kalachek, 1967) who found "no evidence that automation represents a new or serious deterrent to full employment [p. 247]."

But the climate of discussion seems to have calmed somewhat. The *Manpower Report of the President* (United States Department of Labor, 1969a) notes the new methods, machines, and products of the 1950s and 1960s and comments:

> Both experience and forecasts led to the fear that technological improvement would produce drastic job displacement, obsolescence of skills, shrinking opportunities for semiskilled workers, the decline and decay of some industries, and unusual stresses in industrial relations [p. 155].

The Report continues:

> The fear that automation would bring about massive displacement of unskilled workers and a sharp upgrading of the occupa-

tional structure of employment was not, however, borne out [p. 156].

While concern remains about the impact of automation and cybernation on employment and leisure (Childs, 1965; Kahn & Wiener, 1967; Dunnette, in press), labor economists like Wolfbein (1968) have redirected attention to the effects of new technology and on specific industries and types of workers.

Perhaps the differential effects of automation upon various jobs and industries can be clarified by a brief examination of one specific study. Fine (1964) made a functional job analysis of the jobs of 132 workers engaged in several processes in electron tube, computer, and steel manufacturing. He also obtained data from management regarding educational and training requirements. From the workers he secured information concerning their background and experience and their judgments concerning various aspects of the jobs, such as education and training requirements, working conditions, skills needed, and sources of satisfaction. It is not possible to report the findings in detail; however, the following examples may illustrate the point that changes associated with the coming of automation were found to differ for various jobs. The use of Functional Analysis revealed that:

a. "Where the nature of the technological change is from hand assembly to continuous materials processing, three types of jobs emerge [p. 3]." These were the "feeders" who are machine paced; machine tenders and utility operators; and attendants who understand the machine sufficiently to keep it at maximum operating condition.

b. "Where the nature of technological change is from hand testing (an inspection task) to automatic machine testing, there is a sharp change from a major orientation to Data on a low functional level to a major orientation to Things on a low functional level [p. 3]."

c. On the matter of changes in education and training requirements resulting from automation, five differences were found. Two examples are (*a*) feeding and tending jobs under automation required the same or less education than the old hand assembling and testing jobs, but (*b*) since the new automated equipment typically includes electronic and hydraulic devices, the maintenance/repairman often needed high school graduation in order to keep training periods on the job relatively short.

Important differences in worker perceptions, aspirations, and orientations toward automated technology were found between high functional and low functional level workers.

On the basis of findings such as these (only partially reported here), it seems necessary to dismiss easy generalizations regarding automation and to wait for the accumulation of research evidence from studies of specific jobs or job families in various industries.

The Mobility of Workers

There are at least three aspects of mobility which have important implications for vocational guidance. One is simply movement from place to place—geographic mobility. This may mean movement of workers from one part of a city to another, from one city to another, from inner city to suburbs, or from one state to another. While it is probably true that high school graduates and dropouts are apt to find their first employment in or near their home communities, a considerable number of these may become quite mobile geographically as they gain experience and seek advancement. One illustration of such mobility is the transfer of employees of large companies to other work situations. The second aspect of mobility is job mobility—movement from one job to another. This may involve change of occupation or geographic mobility, but it need not. It is important because there are so many who move from job to job. Job mobility is an important consideration in vocational guidance: a work career often involves a sequence of jobs, and the outlook for the future seems to be that more and more persons will be involved in serial careers, or to use Super's term, "multiple-trial" careers, especially at the semiskilled level (Super, 1967, p. 6). The third aspect of mobility which might be called status mobility involves some kind of prestige scale in a stratified society. Such movement, of course, is not independent of job mobility; in fact, the latter is almost implied. As any counselor knows, the counselee's perceptions of occupational prestige enter (at least for many) into the very early stages of vocational development and often continue as potent influences.

Geographic Mobility

The tradition of moving west is alive today. At the present rate, each year approximately 20 percent of all Americans one year of age or over change residence and about six and one-half percent migrate across county or state lines. Since 1945 the population drain has been heaviest from Southern, Northeastern, and North Central states. By contrast California's net in-migration of over three million people during the 1950s matched the state's total number of births and accounted for about 60 percent of its population increase. Florida's net in-migration during the same ten-year span accounted for more than half of the state's growth in population. Such movement reflects more than blind acceptance of the often quoted advice, "Go West, young man," or romantic fantasies of the sunny beaches of Florida. In general the states showing the greatest population growth rates have been those with rapidly expanding economic and employment opportunities. Hightest (estimated percentage) increases in the labor force between 1960 and 1970 have taken place mainly in the Far West (California), the Southwest (Arizona, New Mexico, Nevada), the Rocky Mountain region (Colorado and Utah), and the Southeast (Florida) (Wolfbein, 1968).

States showing the largest labor force increases have been those offering rapidly expanding employment opportunities in the service fields—government, retirement, tourism, and other leisure activities. Wolfbein (1968) points out that every state with an employment growth rate at least double that of the national average has shown an estimated 100 percent or higher increase in state and local government jobs. Such labor force shifts would hardly have occurred in traditional agriculture, mining, and manufacture. Significant advances in fuel, power, transportation, and information processing technology, however, have allowed industry itself to become more mobile. In the future, population flow patterns and manpower characteristics rather than historical precedent and the physical features of regional geography are likely to influence major shifts in economic and employment opportunity. Both industry and people will become geographically more fluid. Thus, it appears that counselors in a good many places will be working with counselees who will sooner or later seek their occupational opportunities in states other than those of their birth. We are counseling a potentially mobile population.

A special aspect of mobility in recent years is the surge into the suburbs and both into and out of the inner cities. This movement is not only a shift of living locale for a considerable portion of the population, but also involves a definite change in ethnic composition. The basic facts can be stated briefly. Although the proportion of nonwhites in the population has increased only slightly from 1940–1965, the nonwhite population has more than doubled in the inner cities while declining in the suburbs. Much of the change can be accounted for by the movement of blacks (United States Department of Labor, 1967). It should be noted, however, that the movement was not exclusively one of blacks but blacks did constitute by a considerable margin the largest single nonwhite group.

The implications of these movements into and out of the inner cities are far-reaching.

Job Mobility

As in the case of geographic mobility, the tradition of job mobility is part of our heritage. While the factory system with its attendant specialization and division of labor was developing in Europe, the United States was still largely a nation in which employment centered about agriculture. Lebergott (1964) suggests that "The tenor of our development had surely been set by 1860, yet as late as that year less than 15 percent of our labor force was in manufacturing [pp. 114–119]." Many of the skills other than farming were developed by farmers as they carried on supplemental occupations. The blacksmith, mechanic, and carpenter were apt to be farmers, and shipyard workers in the Eastern states were likely to be farmers or fishermen in their primary occupational pursuits. Even early ministers and physicians were also sometimes farmers. Contracts for construction of some sections of the National Road were taken by farmers. For the early American worker, job mobility in the modern sense had little meaning; rather the worker was a generalist doing the job which needed to be done or which was available.

Mass statistics for modern times show differences in employment patterns from one period to another for the work force as a whole. Lebergott brings together some of these statistics and compares the sources and uses of labor in 1900 and 1960. His comparison and the data gathered by the United States Department of Labor (1970) emphasize the decline of employment in domestic services and on farms and the rapid growth of positions in government and also in personal, professional, business, and financial services. Valuable as such information may be for understanding the ways and extent to which we have departed from our heritage, and for manpower development and training efforts, this is not the kind of job mobility information most needed by counselors as they work with individuals. What is needed is information which will help establish the degree of probability that a particular individual with a given background and certain characteristics may anticipate changing from one job to another. And if the probability is high, what kinds of job sequences may be expected? In short, what are the probabilities of certain career patterns as against others for a particular individual? Group predictions are not enough.

The concept of job mobility is of course a very old one, and the phenomenon has probably existed since the coming of industrialization elaborated the division of labor and produced a number of more or less differentiated jobs, each concerned with a related set of tasks. There have been many studies of trends, but the counselor in working with the individual needs something more than trends. He needs a set of probabilities for the individual, as already suggested. But this problem merges into a broader one: should vocational guidance attempt to work from a base of long-range predictions, and if so, to what extent? Or should guidance personnel be content with short-range, step-by-step assistance to the individual in his development? The question has meaning for both vocational guidance and vocational education. Traditionally, vocational guidance has assumed considerable predictability of careers, but then traditional vocational guidance has been single-career oriented and is ill prepared to deal with the emerging problem of serial careers. If we are to achieve a real reconceptualization, it is necessary to reckon with the increasing probability that many will be involved in the kind of job mobility in which the working career consists of sequences of jobs. What then is the role of prediction?

Status Mobility

We can count the people who move from one geographical location to another and people who change from one job to another, thus arriving at some quite objective data. But the matter of status mobility introduces a subjective dimension. If a given change is to be considered a change of status, a judgment of interpretation is involved as made by some individual or group—someone perceives the change as a change of status. Obviously, a variety of factors may be involved in such perceptions.

The literature is replete with studies of occupational status, but this is not the place to undertake a comprehensive review. In general, professional workers, managers, proprietors, and some government officials seem to be accorded highest prestige, while clerical workers and skilled craftsmen stand somewhat lower in the hierarchy, and service workers and laborers occupy the lowest positions on the totem pole. Although there is some variation from time to time, the general pattern of average ratings appears to be remarkably stable, having persisted through several wars and a major depression in the thirties.

The rank-order of occupations in the United States seems to reflect the socioeconomic structure characteristic of this country. Changes in perceptions of the relative prestige of occupations come relatively slowly, even though change may actually be under way. Very young children do not seem much aware of occupational prestige, but by late childhood or early adolescence most seem to be well on their way toward learning and accepting the stereotypes common to the national culture, with some modifications supplied by the particular subculture in which they participate. The Horatio Alger myth and the ideal of hard work as a means of self-fulfillment and the pathway to success will persist for many if not most, even though some of the pyrotechnics currently attributed to youth groups and youth culture may seem to deny this. On the other hand, this ideal of the rise of the individual through his own efforts seems to be in the process of being supplemented by the ideal of the rise of total groups. In the words of Katz (see Chapter 3, this volume),

> there began to materialize in some measure the promise that hard work and productivity would be rewarded not only by a laborer's rise *through* the strata of classes, but also or alternatively by his rise *with* the laboring class. Success—or productivity—in work was expected to raise the level of economic rewards for *all* classes to the extent that all persons would feel pride of accomplishment and satisfaction [p. 99].

The extent to which the ideal of the rise of the individual has been supplemented or perhaps displaced by the group is by no means clear, but it is evident that the ferment is under way.

Typically, studies of occupational prestige have attempted to rank occupations given in a single list, as in the studies by the National Opinion Research Center (Hodge, Siegel, & Rossi, 1964, pp. 290–293). One difficulty in such investigations is the possibility that respondents may be employing different points of view or frames of reference. They may well feel that some of the occupations are so different that they cannot be judged as higher or lower in prestige. An alternative approach is to postulate that various groups may possess their own internal systems of prestige and that the various ranking systems of the groups are to some extent parallel. In this approach, the respondent need not be asked to judge between a radio announcer and a machinist, for example, but each is ranked within his own relevant group. Such an approach employs the concept of "situs" as distinguished from a single continuum of statuses. The concept of situs comes from Benoit-Smullyn (1944), and the method was developed by Hatt (1950). An example of a situs is manual work, which includes skilled mechanics, construction trades, outdoor work, factory work, and unskilled labor. Although the concept of situs may be subject to criticism as involving an element of self-selection, this concept does seem to hold promise in the practical enterprise of vocational guidance. For example, the young person may see that *each* of a number of work areas has its own set of paths for recognition, rewards, and standing *within* the family of occupations. From this point of view, the achievement of prestige within one's own group can become a real goal, and such prestige within one's own group may well be more psychologically meaningful than prestige accorded an occupation in some national but heterogeneous hierarchy.

The idea of status mobility, of "getting ahead," or "amounting to something" is part of the American dream. In the days when our country was largely rural and opportunities for individuals abounded, the dream served well. But in our present highly industrialized economy and urbanized and stratified society, it is easy to understand that the individual, unsupported by a group to carry him with them in the struggle to rise, may feel that the climb is just not worth it or may even be impossible. It is easy to slip into frustration or settle for alienation. And it is indeed a long way from unskilled labor to the upper reaches of the hierarchy if one assumes that there is only one hierarchy. The American dream of sure rewards for individual effort is most apt to become sheer fantasy to the people who are now ranked lowest on the totem pole, and traditional vocational guidance with its orientation to middle-class career and mobility in a single occupation has failed this group most completely. A reinterpretation of status as being within one's own group (situs), a greater appreciation of the struggle of total groups to rise by supporting each other, and a clearer understanding of the probability that a very large number of workers will build their working lives out of sequences of jobs which may or may not add up to neat forward progressions—a consideration of such factors can lead to a view of vocational guidance now only dimly sensed.

Demographic Characteristics of the Work Force

In vocational guidance it is important to understand the composition of work groups. However, the demographic characteristics of work groups do change, and so a continuing assessment is needed. As Wolfbein (1964b, p. 140) points out, demographic factors are important in long-term changes, but overriding forces of other kinds may also produce changes in labor market participation. An earlier study by Wolfbein and Jaffe will serve to illustrate. In this study an attempt was made, using 1890 data, to predict the rates of gainfully employed workers of 1930. On the basis of demographic data alone, the investigators would have predicted a decline in rates for all workers, male and female, married and unmarried. Actually, the rate went down for males only, but whereas the predicted decline was .4 percent, the real decline was 2.5 percent. Predictions for women went even further astray. The predicted decline was 4.6 to 4.0 percent, but the actual change was an increase of 11.7 percent. Wolfbein (1964b) concluded, "Obviously, nondemographic characteristics of the work force exerted dramatic changes [p. 140]."

It is with due caution, then, that we approach the matter of demographic characteristics, and presentation will be limited to the four characteristics of age, sex, race, and marital status. The purpose is to note briefly a few examples which may be helpful as general background for vocational guidance.

Age, Sex, and Race

Information compiled by the Bureau of Labor Statistics in the United States Department of Labor reveals steadily rising unemployment rates among the youngest members of the worker pool (ages 16 to 19) as compared with the rate of workers of age 25 and above, projects a significant rise for the 1970s in the percentage of the labor force falling in the prime 25–34 year age group, and identifies the changing composition of the female and the minority components of the national work force (United States Department of Labor, 1970). Such large-scale employment trends have highly significant implications not only for national manpower and training policy but for the career guidance of potential workers in these population categories.

By 1980 the population over 14 years of age is projected to be almost 174 million. A big change will mark those in the age bracket 14–24. The figure of 8.7 million males in this age group in 1960 has since risen sharply and is expected to swell to 14.8 million by 1980. Beyond the increase which had been estimated for males for the 1960–1970 decade, a new 17.2 percent growth is now seen for 1970–1980. For females the corresponding figures are 4.9 million in 1960, 7.7 million in 1970, and 9.2 million in 1980, representing percentage increases of 54.5 from 1960 to 1970 and 20.1 from 1970 to 1980 (United States Department of Labor, 1967). The job participation rate for the adult population as a whole is not expected to change much—57.4 percent in 1960 as against 58.3 percent projected for 1980. For the near future, the largest gains will involve those under age 35. While only moderate labor force percentage increases are foreseen for the 1970–1980 period for those in middle worklife (ages 35–44) and later worklife (ages 45 and above), the increase forecast for the 16–24 age group is nineteen percent and that for the 25–34 age group a remarkable 49 percent (Department of Labor, 1970).

A paradox is seen in the rising proportions of young people, women, and minority group members in the composition of the nation's potential work force by 1980. While these sectors of the population will make up significantly larger percentages of the labor force, each will probably continue to be the object of selective biases in hiring and upgrading practices and each will likely show disproportionately high unemployment rates. There will surely remain in 1980 a formidable challenge for all who are involved in assisting individuals find useful and satisfying roles in the world of work.

Employment Prospects for Special Populations

Where employment opportunities and work histories are concerned, the demographic variables of age, education, sex, and ethnic background interact in complex ways. Dealing with each group variable independently of the others may therefore yield only a gross and somewhat incomplete picture of the employment rates and career histories of subpopulations within the general labor force. Yet research has shown that there are distinctive and rather stable work-relevant features of different groups, and such characteristics have meaning for career guidance strategy. This concluding section of the chapter briefly presents some of the more pertinent employment conditions and trends as they apply to the young dropout, female, and nonwhite worker categories.

Of all special populations, perhaps none is more handicapped by employment restrictions than young workers, chiefly those in the under-twenty age category. Unemployment among teenagers exceeded 12 percent for every year of the 1960s. Comparatively, joblessness in this group may be worsening rather than improving. In 1960 teenagers seeking work showed an unemployment rate of 3.3 times that of the twenty-five-and-over age group. By 1964 the rate had risen to 4.3 and, by 1970, to 5.5. The overall joblessness rate among the 16–19 age group in 1971 was just under 17 percent, a rise of more than 4.5 percent from 1969 (United States Department of Labor 1972a). A government report has forcast that for the 1970s teenagers will enter the labor force far more slowly than in the previous decade (United States Department of Labor, 1970). Mitigating conditions are seen in the small gains in teenage employment toward the close of 1971 and the growing opportunities for part-time work. The chance to work on a fractional time basis is permitting increased numbers of young people to combine schooling with employment, a fact which may be contributing to the rising percentage of school-age youth who are staying in school today.

That increased years of formal education generally improve the prospects of employment has long been known. Yet the fact that, as noted above, joblessness among young people has increased, although school dropout rates continue to fall, demonstrates that the relationship between education and employment status is not a simple one. Currently overall unemployment among school dropouts is over 23 percent; the rate for nonwhites is about one-fourth higher. Slightly over 80 percent of high school age youth are enrolled in school; a small increase is expected by 1980. By that year better than one-fourth of all persons of college age will be attending college. The rate of enrollment growth will be faster for colleges than for lower school levels (United States Department of Labor, 1970, 1972b). It is anticipated that more schooling will bring higher average lifetime earnings. Taking the period around 1970 as the time base, work-life earnings for men are estimated respectively at less than $300,000 for those with eighth-grade educations, about $375,000 for those with high school diplomas, and close to $600,000 for those with baccalaureate degrees. However, a straight line relationship between education on the one hand and employment status and economic advantage on the other cannot be assumed to exist. With the expansion of subprofessional opportunities in the allied health fields, marketing, information technology, and management services, graduates from occupational sequences in the two-year community colleges frequently find better job opportunities than do four-year college graduates. Judged against the job market, we may now be producing a generation of vocationally overtrained youth. One estimate states that 25 percent of college graduates will be employed in positions for which collegiate experience is unnecessary (*Time*, 1971). Job opportunities for B.A. degree holders in the humanities are expected to remain comparatively scarce. The dreary job market for college-trained workers has led Sophia Travis, among others, to undertake a study of the difficulties encountered by job seekers who have recently moved from college to careers (United States Department of Labor, Manpower Administration, 1971b).

Women are becoming an increasingly potent factor in the labor force. The relaxation of restrictions against entry into occupations traditionally viewed as masculine strongholds, vast changes in the occupational structure which have seen the displacement of many unskilled jobs requiring sheer physical labor by others demanding general education and special skills, the spread of part-time opportunities, the changing attitudes toward family roles, the establishment of child day-care centers—all these emerging conditions and others have brought woman as worker to new prominence and have created a greatly enlarged clientele for serious career guidance. By 1971 over 40 percent of married women with children under age 18 were in the labor force, this figure representing almost a 50 percent increase over 1960 (United States Department of Labor, 1972a). Because society has tended to assume a casual stance toward female career roles, adequate knowledge and techniques relevant to the career planning needs of women are lacking. Currently under way at Ohio State University with federal support is a broad-gauged longitudinal study of the educational and labor market experience of young women (United States Department of Labor, Manpower Administration, 1971a).

The changing work status of ethnic minorities in America, particularly of blacks, is too complex and has too many ramifications for proper treatment within the context of this chapter. It can be noted that while perceptible improvement in opportunities for nonwhites has taken place in both the education and employment areas, rapid and substantial further progress is essential. While the 1960s saw a marked reduction in the percentage of unemployed blacks of high school graduation age, their joblessness rate continues to be roughly double that of whites in the same age range. About 70 percent or more of blacks now leave high school as graduates, but this figure still lags behind that of whites as do the figures for earnings (United States Department of Labor, 1970). Since black youth will enter the labor market in significant numbers in the years immediately ahead, national policy must be shaped to insure appropriate educational and economic gains. In Chapter 2, Donald Blocher analyzes further the career development problems and needs of both women workers and nonwhites and he calls for bold new guidance measures commensurate with the difficult tasks facing the nation and our counselors.

REFERENCES

Benoit-Smullyn, E. Status, status types, and status interpretations. *American Sociological Review*, 1944, **9**, 154–161.

Bingham, W. V. *Aptitudes and aptitude testing.* New York: Harper & Row, 1937.

Borow, H. Milestones: A chronology of notable events in the history of vocational guidance. In H. Borow (Ed.), *Man in a world at work.* Boston: Houghton Mifflin, 1964. (b)

Brewer, J. M. *Education as guidance.* New York: Macmillan, 1932.

Brewer, J. M. *History of vocational guidance.* New York: Harper & Row, 1942.

Buehler, C. *Der menschliche Lebenslauf als psychologisches Problem.* Leipzig: Hirzel, 1933.

Childs, G. B. *Is the work ethic realistic in an age of automation? Phi Delta Kappan,* 1965, **46,** 370–375.

Davis, H. V. *Frank Parsons and vocational guidance.* (Doctoral dissertation, Washington University) Ann Arbor, Mich.: University Microfilms, 1958, No. 12-794.

Davis, J. B. Looking backwards: The problem of vocational guidance stated. Presidential address given at the annual convention of the National Vocational Guidance Association, Oakland, California, August 1915. (*Personnel and Guidance Journal,* 1956, **34,** 420–422.)

Dunnette, M. D. (Ed) *Work and nonwork in the year 2001.* Monterey, Calif.: Brooks/Cole, in press.

Fabun, D. (Ed.) The theory of the leisure masses. *Kaiser Aluminum News,* 1966, **24,** entire issue.

Fine, S. A. *The nature of automated jobs and their educational and training requirements.* McLean, Va.: Human Sciences Research, 1964.

Ginzberg, E., Ginsburg, S. W., Axelrad, S., & Herma, J. L. *Occupational choice: An approach to a general theory.* New York: Columbia University Press, 1951.

Hatt, P. K. Occupation and social stratification. *American Journal of Sociology,* 1950, **55,** 533–543.

Havighurst, R. J. *Human development and education.* New York: Longmans, Green, 1953.

Hodge, R. W., Siegel, P. M., & Rossi, P. H. Occupational prestige in the United States, 1925–1963. *American Journal of Sociology,* 1964, **70,** 286–302.

Hoppock, R. Presidential address given at the annual meeting of the National Vocational Guidance Association, Atlantic City, March 1950. (*Occupations,* 1950, **28,** 497–499.)

Jones, A. J., & Hand, H. C. Guidance and purposive living. In G. M. Whipple (Ed.), *Guidance in educational institutions.* Thirty-seventh Yearbook of the National Society for the Study of Education, Part I. Chicago: University of Chicago Press, 1938.

Kalachek, E. D. Automation and full employment. *Vocational Guidance Quarterly*, 1967, **15,** 242–247.

Krug, E. A. *The shaping of the American high school.* New York: Harper & Row, 1964.

Lebergott, S. *Manpower in economic growth: The American record since 1800.* New York: McGraw-Hill, 1964.

Mann, A. Frank Parsons: The professor as crusader. *Mississippi Valley Historical Review*, 1950, **37,** 479–485.

McCully, C. H. Developments of a decade of VA counseling. *Personnel and Guidance Journal*, 1957, **36,** 21–27.

Michael, D. M. *Cybernation: The silent revolution.* Santa Barbara, Calif.: Center for the Study of Democratic Institutions, 1962.

Miller, D. C., & Form, W. H. *Industrial sociology.* (2nd ed.) New York: Harper & Row, 1964.

National Education Association, Department of the Interior, Bureau of Education. A report of the Commission on the Reorganization of Secondary Education. *Vocational guidance in secondary education.* (Bulletin No. 19) Washington, D.C.: Government Printing Office, 1918.

National Vocational Guidance Association. Report of the policy committee. *Occupations*, 1949, **27,** 270–272.

Parsons, F. *Choosing a vocation.* Boston: Houghton Mifflin, 1909.

Reed, A. Y. *Guidance and personnel services in education.* Ithaca, N. Y.: Cornell University Press, 1944.

Rogers, C. R. *Counseling and psychotherapy.* Boston: Houghton Mifflin, 1942.

Rogers, C. R. *On becoming a person.* Boston: Houghton Mifflin, 1961.

Rogers, C. R., & Wallen, J. L. *Counseling with returned servicemen.* New York: McGraw-Hill, 1946.

Rudy, S. W. *Schools in the age of mass culture.* Englewood Cliffs, N. J.: Prentice-Hall, 1965.

Samler, J. Psycho-social aspects of work: A critique of occupational information. *Personnel and Guidance Journal*, 1961, **39**, 458–465.

Schultz, G. P., & Baldwin, G. B. *Automation: A new dimension to old problems.* Washington, D.C.: Public Affairs Press, 1964.

Stephens, W. R. *Social reform and the origins of vocational guidance.* Washington, D.C.: National Vocational Guidance Association, 1970.

Striner, H. E. United States Senate Committee on Labor and Public Welfare, Hearing before the subcommittee on Employment and Manpower. *Nation's manpower revolution.* (Part 5) Eighty-eighth Congress, First Session, 1963.

Super, D. E. A reconceptualization of vocational guidance. Position paper prepared for *Project Reconceptualization*, National Vocational Guidance Association, Washington, D.C. 1967. (Mimeographed)

Super, D. E., Crites, J. O., Hummel, R. C., Moser, H. P., Overstreet, P. L., & Warnath, C. F. *Vocational development: A framework for research,* New York: Teachers College, Columbia University, 1957.

Time, Graduates and jobs: A grave new world. May 24, 1971, pp. 49–59.

United States Department of Labor, Bureau of Employment Security. *Estimates of worker trait requirements for 4,000 jobs as defined in the dictionary of occupational titles.* Washington, D.C.: Government Printing Office, 1956.

United States Department of Labor, Office of Manpower Automation and Training. *Mobility and worker adaptation to economic change in the United States.* (Manpower Research Bulletin No. 1) Washington, D.C.: Government Printing Office, July, 1963 (Revised)

United States Department of Labor. *Manpower report of the President.* Washington, D.C.: Government Printing Office, 1964.

United States Department of Labor, Manpower Administration. *Dictionary of occupational titles.* (3rd ed.) Vols. I and II. Washington, D.C.: Government Printing Office, 1965.

United States Department of Labor. *Manpower report of the President.* Washington, D.C.: Government Printing Office, 1967.

United States Department of Labor. *Manpower report of the President.* Washington, D.C.: Government Printing Office, 1969. (a)

United States Department of Labor. *Statistics on manpower.* A supplement to the *Manpower report of the President*, March, 1969. Washington, D.C.: Government Printing Office, 1969. (b)

United States Department of Labor. *U.S. manpower in the 1970s: Opportunity and challenge.* Washington, D.C.: Government Printing Office, 1970.

United States Department of Labor, Manpower Administration. *Years for decision, Volume 1.* Manpower Research Monograph No. 24. Washington, D.C.: Government Printing Office, 1971. (a)

United States Department of Labor, Manpower Administration. *Manpower research and development projects.* Washington, D.C.: Government Printing Office, 1971. (b)

United States Department of Labor. *Manpower report of the President.* Washington, D.C.: Government Printing Office, 1972. (a)

United States Department of Labor. *Jobs for the 1970s.* Washington, D.C.: National Audiovisual Center, 1972b. (Series of forty 2 x 2 slides)

U.S. Office of Education, *Report of the national conference on life adjustment education. Chicago, October 16–18.* Washington, D.C.: United States Office of Education, November, 1950. (Mimeographed)

United States Senate, Committee on Unemployment Problems. *Studies in unemployment problems.* Washington, D.C.: Government Printing Office, 1958.

Venn, G. *Man, education and work.* Washington, D.C.: American Council on Education, 1964.

Wiener, N. *The human use of human beings.* New York: Doubleday, 1954.

Williamson, E. G. *Vocational counseling.* New York: McGraw-Hill, 1965.

Wolfbein, S. L. *Employment and unemployment in the United States.* Chicago: Science Research Associates, 1964. (a)

Wolfbein, S. L. Labor trends, manpower, and automation. In H. Borow (Ed.), *Man in a world at work.* Boston: Houghton Mifflin, 1964. (b)

Wolfbein, S. L. *Occupational information: A career guidance view.* New York: Random House, 1968.

Wrenn, C. G. *The counselor in a changing world.* Washington, D.C.: American Personnel and Guidance Association, 1962.

Wrenn, C. G. Human values and work in American life. In H. Borow (Ed.), *Man in a world at work.* Boston: Houghton Mifflin, 1964.

2

social change and the future of vocational guidance

DONALD H. BLOCHER
University of Minnesota

While the conjugal family remains a dominant social unit, Donald Blocher notes that it has largely ceased to function as the principal organizational mechanism for the production of economic goods. The locus of production long ago shifted to industrial establishments, and parental roles have become increasingly diffused. The transmission of specific work knowledge and skills from parent to child is no longer common. Familial responsibility for teaching the child about occupational life now appears to center on developing competence in interpersonal relations, and although this relatively non-specific objective of child rearing can still hold significance for youth's potential work role, its importance is lost upon many families.

Pervasive social change poses formidable challenges for vocational guidance as it concerns the emerging needs of women, minority groups, and the youth culture. Earlier marriage and completion of child-bearing activity, coupled with the relaxation of restrictions against occupational entry, now allow women to combine domestic and work functions in many ways. The trend away from rigid sex-typing of traditional masculine vocations has broadened women's job opportunities, and the converse seems also to be becoming a reality for men. Such extended horizons need to be made fully visible through career guidance. Similarly, in their work with minority group clients, counselors must grasp the significance of crumbling barriers to employment which the human rights thrust is bringing about. But, Blocher argues, they cannot adopt a detached position toward the equal opportunity movement, and he urges an activist role for guidance practitioners. Counselors need, furthermore, to begin by reexamining their own latent attitudes, and they must help minority group clients establish their own identities and personal values.

Many members of today's youth culture are the offspring of an affluent society which deprecates their economic worth. They are captives of a protracted adolescence, bound together in a leisure-oriented subculture, and "excluded by law and custom from becoming economically productive." Blocher concedes that many young people sense the importance of work as a means to achieving autonomy and self-regard, but are often thwarted by the adult world. That they develop negative attitudes toward the servile, unappealing jobs they are allowed to hold is a measure of their assimilation of the status-centered values of the controlling society. It is improper, contends Blocher, to hold out to all youth the prospect of self-actualization through work when, for many, the odds against realizing such a psychological goal are long. The mission of career guidance is to assist youth to render to awareness their own values, to show them how these relate to the world as it actually is, not as it is idealized, and further, to assume an interventionist stance to make the world of work more humane.

Blocher proposes the principles of discontinuity, life stages, life style, and life space as conceptual elements in any viable new strategy to foster career development. Traditional insight-oriented counseling alone may not be adequate. In his two-dimensional vocational guidance model, a variety of both direct and indirect interventions are summoned. On the plea that career guidance must leaven the bread of idealism with the demands of reality, Blocher concludes his chapter with a broad-net reconceptualization of vocational guidance which encompasses and summarizes his major propositions.

H. B.

We live in a world where the ultimate certainty has become that of the inevitability of change. Counseling and guidance practitioners are engaged in helping others think about and plan their futures in a world in which a third of the population was unborn a scant fifteen years ago. Major industries such as television, computer, aerospace, and atomic energy were in the realm of science fiction four decades ago. Dynamic centers of dramatic industrial and population growth were rural by-ways twenty years ago. Movements of people—from farm to city, from city to suburb, from North to South, and from East to West—dwarf the great migrations of ancient times and proceed almost unnoticed. Social and cultural revolutions in sexual mores, human rights, and family relationships are the rules rather than the exceptions of our time.

We live in the midst of a second industrial revolution called cybernation that multiplies technological changes at exponential rates. We launch a desperate effort to save the very air and water that we so exuberantly learned how to poison a few short years ago. The word *ecology* has moved in a matter of months from an esoteric burial ground of the college textbook to the bandwagon world of political sloganeering.

Decisions of national and international policy that profoundly influence the working lives and futures of millions are made daily. Plans for space explorations, supersonic transports, anti-ballistic missiles, brushfire wars, and prime interest rates are made and changed, and the most confident predictions about employment outlooks in a dozen major occupations are suddenly, dramatically altered.

One striking illustration is to be found in personnel supply and demand projections of highly trained scientists. The President's Manpower Report to the Congress submitted in March, 1970, contained the following statement. "The requirements for science doctorates will greatly exceed the probable supply available to the colleges throughout most of the period [of the 1970s] [p. 173]." Yet by the end of 1970 the surplus of high-level people in the sciences had reached such dramatic proportions that feature articles about it were appearing almost daily in the public press (New York *Times*, Nov. 1). Newer strategies for prediction are being developed that hold some hope for improving our ability to anticipate future events (Kahn & Wiener, 1967).

In the face of transformation occurring with this kind of rapidity and permeating so many aspects of our life, what is the future of the vocational guidance enterprise? If the assumptions and strategies that underlie our models of decision making, actuarial prediction, and matching of men and jobs are, indeed, already suspect, where do we go, what are our directions? What kinds of long-term cultural and social shifts are at work that will have an impact on vocational guidance? How will such factors force the reshaping of our professional practices? What are some of the newer concepts and understandings which vocational guidance can utilize in meeting the challenge of change?

Several major areas of social and cultural development are discussed in the following pages, and their implications for vocational guidance are explored. Out of this discussion a tentative framework for redefining and reorienting the vocational guidance enterprise is attempted.

The Impact of Social Change

Just as technical and industrial changes are transforming the economic world in which people work, and demographic changes are altering the characteristics of the working population itself, so too have dramatic social changes affected the psychological milieu within which contemporary Americans grow, live, and work.

Human behavior is very much a social product. People exercise selective perceptions, organize their experiences, attach meaning to events, and build expectations about the future on the basis of social learning. Values, attitudes, interests, and stereotypes are acquired primarily through interactions with those significant others with whom we share membership or reference groups. In periods of very rapid social change, intergroup and intergenerational differences in social learning become so great that relationships, communication, and understanding among individuals with differing backgrounds may become difficult.

Vocational counselors and others who have responsibility for furthering the career development of the individual are among those in the society who are directly concerned with bridging the communication and relationship gaps among generations, races, and social classes. If these professionals are to discharge these obligations, they will need to understand and appreciate the impact of cultural and social changes as they now impinge upon the lives of people. Significant numbers of people of all ages are presently questioning basic social values and are in the process of committing themselves to what is called the counter culture (Keniston, 1970).

The family is obviously the primary group which has the earliest and perhaps most profound impact upon developing human beings. Changes in patterns of family organization, nature of family relationships, and ideals and expectations about family functioning will inevitably produce important effects on the development of children in terms of their values, attitudes, and aspirations.

Several relatively long-term changes in family patterns are of particular relevance. Historically, the family as a stable social institution emerged very largely out of economic necessity. In Western civilization, division of labor dictated by physical and psychological differences between men and women furnished a basis for family development that persisted until the beginning of the present century. In this country, with the decline of subsistence farming as the modal means of family support, profound changes in family patterns were set in motion.

As Hill (1960) has observed, in the years from 1890 to 1960 the proportion of American families subsisting from farming changed from almost one-half to less than one-tenth. As this change occurred, the primary pattern of family organization changed from an economic to a social model.

When the family ceased to function as an organization whose primary mission was the production of economic goods, the role of the father as a kind of "shop foreman" changed. The father left the home to earn the living. The economic self-sufficiency of the family broke down. The family became economically dependent upon the availability of jobs, and dependent on the society for an increasing variety of social services, including education for the children.

The role variability of women within and outside the family increased rapidly. As the father spent most of his waking hours outside the home, the mother assumed increasing responsibility for decision making of all kinds. In situations where the father's earning capacity was low, the mother more and more frequently left the home to augment the family income through outside work.

The result of the breakdown of the family as a self-contained, nearly independent economic unit has been the gradual emergence of a new model upon which to sustain family cohesion. Some sociologists term this family pattern the "conjugal family" (Goode, 1971) or the "companionship model" (Burgess & Locke, 1945).

In this model, the old unifying forces of paternal authority, rigid discipline, and economic necessity tended to be replaced by cohesive factors inherent in the interpersonal relationships among family members. Mutual affection, sympathetic understanding, emotional support, and comradeship became the central cohesive factors in the family.

The focus within this family pattern is on the optimum development of family members, rather than on the accumulation of material wealth for its own sake or even the establishment of some minimum degree of economic security. This contemporary model of marriage and family has tended to work well in middle- and upper-class groups where levels of formal education and economic affluence are relatively high. Divorce rates of college educated people are about one-half those of people with grammar school educations and are lowest of all among professional workers (Hill, 1960).

Along with the shift to the companionship model have been trends in numbers and spacing of children which have further reduced sex role differences in marriage. As the number of children in the family declines, and as the arrival of children tends increasingly to be confined to the early years of marriage, more and more wives resume career patterns that are interrupted rather than terminated by marriage and childbearing (Useem, 1960).

These changes have resulted in an increasing democratization of family life in which roles and responsibilities within the marriage tend to be shared on a flexible and dynamic partnership basis. Clear-cut lines of sex role-appropriate behavior become increasingly blurred. Mother washes the car as well as the dishes, dresses appropriately in masculine garb, and often uses a vocabulary appropriate to the frustrations of the task.

Marriage within this model is thus viewed increasingly as a kind of joint career for which preparation can provide the skills and insights necessary for success. The index of the quality of marriage within this model appears to be the mutual contribution the marriage makes to the development of the marital partners. The degree of matching that is maintained in the rate and direction of this mutual development is also a vital factor. The simple test of this matching factor is probably in what, and how, husband and wife communicate.

The focus in this family model, then, is upon the quality of an interpersonal relationship and the interpersonal skills of communication necessary to develop and to maintain it. As marital partners develop their marriage around such relationships, they are also fundamentally redefining the way in which the family assumes responsibility for the development of its children. The modern family's contribution to the educational development of the child lies primarily in the area of human relations training. The conjugal family has largely given up the formalized "vocational training" role that characterized family functioning as an economic unit. Parents are likely to be aware that they can contribute little to the direct job training of a child in the vastly complex and changing industrial world.

Within the companionship or conjugal model, however, parents are undertaking once again to prepare the child for the world of work, not by instructing him in technical skills, but in helping him develop competence in the area of interpersonal relations. Such parents, often by virtue of their own patterns of marital interaction, are aware that their children must learn to be sensitive to the nuances of interpersonal relationships in order to function in the large and complex organizations of industry, business, and government.

The conjugal family at its best, then, is a vitally important crucible within which the vocational development of the child occurs. The fact that interpersonal skills are vital to the vocational success of workers in almost every field is well known. The conjugal family places greatest emphasis on preparing children to "get along" with others. It provides human relations role models for children in terms of the communication patterns existent between mother and father, and helps establish aspirations to seek out opportunities for deeply involving relationships in both career and marriage. The family model of a relationship in which mutual growth and development is the primary goal helps provide the aspiration to see careers as a similar kind of vehicle for self-actualization, rather than merely a means of providing economic security.

The conjugal model of marriage and family is not, of course, free of problems. Its very focus on the quality of human relationships may serve to deny important values of individual freedom and creativity. Much of the socialization emphasis in this family model may be placed upon external and in some ways superficial patterns of interpersonal behavior. Cleanliness, grooming, acceptability of language patterns, control and even constriction of impulses and spontaneity may become values that are constantly impressed upon the growing child. Any behavior that can be seen as socially abrasive, however honest, may be inhibited.

The central ethic of this kind of socialization process too often becomes the one epitomized by the ubiquitous deodorant commercial, "Thou shalt not offend thy neighbor." In the face of this kind of preoccupation with interpersonal acceptability, rather than interpersonal involvement, important values of honesty, caring, and empathy may well be obscured. The reaction of adolescents to this superficiality has been beautifully illustrated in the intergenerational warfare of our times. The long-haired "unantiseptic" flower child has almost perfectly captured the antithesis of the socialization goals of many middle-class families and in doing so has accomplished a masterpiece of passive resistance, but often at a terrible cost to his own acceptance and freedom in society.

Where the conjugal model is not externalized and does not focus solely on surface level values, it does provide for a kind of affective development not readily available elsewhere in a depersonalized, emotionally malnourished society. The increasing incidence of experimentation among young people with communal or other multi-partner marriage models indicates their impatience with the failures that they perceive in the most superficial applications of the companionship model and, ultimately, their repudiation of the model Mead (1971).

The conjugal family is a small, nuclear unit centered almost entirely in the marriage relationship. The decline of kinship as an important factor in American family life is well known. The extended family which includes close relationships and common living arrangements between generations and across broad family constellations is an increasing rarity in middle-class America. The nuclear family of husband, wife, and children is particularly adapted to high degrees of geographic, social, and economic mobility. This kind of family is free to move where opportunity exists, and its upward social aspirations are not tied to those which are residual to a previous generation or to the status levels of the least successful or lowest aspiring relatives. One reason that education is so highly valued in the conjugal family is that it is seen as a primary vehicle for upward mobility, and the horizons of this family are not limited by the achievements, or lack thereof, of past generations or contemporary relations.

The conjugal or companionship model of family organization is, then, designed to facilitate the development of its members through a network of close interpersonal relationships. Its primary goal is not the accumulation of material wealth, but the nurturance of members exposed to the frequently dehumanizing effects of a complex and impersonal urban society. This family model provides great freedom and mobility for its members when it functions optimally. Since its sole anchor is the marital relationship, however, its members are extremely vulnerable to any disruption in that relationship.

One very important consideration must be attached to this discussion of change in American family life. The data on which the development of the conjugal model is based have been gathered in studies of middle-class families. Mirra Komarovsky (1962), in one of the relatively few comprehensive studies of marriage and family relationships among working-class people, points out that many of the trends that define the companionship or conjugal family are not so apparent in working-class marriages. Among the latter, patterns of verbal communication between husband and wife are much more limited and relatively impoverished. The extended family is more important. Wives tend to seek advice from female relatives more frequently. Recreational and social activities are less frequently heterosexual in nature. Quite generally, marital partners meet fewer of their needs in the marriage relationship than do middle-class partners. Gans (1962) describes similar phenomena in his classic study, *The Urban Villagers.*

The difference between working-class cultures in respect to the emergence of the companionship model in marriage is even more striking in studies of lower-class black families. Jessie Bernard (1966) mentions that the movement toward the conjugal model has in fact been almost precisely reversed in patterns of family organization among lower-class groups. A study of what Bernard terms the "marriage trajectory" indicates that, in the ghetto culture, proportionately fewer and fewer families are organized around stable long-term marital relationships.

The implications of those striking differences between the norms for family organization and functioning between the predominantly middle-class society and increasingly alienated groups are great. When these differences are still further intensified by minority group membership, the pressures toward alienation are indeed profound (Gans, 1968). Among the implications of such differences are the effects which they have on the vocational development of young people (Himes, 1964; Wilcox, 1972).

As noted previously, the contemporary family at all strata of society is relatively incapable of providing vocational preparation of a technical nature. Such preparation is necessarily one of those services which must be provided outside the home. In those family situations where the conjugal family model functions well, however, children are being provided with an invaluable kind of vocational preparation that immeasurably enhances their vocational development. In such families children grow and develop in the midst of a network of human relationships characterized by high levels of personal investment and ego-involvement. They internalize expectations and aspirations that encompass a future filled with similar kinds of relationships with attendant satisfactions. Such aspirations apply to both career and marriage. These children do not find it difficult to envision themselves making lifelong commitments of the most deeply ego-involving nature in both career and marriage. Their levels of aspiration for themselves are unfettered by the negative experiences of economically and socially unsuccessful relatives. They are extremely mobile geographically and feel free to seek out opportunity wherever it may be found. Narrow perceptions of sex role-appropriate behaviors do not limit their occupational values or stereotypes. Boys from such families can readily aspire to careers in the arts or social services, while girls are increasingly able to envision careers in science and engineering (McClelland, 1967).

Conversely, however, millions of young people in our society develop within family patterns which do not share these characteristics. In middle-class families where death, divorce, or extended separations have occurred, children may be extremely vulnerable emotionally because of lack of support from an extended family or even a stable neighborhood environment. Where the middle-class family has obsessively pushed superficial values of externalized acceptability, it has produced a generation of rebels, with a deeply felt but dimly articulated sense of the hypocrisy and injustices they have experienced. Lower-class children, particularly those from minority groups, frequently do not experience or even observe close, stable, and long-term interpersonal relationships of any kind. Children from these homes have available few, if any, models of commitment or involvement to career or family. Verbal communication patterns, particularly on the level of affect, are absent or impoverished. Heterosexual interactions in recreation are limited, and sex-appropriate roles are sharply differentiated. Aspiration levels are often tied to the experiences of the least adequate members of an extended family or decaying neighborhood. Because of ties to the extended family, geographical mobility may involve great emotional trauma unless some contact with relatives can be maintained.

For both the alienated lower-class and the rebellious middle-class youngsters, few family resources exist to enhance vocational development. Social and educational services aimed at equipping such children for adequate vocational functioning cannot assume that the family has developed in these children the same kinds of interpersonal and communication skills or the same kinds of attitudes and aspirations toward work, institutionalized authority, or personal responsibility as those which are transmitted in the most successful middle-class families (Kvaraceus, Gibson, & Curtin, 1967).

The Changing Role of Women

Another extremely important aspect of social change already alluded to in this discussion concerns changes in the role opportunities and prescriptions for women in contemporary American society. Part of this change stems from the current patterns of family size and spacing of children in that society. Control of and planning for conception have become a middle-class cultural norm. As this kind of control is exercised, role prescriptions for women that evolved purely as a product of their childbearing functions are rapidly giving way. More women are completing their childbearing in the early years of marriage. This, coupled with a tendency to marry at earlier ages, has produced a dramatic change in the career patterns and possibilities for married women. For increasing thousands of young women the choice is no longer between family and career, but toward alternatives involving complex career patterns which combine marriage and family responsibilities with very real, if interrupted, commitments to vocational opportunities outside the home (Epstein, 1971).

For many women, the articulation of these kinds of serial career patterns will involve continuous vocational planning if they are to reach optimum levels of satisfaction and contribution. Educational planning for such women will involve critical attention to flexibility and storability of vocational skills and understandings.

Perhaps of even greater impact on the role of women than changes in childbearing patterns has been the breakdown of cultural taboos that have long limited the vocational opportunities of women in our society. Factors such as industrialization, urbanization and suburbanization, and geographic and social mobility, as well as changes in marriage and family patterns, have finally weakened traditionally arbitrary and irrational attitudes toward roles of women. Rigid sex role differentiations based more on tribal lore than on twentieth century reality are finally crumbling in ways that are vastly expanding the social, political, and vocational opportunity structure available to women. The result for society will be the release of a vast reservoir of untapped human resources. The result for both men and women will be a broadening of career opportunities and the chance to plan a career on the basis of valid individual differences rather than sex mythology (Epstein & Goode, 1971).

These cultural changes are obviously not occurring without stresses and strains. Militant groups of women are demanding more rapid acceleration of changes in opportunities. Other groups of both men and women are threatened by the pace of changes already occurring (Millet, 1970).

A vocational guidance enterprise truly committed to the optimum fulfillment of human potential and satisfaction must help to move the society through the transition toward full vocational opportunity and commitment for women. Vocational guidance must make available help to individual women to develop the kinds of life styles and vocational commitments that will enhance their own actualization and development. At the same time vocational guidance must help the society rid itself of primitive and irrational attitudes that impede the implementation of such life styles for both men and women.

Changing Opportunities for Minority Groups

Another vastly important process under way in contemporary American society is the revolution in human rights. This major restructuring of the society is, of course, centered around the struggle of black Americans to assert their fundamental rights of citizenship. It is far from limited to that struggle, however. The total movement is resulting in marked changes in relationships between many different groups and the larger society. Minority groups such as American Indians, Puerto Ricans, and Mexican-

Americans are also profoundly affected. All of those Americans who dwell in the subcultures of rural and urban poverty are involved. That whole segment of American society which Michael Harrington (1962) referred to as "the Other America" is in the process of stirring restlessly in anticipation of long-awaited opportunities to actualize potentials as fully human beings. The opportunity structure within American society is expanding rapidly (although undoubtedly not rapidly enough) to include those who have long been shut out because of racial and ethnic prejudices, systematic deprivation of educational and cultural advantages, or geographical and social isolation (Wilcox, 1971).

As these new opportunities become realities, it is vitally important that means be found to communicate them to those who have long abandoned the will even to hope for a better life for themselves and their children (Lewis, 1966).

Major efforts at communication with socially alienated groups must be undertaken if the potentials inherent in the revolution in human rights are to be realized. This revolution in rights is a fragile one. Human rights must be exercised to be maintained. In the broadest terms the challenge to vocational guidance is to help individuals step through the opening doors of educational and vocational opportunity to the higher levels of human development that lie beyond.

Vocational guidance practitioners cannot remain neutral in any sense in this struggle for full opportunity. They must be willing to battle the forces that deny opportunity and dignity to any group. Active engagement in social issues is a heritage from the past that guidance cannot disown without forfeiting its very reason for existence (Stephens, 1970).

Vocational guidance is obviously very much in the center of the emerging dialogues between the "two Americas." There is great danger that vocational guidance will merely reflect the smug and unlistening attitudes of hypocrisy, paternalism, and self-righteousness that characterize much of the approach of white, middle-class America to black America and to other disadvantaged minority groups.

The role of vocational guidance with minorities is not to convert them into carbon copies of white, middle-class "virtue." It is rather to help these Americans to develop their own identities, their own unique talents, and their own values—and to help create a society that can accept, value, and utilize these talents to build a better America.

The first step for vocational guidance workers in beginning their encounters with minority groups is not merely to determine the kind of help that can be offered to those who are culturally different. The first step, rather, is for the professional to look at himself, his attitudes and his values, to determine the kind of help he may need in order to become a more sensitive, understanding, and committed person.

Until vocational guidance can enter into a two-way, mutually growth-producing dialogue between its own professionals and the members of culturally alienated groups, it will make little contribution to the development of a united and fully integrated society.

The Youth Culture

Age bases for differentiating subcultures, while often tacitly recognized in terms of norms for styles of dress and other age-appropriate behaviors, are usually not recognized at quite the same level of awareness as are other kinds of subcultural differences. Perhaps this is because, in a sense, the members of an age-defined subculture are merely "passing through" rather than permanently residing in the subculture.

Our society has, however, for a variety of reasons produced a highly visible youth culture that can hardly be ignored. Coleman (1961), in his classical study of the youth culture—or as he terms it, the "Adolescent Society"—believes that the complexity, mobility, and specialization inherent in our highly industrialized and urbanized society have made the youth cultural phenomenon inevitable. The essential characteristic of the youth culture as a social phenomenon is that the behavior of its members is more directly and influentially determined by dynamics operating from within it than by the social forces operating in the society at large.

Adolescence in all societies has, of course, long been noted as a particularly stormy stage of human development. Intergenerational conflict is probably as old as organized human society. Several factors, however, operate in contemporary society to aggravate problems of intergenerational communication.

According to Bernard (1961), the youth culture is predominantly a product of the affluent state of our society. Our society is wealthy enough to keep a rather high percentage of its youth together for a longer period of time and with a greater amount of leisure than any previous society. The close proximity of youth brought together within purely educational institutions for long periods of time, almost completely divorced from the mainstream of economic activity and in many ways cherished as visible objects of their elders' upward mobility and affluence, has given rise to many of the behavior patterns which define the subculture.

In many respects the youth culture—especially the elite element that determines the tastes, values, and mores of the total group—represents an affluent leisure class within the larger society that is excluded by law and custom from becoming economically productive, has little general responsibility for the maintenance of social values, and is expected to reflect the dream of contentment and well-being that sustains the mythology of an insecure and materialistic adult society.

When youth do not communicate contentment with, or appreciation for, their status as lapdogs of the adult society, they incur the wrath of that society. The battle of generations is often occasioned by the inability of adults to understand the restlessness and impatience that adolescents feel toward the contradictions and flaws they see in the adult society. Conflict is often generated by the total reversal of role expectations between generations. Instead of reducing the tensions and anxieties of a stressful adult world, adolescents become its severest critics.

One of the obvious factors that has given rise to the youth culture is its relative removal from the work activity that furnishes the principal structure for most adult life in our society. It is hardly remarkable that many of the distinctive values, tastes, and mores of the youth culture center around leisure activities. The youth culture is virtually defined by particular styles of dress and grooming, tastes in music and entertainment, paraphernalia for sports and recreation, and preferences for hangouts and activities. In fact, supplying the youth culture with its accoutrements—from cosmetics to surf boards—has become a major industry upon which the economy is heavily dependent.

The fixation with fun and games with which the youth culture is preoccupied is as much imposed by the adult society as it is chosen from within by youth themselves. Obviously, very many youth do work—some from economic necessity, some for additional spending money to maintain themselves in the status system, many from the realization that work experience is an invaluable part of the maturation process. Many youth are acutely aware of the value of work experience in providing the foundations for feelings of independence and self-worth, in learning to function in sex-appropriate roles, in achieving new relationships, and in learning socially responsible behaviors, as well as in selecting and preparing for an occupation.

Unfortunately, despite the fact that many young people strongly desire and seek out work opportunities, the society is often extremely ambivalent about affording them such opportunities. Except in times of war or other unusual economic activity, the employment of youth is generally not wanted. So-called child labor laws and other labor standards legislation, employment and union practices, and licensure procedures often contain provisions that systematically limit the work opportunities of young people. Such limitations are often imposed under the guise of welfare and protection, but are actually motivated by the desire to limit the competition of young people with older workers.

Further limitations occur because of negative and inaccurate stereotyping of young workers. From the standpoint of negative social stereotyping that limits opportunity, young people in our society constitute a minority group subject to bias and discrimination on at least as widespread a scale as that which confronts racial minorities. Typical stereotypes of the "teenager," which are widely disseminated in the mass media and apparently well-internalized in the middle-class adult population, exaggerate characteristics of impulsiveness, mood swing, and sexuality and almost totally ignore equally striking characteristics of psychological openness, willingness to make commitments, altruism, and industriousness that are present in the vast majority of youth.

Many youth want and need to be taken into partnership with the adult society. Their eagerness to participate in social action causes such as the Civil Rights Movement, VISTA, and the Peace Corps give ample evidence of this yearning for involvement. Vocationally, again many youth share the same values that motivate the adult population. They want psychologically meaningful and fulfilling jobs. They are also very much aware of the status and prestige hierarchies that are established around occupations.

In point of fact, most of the job opportunities that are available to youth are open precisely because they are unattractive to adults. Much of the menial, routine, and unattractive work, particularly in small business organizations and in industries such as food service and distributive concerns, is done by young people. That they are often very dissatisfied when their opportunities are limited to these kinds of jobs is merely proof that they have internalized the values of the larger society.

Young people need job opportunities that allow them to find some meaning in work, that allow them to experience and maintain appropriate levels of responsibility, and that give positive reinforcement to effective vocational behaviors. Vocational guidance must communicate such needs to the society.

One of the dangers inherent in the youth culture concept itself is that the youth culture shares the same kind of overgeneralization and oversimplification represented in social stereotyping generally. When we talk about "Youth," either as the product of a generational subculture or as a composite caricature of a set of distorted social perceptions, we obscure the many social and individual differences that remain vitally important to understanding them as individual human beings.

When we refer to "Youth" we must always define which group of youth we mean. The stability or meaning of trends in the adolescent and young adult population, no matter how dramatic they seem, is far from clear. The decade of the 1950s brought with it cries of alarm about the lack of adventure and idealism in "Youth." Pension plans, fringe benefits, vacation time, and material security were supposedly corrupting and defiling the idealism and social consciences of the young. Scarcely a decade later we heard the anguished screams of many of the same perennial critics about the irresponsibility and lack of commitment of the "dropout" generation.

Little real evidence exists to assess the permanence, direction, or significance of widely advertised but poorly analyzed trends among the young people of our society. The task of vocational guidance workers is to understand the social forces operating in the life space of adolescents without stereotyping them in terms of the overdramatized myths that permeate the adult society.

The Impact of Changing Values

Values are socially learned constructs through which people view events and assign meaning and significance to experiences. They encompass aesthetic, moral, ethical, and utilitarian or material dimensions. Values consequently become the navigational aids through which individuals and, to some extent, whole societies give direction to life. Values tend to activate human motivation, elicit commitment, and channel behavior. To a large degree, value judgments determine how people mobilize their resources to cope with or master the environment (Firth, 1970).

Consensus about basic values within a society is a powerful stabilizing factor that enhances group cohesiveness. Changes in value systems are inevitable, however, and represent desirable aspects of the society's capacity to cope with change. Social values are not timeless, but rather are culturally relative adaptations to the nature of the world as perceived by a given group of people at a particular point in time.

Typically in the history of human events, changes in social values have tended to proceed at rates which make them more or less inconspicuous to members of any single generation. For most generations the slow pace of social change has made possible the comforting illusion that their contemporary social values were universal and timeless, and that consensus was the norm among mature, right-thinking members of the society.

As social and technological changes have accelerated in recent years, and as travel and mass media of communication have disseminated and amplified the consequences of these changes, such comforting but naïve delusions about the permanence of values have been slowly eroded. Many traditionally accepted values have been challenged, and some have most certainly been replaced by emerging values better suited to the changing world as seen in contemporary perspective.

As intergroup and intergenerational differences become apparent, they tend to introduce stresses into the fabric of society. At the same time, they provide the ingredients for new and potentially more effective adaptations to environmental demands.

Many people tend to view with alarm all evidence that their own cherished values may be modified or swept aside in the process of social change. Vocational guidance is, of course, very directly concerned with values and changes in values. Those concerned with vocational guidance cannot afford to react to value changes with rigid defensiveness or automatic rejection, nor can they merely ignore such changes in the hope that they will go away.

Work Values

Profound changes in values are occurring in every segment of society and every phase of life. Not the least of these changes concerns values held in relation to work. The centrality of work as the primary source of self-esteem and personal identity is increasingly subject to challenge, particularly among blue-collar workers. The "Protestant Ethic" as the source for work morality has long been on the wane. As Murphy points out, work as a symbol of the expiation of original sin is hardly a belief compatible with contemporary attitudes. Similarly, the obvious relevance of work simply as a necessity for economic survival is, as Levenstein persuasively contends, simply not congruent with the facts of life in an increasingly automated economy, an affluent society, and a welfare state. (See chapters 4 and 5 by Aaron Levenstein and Gardner Murphy in this volume.)

As work-oriented value systems are no longer structured solely around either religious sanctions or economic necessity, the psychological aspects of man's relation to work become increasingly a determinant of the values through which he involves himself in work. Work is increasingly valued or devalued not in terms of a moral imperative to work, not alone as an unfortunate but necessary means for economic survival, but as a way of organizing life in some psychologically meaningful and need-fulfilling way.

Value systems relevant to work increasingly encompass dimensions of status, prestige, independence, power, dignity, and opportunity for satisfying interpersonal relationships. Increasingly, work tends to be valued in terms of its opportunities for facilitating optimal personal development of the worker. In many ways the institution of work has undergone a revolution similar to that previously discussed in relation to marriage. The economic survival motive is being replaced by a higher order need which, in Maslow's term, can be called "self-actualization."

The significance of psychologically relevant values in relation to work was described years ago by Caplow (1954), who pointed out that contemporary societal values tend to rate white-collar work, self-employment, and "clean" occupations as superior; to attach the importance of a business occupation to the size of the organization; and to regard personal service as degrading. Other psychologically relevant values embraced by contemporary society include the belief that the length of formal education required for a job is a direct indicator of its worth and that the number of people supervised is a measure of the importance of a job.

To some extent, such values may be socially adaptive in an economy that demands increasing technological specialization, organizational complexity, and interpersonal competence. For those who increasingly aspire to relate themselves to the world of work in psychologically fulfilling ways, however, risks of failure or perceived failure increase rapidly. When expectations for fulfillment from work are very high, many people are likely to experience frustration and defeat. A societal model of work as a means of self-actualization for all is an exceedingly ambitious one to fulfill.

Social critics like Paul Goodman (1960) have suggested that work in contemporary society is increasingly bereft of psychological meaning for a very large segment of the population. When the society installs a value system based upon an evaluation of work primarily in terms of its opportunity for psychological self-fulfillment, it creates a very high level of expectation. However, when large numbers of people in the society—because of cultural or educational deprivation or sheer lack of ego-involving jobs—are prevented from relating to work in psychologically meaningful ways, it is not surprising that work is devalued, commitment is kept minimal, and alienation from the world of work is profound.

We are presently confronted with a generation of young people who are increasingly challenging and questioning the predominant social values regarding work. Large numbers of these young people are "dropping out" of what they perceive as meaningless, degrading, and unfulfilling pursuits.

Often they seem unable to define or articulate (at least to their elders) the kinds of goals and aspirations to which they are willing to commit themselves. One of the crucial challenges of modern vocational guidance is to open genuine channels of communication with these young people and help them to articulate their *own* values and relate them to the world of work as it now exists; at the same time vocational guidance should attempt to help the society change that world to engage the energies and abilities of youth who seek ways of implementing emerging values and alternative life styles.

It seems of little use for vocational guidance, then, to array itself against the rising tide of vocational expectations generated in the society. Instead, tremendous challenge exists in the tasks of helping individuals learn to maximize their potential for obtaining self-fulfillment through work and of communicating in the society the urgency of restructuring work and work opportunities to provide the greatest possible source of psychological fulfillment to people from all walks of life. If contemporary work values are to become viable sources of cohesiveness rather than divisiveness within the society, that society must learn to organize the institution of work in ways that allow all members to relate to it in the broadest terms as a way of developing self-fulfillment through a valid social contribution.

What are the implications for vocational guidance of the social, cultural, and economic changes that have been discussed in the preceding pages? Are the concepts that have nourished and sustained vocational guidance in the past adequate for meeting the challenge of change? Will the epitaph of vocational guidance indeed be: "Born 1909; Died 1980 of Future Shock"?

The author's firm belief is that vocational guidance will indeed survive the decade of the seventies and can emerge healthier and more vital than ever before. Like all predictions, however, this one is based upon some key assumptions. The most central of these is that vocational guidance will be able to renew itself through the adoption of several basic substantive changes in its conceptual foundations. Fortunately a number of these changes are already well under way.

Implications for Vocational Guidance Strategies and Processes

One of the most influential and pervasive forces to influence the direction of vocational guidance concepts has been the steadily broadening emphasis which has expanded from providing assistance with specific vocational decisions to include concern with facilitating vocational development. The latter emphasis has been broadened from a narrow concern for working with youth only at that time period associated with school leaving and initial entry into the labor market, to include planned interventions at life stages ranging from preschool through retirement. Similarly, the thrust of vocational guidance processes has deepened in terms of the social and psychological dimensions with which these processes are concerned. For many years the recognition has been clear that vocational guidance interventions must necessarily be designed in terms of the total context of psychological characteristics and social backgrounds of individuals.

Just as education generally has been engaged in learning to think in terms of the "whole child," so has vocational guidance been confronted with the challenge of attempting to conceptualize its interventions and processes in terms that respect the psychosocial integrity of human experience, but in terms which are not so global and abstract as to lose all meaning at the level of practical application. As we attempt to conceptualize vocational guidance strategies and processes in terms of their impact upon human growth and human functioning, a number of conceptual tools appear to be useful for the facilitation of vocational development.

The Concept of Discontinuity

One of the primary principles that has been generated by contemporary behavioral science is that the process of human development represents a dynamic interaction between a set of biological tendencies inherent in the genetic structure of the organism and the cultural and social conditions present in its environment. In very simple, primitive societies, cultural influences may impinge on developing individuals at rates that closely approximate the biologically regulated processes which determine readiness for such cultural experiences. For example, preparation for economic self-sufficiency or work proceeds at approximately the same pace as the development of physical strength. As the child becomes physically able to perform work tasks in the family and society, he is given increasingly difficult and important responsibilities. Thus he experiences *continuity* between his physical and vocational development. In simple societies, biological clocks and cultural clocks keep the same time.

In complex industrial societies, however, there are many cultural clocks, none of which necessarily keeps the same time as the biological clocks that govern development. Nor do the various cultural clocks always agree with one another. Attaining adulthood in a Western industrial society, for example, is not a simple matter of the biological onset of puberty and an accompanying tribal ritual. Instead, the attainment of adult status is variously measured by a number of cultural timetables that are read in terms of measures such as school-leaving age, working age, marriage age, drinking age, driving age, military age, voting age, and a host of other even less standardized schedules, none of which is necessarily adjusted to the biological state of any particular individual (Drucker, 1969).

In industrialized societies, then, individuals experience *discontinuity* between aspects of their development. At various stages of development, discontinuity is virtually built into the biosocial interaction process. Entry into school, entry into the labor market, marriage, parenthood, and compulsory retirement are all examples of events which may be accompanied by great discontinuity and resulting psychological stress and maladaptive behaviors. Complex societies often build institutions aimed at reducing discontinuities and facilitating the smooth development of individuals. Obvious examples of such educational institutions are the kindergarten and the junior high school. Both were developed to bridge discontinuities between social expectations and biological readiness.

It is possible to conceptualize vocational guidance as another societal function aimed at reducing discontinuities in vocational development. Such discontinuities are the inevitable product of tremendously complex divisions of labor, rapid urbanization, and long periods of formal education. As we have seen, the modern family can contribute relatively little to the development of strictly vocational skills in a vastly complex industrial society. Many families are even unable to provide the kinds of environment in which children can learn positive attitudes toward work and the basic interpersonal skills necessary for effective work-related behaviors.

The youth culture, which is the dominant socialization agent in adolescence, is primarily leisure oriented, rather than work oriented. Entry into the world of work upon school leaving is thus frequently an event that introduces great discontinuity into the lives of young people. Rapid technological and social changes similarly inject discontinuities into the lives of older workers. Women who complete childbearing in their late twenties and who seek to resume careers in the labor market find the transition difficult in many ways. Middle-aged men find themselves displaced by technological changes or find their mobility reduced by hiring practices that exclude workers over 45 with little regard for either their capacity for continued productivity or their preparation for retirement. The tremendous rapidity of social change discussed in the first section of this chapter magnifies greatly the discontinuities faced by nearly everyone living in such a society.

When vocational guidance strategies are conceptualized in terms of bridging discontinuities, one psychologically relevant dimension involves the area of motivation. Motivation is, of course, the psychological construct that we use to explain purposeful or goal-directed behavior. No living organism is ever really unmotivated. Instead, what we term motivation is the ability to schedule need satisfactions in ways that maximize possibilities for attainment of high-priority goals. In a complex society, most need satisfactions are tied to a set of contingencies for behavior that must be met before gratifications can be obtained. Most of these contingencies involve some degree of gratification deferral. The ability to defer gratifications and to behave in a purposeful way that will lead to eventual gratification is *learned.* Infants obviously have little ability to defer gratifications. The motivational structure of the infant is, in the words of the popular song, "I Want What I Want When I Want It." Optimum vocational development obviously involves the acquisition of strong, yet flexible motivational structures that allow individuals to schedule gratifications in ways that will maximize their overall, long-term need fulfillment.

Many sharp discontinuities are built into the socialization of children as they develop—or fail to develop—effective motivational patterns. Some of these occur very early (in the family) in terms of child-rearing patterns with regard to weaning and toilet training. Many others occur outside the family, however, with entry into school, demands for attention and concentration in school work, entry into paid work, entry into high school and college, and so forth.

For some children, the discontinuities that are built into their development in regard to gratification deferral will be too great to be coped with effectively. For them, crippled educational skills, premature school leaving, and a job history of repeated failures may spell inadequate vocational development. Conversely, other individuals may be so "successful" in learning to defer gratifications in rigid and nonadaptive ways that they are unable to function effectively in marital and parental roles or to cope with the healthy use of leisure time or retirement.

Vocational guidance strategies and processes need to be geared to those cultural transition points where discontinuities are so great as to threaten optimum development. Such transition points can often be converted into settings for developmental crises which, when resolved, can lead to the development of new and higher levels of effectiveness. Fortunately, the society has begun to help some disadvantaged groups cope with extreme discontinuity by means of such programs as Head Start and the Job Corps. Vocational guidance processes conceptualized around goals of bridging discontinuities in development can facilitate smooth and healthy vocational development of individuals at all life stages.

The Concept of Life Stages

A key concept in the reformulation of vocational guidance processes involves the assignment of those events which define vocational development to a sequence of life stages, each characterized by a developmental theme that dominates the strivings of its particular period.

Central to the life-stages approach to human development is the notion that development in a complex, industrial society can never be completely smooth and continuous, but that the culture inevitably imposes a framework within which development is regulated and circumscribed. Thus, in a sense, the relevance of a life-stages approach is derived at least in part from the existence of discontinuities.

There have been many life-stage schemas proposed to elaborate the processes of development. The one chosen here has been more fully described by Blocher (1966). This particular schema analyzes development in five major stages, some of which are divided into substages. The life-stages approach assumes that one crucial dimension in individual differences is the age factor, and that behavior can be neither fully understood nor appropriately modified without reference to the life-stage context within which that behavior occurs.

The usefulness of a life-stages approach for formulating vocational guidance objectives and processes hinges heavily on the fact that each life stage involves characteristic *developmental tasks* which must be recognized, confronted, and met and mastered by the individual if future development is to proceed optimally. Havighurst (1953) defines developmental tasks in this way:

> A developmental task is a task which arises at or about a certain period in the life of the individual, successful achievement of which leads to his happiness and to success with later tasks, while failure leads to unhappiness in the individual, disapproval by the society and difficulty with later tasks [p. 2].

Many developmental tasks are obvious and simple to define. Learning to read, for example, is an obvious developmental task of education in the early elementary school years. Failure to achieve this task in this particular period is certain to increase the probability of failure with all kinds of later school-related tasks, with resulting personal unhappiness and social disapproval.

Much of the function of facilitating vocational development involves helping individuals identify and master developmental tasks related to the enhancement of vocational effectiveness. Unfortunately, far too little is presently known about the precise nature of key vocational development tasks at various life stages. Normative data on levels of vocational maturity at particular ages are sketchy. Knowledge about the nature of instrumental behaviors needed for vocational effectiveness is similarly lacking. Lines of research developed by Super and his associates (1963), Tiedeman and O'Hara (1963), Gribbons and Lohnes (1968), and Crites (1969) have begun to provide the kind of elaboration needed to define vocational guidance processes geared to the requirements of a truly developmental framework.

Havighurst (1964, p. 216) attempted to define the sequence of developmental tasks that eventuate in vocational maturity within a set of four central stages which are summarized in Table 1.

Obviously, we need to break down important developmental tasks into smaller and more specific units. We also need to understand more about the differences in developmental tasks imposed by differing socioeconomic and subcultural backgrounds, career patterns, and life styles. Even in our present state of incomplete knowledge, however, the concept of helping individuals master key developmental tasks is a useful one around which to conceptualize vocational guidance processes.

The Concept of Life Style

Another fundamental concept for formulating the nature of vocational guidance processes is that of life style. One of the basic factors in human behavior, systematically ignored by psychology, is that basic unity inheres in every human life. For many years the late Gordon Allport pleaded for the development of an idiographic psychology which could concern itself with the unities that describe an individual human life.

Robert White (1966) describes eloquently the need for the study of lives when he writes:

> Much as we have come to know about personality, there is a serious gap at the very center of the subject. Individual lives moving forward normally amid natural circumstances have received almost no systematic study and have played almost no part in our current understanding. . . . The psychologist . . . has almost never studied ordinary people as they increase their mastery of the ordinary problems of daily life. . . . The natural growth of personality and the higher flights of human achievement have been given poor representation in man's current ideas about himself [p. 2].

Vocational guidance is concerned very directly and very immediately with the study of ordinary human lives. Vocational guidance processes have relevance only as they influence and contribute to such lives. The concept of life style, then, refers to the unique combination of values, choices, strategies, mechanisms, and behavior patterns through which the individual establishes personal goals and both copes with stress in, and strives for mastery over, his environment.

The concept of styles of coping was introduced by Lois Murphy (1962) in the study of children's reactions to difficult or stressful situations. She found that individual children tended to develop distinctive styles or strategies for coping with problematic situations. In our usage, the concept of coping is extended to include mastery-oriented behaviors that are intended to establish control over the environment as well as to protect the individual from stress.

Kroeber (1964, pp. 178–198) defines coping behaviors as patterns used by active, effective people in dealing with biological, psychological, or social demands presented in their environment. Since vocational guidance processes are aimed at helping people relate work to life styles that are satisfying and effective, coping and mastery behaviors are in a real sense the potential

Table 1
Vocational Development: A Lifelong Process

Stages of Vocational Development	Ages
I. *Identification with a Worker* Father, mother, other significant persons. The concept of working becomes an essential part of the ego-ideal.	5–10
II. *Acquiring the Basic Habits of Industry* Learning to organize one's time and energy to get a piece of work done. School work, chores. Learning to put work ahead of play in appropriate situations.	10–15
III. *Acquiring Identity as a Worker in the Occupational Structure* Choosing and preparing for an occupation. Getting work experience as a basis for occupational choice and for assurance of economic independence.	15–25
IV. *Becoming a Productive Person* Mastering the skills of one's occupation. Moving up the ladder in one's occupation.	25–40

products of vocational guidance. At the upper limits of human performance, life styles are characterized by what Gardner Murphy terms "progressive mastery" (see Chapter 5 by Gardner Murphy in this volume). That is, the life style leads to a process by which engagement in complex tasks or activities produces progressively greater control over, or appreciation of, the phenomenon which is being explored or manipulated. The process itself becomes intrinsically rewarding because each successive level of mastery unveils new and hitherto unsuspected mysteries and challenges. Without such a concept, the motivation that sustains many individuals in a lifetime devoted to the pursuit of a particular goal is hardly understandable.

The Concept of Life Space

Most human behavior can be understood only in terms of its interaction with other significant individuals and with social groups. Each human being lives and grows in a world of psychological as well as physical space. Psychological space is described by a geography whose rivers and mountains are constituted by interpersonal roles and relationships.

The social and interpersonal interactions of people help to define their life space and determine the nature of the transactions that they conduct with the environment. The life space of a street corner gang of angry and alienated young delinquents is as different from the life space of the group attending the Rotary Club luncheon as the environment of an astronaut landing on the moon is from that of a golfer playing the front nine at a Palm Springs country club.

To be relevant to the full range of human beings in a vast, complex, and highly diversified society, vocational guidance processes must be able to navigate the life space of human beings whose social group memberships and social roles vary tremendously. Calia (1966) points out that traditional conceptualizations of counseling processes are often inappropriate for work with those whom we rather self-righteously term the "culturally deprived." Guidance and counseling processes based

Table 2
Principal Developmental Tasks and Coping Behaviors by Life Stages

Life Stages	Social Roles	Developmental Tasks	Coping Behaviors
Infancy (Birth–3 years)	Love-object roles; receiving and pleasing	Trust: Learning to eat solid food and feed self, control elimination, manipulate objects, walk, explore immediate environment, communicate, relate to family, accommodate to a daily life rhythm.	Approaching Receiving Accepting
Early Childhood (3–6 years)	Sibling, playmate, sex-appropriate roles	Autonomy: Sense of Separateness: Developing sense of self, sense of mutuality, realistic concepts of world. Learning to be a boy or girl, manage aggression and frustration, follow verbal instructions, pay attention, become independent.	Approaching Receiving Accepting
Later Childhood (6–12 years)	Student, helper, big brother, or big sister roles	Initiative-Industry: Learning to read and calculate, value self and be valued, delay gratification, control emotional reactions, deal with abstract concepts, give self to others, formulate values.	Environmental-mastering Value-relevant Work-relevant
Organization Early Adolescence (12–14 years)	Peer roles, Hetero-sexual roles	Identity Development: Learning to be masculine or feminine, belong in various relationships, control impulses, be positive toward work, study, organize time, develop relevant value hierarchy.	Social Sex-appropriate Achievement-oriented
Later Adolescence (15–19 years)	Peer roles, Hetero-sexual roles	Identity as a Potential Worker: Learning to move from group to individual relationship, achieve emotional autonomy, produce in work situations.	Reciprocal Cooperating Mutuality

Exploration Young Adulthood (20–30 years)	Marriage roles, Career roles	Intimacy and Commitment: Generativity: Learning to commit self to goals, career, partner; be adequate parent; give unilaterally.	Sexual Risk-taking Value-consistent
Realization (30–50 years)	Leadership, helping, creative, accomplishment roles	Ego-integrity: Learning to be inner-directed, be interdependent, handle cognitive dissonance, or be flexible and effective emotionally, develop creative thought processes, develop effective problem-solving techniques.	Objectivity, intellectual, logical analysis, concentration, empathy, tolerance of ambiguity, playfulness, sublimation, substitution, suppression
Stabilization (50–65 years)	Leadership, helping, managing, creative, accomplishment, authority, prestige roles	Learning to be aware of change, have attitude of tentativeness, develop broad intellectual curiosity, develop realistic idealism, develop time perspective.	Change-oriented Value-relevant Sensitivity
Examination (65 + years)	Retirement roles Nonworker roles Nonauthority roles	Learning to cope with death, cope with retirement, affiliate with peers, cope with reduced physical vigor, cope with changed living conditions, use leisure time, care for the aging body.	Affiliative Productive leisure time Personal enhancement

upon the concept of self-referral as the only possible framework for initiating contacts, or upon a belief in self-exploration through passive, sedentary talk as the only model for learning about oneself, may be hopelessly inadequate to the challenges confronted by vocational guidance.

Table 2 represents an attempt at synthesizing life stage, life style, and life space dimensions in terms of their relevance to developmental counseling.

Vocational guidance processes should be geared to take advantage of the best that exists in traditional practices, and should also involve a willingness to venture beyond those practices to build broader and more powerful technologies for enhancing human effectiveness. For example, vocational guidance processes must go beyond a technology built around traditional theories of insight-oriented counseling. Such processes have shown promising, but very limited, potentials for effectiveness, even with middle-class clientele. Vocational guidance should be ready to move beyond the present state of counseling theory to explore the relevance of other technologies. It is useless to undertake programs aimed at providing sophisticated levels of understanding about groups of people who vary widely on life stage, life style, and life space dimensions unless we also undertake to create intervention processes that are flexible enough to encompass the differences in needs and characteristics revealed by such understandings.

A Two-dimensional Model of Vocational Guidance Processes

As an example of efforts to expand the conceptualization of vocational guidance processes, a two-dimensional model of intervention with two or more options in each dimension is presented here. This model obviously represents an initial and tentative step in the effort to expand process concepts which might better meet the needs of the full range of social, cultural, and individual differences.

The two-dimensional model is articulated in terms of (*a*) "direct interventions" and (*b*) "indirect interventions."

Direct Intervention

The direct intervention has traditionally been associated with the counseling interview. As usually conceived, it has involved the establishment of a direct relationship between counselor and client which is presumed therapeutic and which typically involves talk about the client's behavior, with at least a partial focus upon self-exploration.

There is no attempt here to deprecate the importance of vocational counseling models of intervention. Recent research and conceptualizations about counseling interventions (Carkhuff, 1972) represent promising developments for the improvement of counseling effectiveness. Individual counseling, however, is no longer the sole model within which vocational guidance processes can be conceptualized, nor is individual counseling even necessary for the most potent or viable kind of intervention in every situation.

In recent years much new knowledge about group dynamics has generated the development of group counseling models that may offer potentials for changing human behavior which at times exceed those of individual counseling models. Group models are no longer conceived merely as less expensive substitutes for individual counseling whose choice is dictated by reasons of cost or other expediencies. Instead, the harnessing of powerful dynamics for change that exist within group interactions makes group procedures very promising models of intervention.

Another model of direct intervention that has always existed, but which has been generally neglected, is the teaching process itself. Many of the goals of vocational guidance can be implemented by teachers within the formal curriculum. Vocational guidance processes that do not include teaching within the formal curriculum ignore the single most extensive educational medium available. Almost every area of the formal curriculum can deal with vocationally relevant learning experiences. Such experiences are centered upon both the "cognitive" and "affective" domains of curriculum. Vocational guidance processes should permeate rather than proliferate the curriculum. Rather than relying solely on courses or units in occupational information, vocational guidance needs to identify and explicate the vocational relevance of every course and unit in the formal curriculum. Teachers can be helped to recognize and implement their roles as workers in facilitating vocational development to the same degree that they are committed to facilitating other aspects of cognitive or emotional growth and maturity. Such an involvement of vocational guidance with basic educational processes is not an abdication of responsibility for providing specialized services, but rather is an extension of such services.

Indirect Intervention

The second dimension of vocational guidance processes is termed an "indirect" dimension. There are many important and legitimate vocational guidance processes that do not involve direct, face-to-face contacts with clients.

One aspect of this dimension is somewhat analogous to the mental health concept of "milieu therapy." Vocational guidance personnel can make substantial contributions to the sound vocational development of individuals by addressing their efforts to the improvement of school, family, and community environments. The vocational guidance worker—acting as a consultant or agent of change within the school, family, or community—can often produce results of far greater impact than those to be gained through hours of direct intervention with clients.

Examples of important indirect interventions include the development of part-time work experiences through work-study and cooperative vocational education programs, the implementation of volunteer work experience opportunities, and the establishment of programs of continuing and adult education. The provision of stimulating summer employment opportunities, efforts to eliminate arbitrary or irrational entry requirements in employment, assistance in the transition from school to job and constant vigilance to combat discrimination in hiring practices or exploitation of youth in fraudulent training programs are similar instances.

The full scope of vocational guidance activities must also be conceptualized to include large-scale interventions in the society in the form of public information programs through the mass media, efforts to influence legislation and administration at all levels of government, and efforts to improve the articulation and coordination of inter-agency and inter-professional relationships.

Goals for the "New Vocational Guidance"

What are the goals of a vocational guidance enterprise founded upon the ideas described in this chapter? Several can be identified rather clearly at this point:

a. Helping all individuals become more aware of the vocational alternatives available to them at particular stages of their development and to understand the probable consequences of those alternatives.

b. Helping all individuals to achieve a satisfying vocational identity that allows them to relate a productive work life to an acceptable life style.

c. Helping all individuals to acquire a set of work-relevant coping and mastery behaviors that enable them to engage the world with dignity, self-esteem, independence, and effectiveness.

d. Helping the total society to conceive of and organize the institution of work in ways that satisfy legitimate human needs in fully human ways.

e. Helping the total society to build an opportunity structure that is devoid of racial, ethnic, sexual, and social prejudice and that is based upon recognition of the talent and potential inherent in all its members.

The goals defined above may seem grandiose, pretentious, or utopian. The adjective "all" has been used frequently and with intent. As we have seen, the rate of social and technological change within our own culture has accelerated with unprecedented speed. Vocational guidance must react to the challenge of change and the rising tide of human expectations with a healthy idealism tempered with continuous testing of reality.

As the philosophical and theoretical foundations of the movement have expanded to reflect new conditions and needs, and as the field broadens its concerns, the roles and competencies of professional workers inevitably grow. The career guidance function is now seen to pervade the work of many professionals in the helping occupations. Old roles and relationships must be reevaluated and new concepts and definitions provided.

In terms of this need for reconceptualization, the following framework for viewing a new vocational guidance is proposed:

Vocational guidance is a broad social function concerned with applying scientific knowledge and human understanding toward the development of social processes and individual learning experiences. Its purpose is to promote the maximum realization of human potential for social contribution and self-fulfillment through work. Vocational guidance seeks to contribute to the effective functioning of a society which attempts to provide opportunities for all its members to meet material and psychological needs in socially constructive ways. It is intended to help individuals relate themselves to work within the framework of a life style that is personally satisfying, socially constructive, and economically productive. Since each individual interacts with his particular social, cultural, and physical environment in a unique way, vocational guidance recognizes that work will not have the same meaning, nor even the same centrality, for human beings with differing needs, perceptions, and characteristics. The concerns, processes, and functions of vocational guidance are defined by the total range of human needs and problems within the society, and by the state of development of supporting sciences and disciplines.

REFERENCES

Bernard, J. Teen-age culture—an overview. In J. Bernard (Ed.), *Teen-age culture.* Philadelphia: American Academy of Political and Social Science, 1961.

Bernard, J. *Marriage and family among Negroes.* Englewood Cliffs, New Jersey: Prentice-Hall, 1966.

Blocher, D. H. *Developmental counseling.* New York: Ronald Press, 1966.

Burgess, E. W., & Locke, H. J. *The family: From institution to companionship.* New York: American Book, 1945.

Calia, V. The culturally deprived client: A reformation of the counselor's role. *Journal of Counseling Psychology,* 1966, **13,** 100–105.

Caplow, T. *The sociology of work.* Minneapolis: University of Minnesota Press, 1954.

Carkhuff, R. The development of systematic human resource development models. *The Counseling Psychologist,* 1972, **3** (3), 4–11.

Coleman, J. *The adolescent society.* Glencoe, Illinois: Free Press, 1961.

Crites, J. O. *The maturity of vocational attitudes in adolescence.* Iowa City, University of Iowa, 1969.

Drucker, P. F. *Age of discontinuity: Guidelines to our changing society.* New York: Harper & Row, 1969.

Epstein, C. F. *Woman's place: Options and limits in professional careers.* Chicago: University of California Press, 1971.

Epstein, C. & Goode, W. (Ed.), *Other half: Roads to women's equality.* Englewood Cliffs, N.J.: Prentice-Hall, 1971.

Firth, R. Essays on social organization and values. *Monographs on Social Anthropology,* 1970, No. 28.

Gans, H. J. *People and plans: Essays on urban problems and solutions.* New York: Basic Books, 1968.

Gans, H. J. *The urban villagers.* New York: Free Press, 1962.

Goode, W. J. *World revolution and family patterns.* New York: Free Press, 1963.

Goodman, P. *Growing up absurd.* New York: Random House, 1960.

Gribbons, W. D., & Lohnes, P. R. *Emerging careers.* New York: Teachers College Press, Columbia University, 1968.

Harrington, M. *The other America.* Baltimore: Penguin, 1962.

Havighurst, R. J. *Human development and education.* New York: Longmans, Green, 1953.

Havighurst, R. J. Youth in exploration and man emergent. In H. Borow (Ed.), *Man in a world at work.* Boston: Houghton Mifflin, 1964.

Hill, R. The American family today. In E. Ginzberg (Ed.), *The nation's children.* Vol. 1. *The family and social change.* New York: Columbia University Press, 1960.

Himes, J. S. Some work-related cultural deprivations of lower-class Negro youths. *Journal of Marriage and the Family,* 1964, **26,** 447–449.

Kahn, H., & Wiener, A. *The year two-thousand: A framework for speculation in the next thirty-three years.* New York: Macmillan, 1967.

Keniston, K. *The uncommitted.* New York: Dell, 1970.

Komarovsky, M. *Blue-collar marriage.* New York: Random House, 1962.

Kroeber, L. C. The coping functions of the ego mechanism. In R. H. White (Ed.), *A study of lives.* New York: Atherton Press, 1964.

Kvaraceus, W. C., Gibson, J. S., & Curtin, T. J. *Poverty, education and race relations.* Boston: Allyn and Bacon, 1967.

Lewis, O. *Vida: a Puerto Rican Family in the culture of poverty, San Juan and New York.* New York: Random House, 1966.

McClelland, D. C. The *achieving society.* New York: Free Press, 1967.

Mead, M. *Family.* New York: Macmillan, 1971.

Millet, K. *Sexual politics.* Garden City, New York: Doubleday, 1970.

Murphy, L. *The widening world of childhood.* New York: Basic Books, 1962.

Rice, B. Down and out along route 128. New York *Times.* November 1, 1970.

Stephens, R. *Social reform and the origins of vocational guidance.* Washington, D.C.: National Vocational Guidance Association, 1970.

Super, D. E., Starishevsky, R., Matlin, N., & Jordan, J. P. *Career development: Self-concept theory.* New York: College Entrance Examination Board, 1963.

Tiedeman, D. V., & O'Hara, R. P. *Career development: Choice and adjustment.* New York: College Entrance Examination Board, 1963.

United States Department of Labor. *Manpower report of the President.* Washington, D.C.: United States Government Printing Office, 1970.

Useem, R. H. Changing cultural concepts in women's lives. *Journal of the National Association of Women Deans and Counselors,* 1960, **24,** 29–34.

White, R. W. *Lives in progress.* (2nd ed.) New York: Holt, Rinehart and Winston, 1966.

Wilcox, R. (Ed.) Psychological consequences of being a black American: A collection of research by black psychologists. New York: Wiley, 1971.

3

the name and nature of vocational guidance

MARTIN R. KATZ
Educational Testing Service

In his 1957 standard work, *The Psychology of Careers,* Donald Super presented a convincing case against long-established but obsolescing conceptions of vocational guidance, and he proposed a new definition which emphasized the developmental, insight broadening, and reality testing functions of the occupational helping relationship. What new problems and challenges are posed by the sweep of recent economic and social history? In Chapter 3, Martin Katz constructs a meticulously detailed reinterpretation of vocational guidance set against both the national forces which spawned and nourished it and the perplexities of today's fluid world of work.

Noting that there must first be options and that individuals must then be free to choose among them, Katz declares that the principal objective of guidance is "to foster freedom and competence." Having thus framed his target, he moves to a methodical analysis of the substance of vocational guidance, although aims and content are obviously intertwined. The content of the field may be specified in the form of a "curriculum for vocational guidance." Katz's curriculum begins with the person's appreciation of his own responsibility for making career choices and then moves on to embrace an array of understandings and skills prerequisite to rational decision making.

On the problem of nomenclature, Katz concedes that the term "career guidance" has the virtue of comprehensiveness in relating to a variety of work and nonwork choice situations, but he prefers to retain the historically rooted "vocational guidance." While terms like vocation, occupation, job, and position are often used loosely and interchangeably, Katz finds utility in preserving the connotative distinctions among them. "Vocation," either in its original sense of a spiritual calling or its more recently acquired flavor of a secular calling, should be reserved for the work of those who have a profound commitment to it, who have relatively great autonomy in performing it, and who derive feelings of importance from it and find it intrinsically rewarding. An "occupation" requires specialized training and personal application but involves less autonomy, stability, and self-fulfillment. "Employment" refers to Havighurst's society-maintaining work, involving little emotional attachment, no special skill, and few intrinsic rewards. The work life styles of individuals in the three categories differ dramatically, a reality of which both the counselor and his client must be aware.

While the strong positive values which have generally been thought to inhere in work since the Reformation may be eroding, and certainly they cannot be claimed to hold for those groups who have been denied opportunity for upward socioeconomic mobility through career, work as a mechanism for improving one's social class status has still been powerful enough, Katz concludes, to function as "a major tenet of the American ethic." Thus, vocational training and vocational guidance programs have had significant roles to play in times of national crisis and dislocation—the depression of the 1930s, World War II and the ensuing period of peace immediately beyond, the post-Sputnik years, and the War on Poverty in the 1960s. In the last-named instance, Katz reminds us that the nation, in effect, waged a war on nonwork. The continuing clamor for welfare reform inevitably carries the stipulation that the economically disenfranchised be restored to productive status in society by means of work incentive programs.

The unstable nature and growing complexities of the world of work now make the task of vocational guidance difficult but hardly lessen its importance. Increasing numbers of workers must anticipate serial careers rather than single-job work histories. It is the task of guidance to help equip them to prepare for and accommodate change. Many youths now question the relevance of work to personal values. Yet, vocational guidance potentially has a service to render them, since most of the options which the counterculture considers meaningful are still within its content range. Perhaps the most formidable problem of all centers on the distressing incompatibility between available jobs in the present economy and the needs and values of job applicants. Is there a solution? Katz suggests there is, and he raises it in the form of a bold question of his own—"cannot . . . society create vocations and occupations that emphasize individual values even at the expense of economic values?"

H. B.

Charting the Terrain: An Explication

Participation in vocational guidance is structured into two roles: one participant, the counselor, helps another, the client. While the persons cast in these two roles have important speaking parts, they are by no means the only actors: the client's parents, teachers, ministers, friends, relatives, employers, fellow students, fellow workers, and so on also have featured parts—to say nothing of assorted spear-carriers comprising, literally, a cast of thousands. Each member of this cast is the star of his own show, but as in a good repertory company everyone is prepared to accept a supporting role in the drama of every other person's career development. (Or almost everyone. Now and then someone cast in a subordinate role—for example, parent—succeeds in stealing a scene or two, and may even dominate the whole play.)

The part of the counselor varies greatly in importance from one play to another. Sometimes, he may play the "second lead." Occasionally, he is the *deus ex machina* who resolves the dilemma and makes the plot come out right. More often, his lines are short and seemingly trivial. (But we must not underestimate the power of some counselors to make a *tour de force* out of "Mmhmm.") Regardless of the size of his role, however, the counselor is also the *raisonneur* of each drama. He is presumably the one who understands what is going on and can make some attempt to explain it.

Now and then, veterans of such parts get carried away by their virtuosity in understanding and explaining individual dramas. They retire from the stage and become critics; that is, they try to generalize about the individual dramas of career development in which they have participated. If given any modicum of encouragement, they may go on to define, to classify, to compare, to analyze, to evaluate—and eventually to derive universal principles and to make sweeping recommendations for practice.

In any such attempt to reconceptualize or redefine vocational guidance and reappraise its direction for the future, it is necessary to pontificate a bit; to quibble over terms (for surely names affect practices), to interpolate opinions among data (for when are data sufficient to answer questions of policy?), and to extrapolate tendencies (for how else can we anticipate where things are going?). One also assumes license to pull together many observations, ideas, bits of history, argumentation, and even some crystal ball gazing in order to synthesize a statement of principles which will be meaningful to other theorists and to practitioners alike.

Logically, a proper reconstruction and synthesis should be preceded by an analysis of the present state of vocational guidance. This analysis requires that various elements of vocational guidance be singled out for discussion—for the same reason the drama critic may treat sequentially such topics as plot, characterization, theme, setting, and so on. Although the elements have no independent existence, they are useful for critical analysis simply because it is easier to talk about one thing at a time, rather than everything at once. The term vocational guidance implies several such elements for analysis. One is content (vocational); another is process (guidance) which involves participants and (we may assume) a setting. It is reasonable to assume also that this process, involving this content and these participants, has a purpose. This chapter will focus on the first of these elements—content.

Discussing what vocational guidance is about (content) will also involve, by necessity, what vocational guidance does (process), what it is for (purpose), who is involved (participants), and in what place and at what time (setting). (See Katz, 1963, 1966b, 1969a, 1969b, 1969c for discussion of these various other elements.) Identifying and labeling these elements may help to sort out some of the issues, even though vocational guidance itself cannot be cut into separate slices that can be buttered and eaten one at a time. A discussion of content will incorporate parts of all other elements, taking bites out of process, purpose, and the rest.

Starting with content seems appropriate from a historical

point of view. Brewer (1942) has suggested that four conditions led to the rise of the vocational guidance movement. The first two of these conditions were economic and apply directly to what we are calling the content of vocational guidance. They were the growth of technology and the increasing division of labor. These twin phenomena of the rise of industrialism made the world of work much more complex: occupations increased in number and variety; they became both more specialized and less visible. Information about occupations, consequently, became less accessible and more difficult to relate to common childhood experiences and observations. Formal methods of preparing and presenting occupational information were needed, and such information came to represent a substantial part of the content of vocational guidance.

The growth of technology and the demand for specialized labor led to the third condition mentioned by Brewer—the spread of vocational education. Stephens (1970) emphasizes much more than Brewer the close kinship between vocational education and vocational guidance. He points out that early leaders of the National Society for the Promotion of Industrial Education, which worked hard to put vocational education into the public schools, were greatly concerned with vocational guidance, and, indeed, "officiated at the birth" of the National Vocational Guidance Association. Clearly, the rise of vocational education influenced the setting of vocational guidance: vocationally oriented decisions had to be made by students in the schools. That students could choose curriculum paths with various vocational ramifications meant that the content of vocational guidance was extended to decisions about education. Thus, there is no doubt that vocational education and vocational guidance were closely linked. Vocational education provided opportunities for students to try out abilities and interests that were presumably relevant for occupational options. Such exploratory experience is a very special case of occupational information and may even be regarded as a distinctive addition to the content of vocational guidance. As Brewer (1942) says, "Educationally, they [vocational guidance and vocational education] supplement each other, vocational guidance being both the vestibule and the back porch for vocational education [p. 5]." Thus, vocational guidance helped students first to make an informed and rational choice of curriculum, and then to relate the additional knowledge of their own abilities and interests gained from that curriculum experience to choice of an occupation.

But Brewer insists that these three conditions—the growth of technology, the division of labor, and the spread of vocational education—would not have sufficed to start a vocational guidance movement had they not been abetted by concurrent ideological forces. Thus, Brewer sees as fourth condition—the spread of modern forms of democracy, particularly freedom to choose and all that it implies. We may, without undue strain, take this ideological force to include various aspects of humanitarianism and reform. Quite specifically, for example, the commitment to "preparing children for participation in democratic procedures" (Brewer, 1942, p. 7) can be associated with attempts to stamp out child labor and extend the period of universal education. As Rockwell and Rothney (1961) point out, the pioneers in the vocational guidance movement possessed a strong belief in the "improvability" of man and of society: they had "faith in man's ability to control his evolution [p. 350]." Stephens (1970) also emphasizes the role of the reform movement, particularly "urban Progressivism," in the shaping of vocational guidance during the early years of the century. These ideological forces seem to bear primarily on the purpose of vocational guidance. Hofstadter (1955) suggests that an aim of the reform movement was to restore "economic individualism and political democracy," and Stephens goes on to urge that contemporary guidance rededicate itself to "changing the conditions of work, society, and education." But Stephens begs the question of specifying what content of vocational guidance is suitable for this militant purpose. Brewer (1942) has no such hesitancy in identifying vocational guidance as a "necessity to democracy," implying that vocational decisions, freely and intelligently made, may serve as a paradigm for the many decisions—"in ever widening circles of activity [p. 8]"—that comprise democracy in government. Thus, Brewer extends the content of vocational guidance to include decisions about other matters as well as about education and occupation.

In addition, developments in psychology, particularly in measurement but also in clinical work, had a strong impact on the process of vocational guidance. Indeed, psychological measurement grew up along with vocational guidance, and by the end of World War I began providing it with tests and other techniques. As the use of clinical and psychometric techniques came to be applied particularly to attributes that were deemed to be isomorphic with the requirements and characteristics of occupations, or occupationally relevant choices, the appraisal of the individual began to be absorbed into the content of vocational guidance.

Thus, the vocational guidance movement was fathered by economics, mothered by ideologies, housed (at least part of the time) by education, and befriended by psychology. Its content retains traces of all these relationships. But of course none of these forces is static: as economics, political and social ideologies, education, and psychology change, their influences change; and as vocational guidance has matured, it has tended toward more purposeful control of its own destiny.

Thus, the maturation of vocational guidance seems to recapitulate the career development of an individual. The individual starts with a genetic inheritance and is shaped by family culture, and other environmental forces, which are themselves subject to change; as he approaches maturity, however, he gains in freedom and competence to formulate, express, and realize his own intentions. If a major purpose of guidance is to foster that freedom and that competence in all individuals, on what content should it focus? It is suggested here that an appropriate content is based on opportunities for choosing, with specific emphasis on the functional knowledge required for informed and rational career decision making. In the absence of opportunities for choice, the concept of vocational guidance loses distinctive meaning.

Opportunities for Choice

The content of vocational guidance is defined as the opportunities for choice that society permits among educational and occupational options. Most people are confronted with a sequence of such choices, qualified and timed according to the dictates of the educational system, labor laws, labor market conditions, certification and licensing requirements, union regulations, employers' personnel policies, the state of the economy, military service obligations, family pressures, ethnic or religious affiliations, and other such cultural constraints. The options are not limited to occupational titles or educational programs. They span such highly specific arrays as places of possible employment and such broad concerns as the relative desirability of work or formal education or "dropping out" at a given age. This definition recognizes that the number and nature of choices vary from one individual to another.

Some persons seem to make no choices, perhaps have no opportunity to do so. Guidance cannot give them the opportunity; society must do that. Guidance practitioners should be particularly sensitive to the limits on opportunity in some sectors of society. The unwarranted restrictions that have prevailed for years on choices open to blacks, Chicanos, American Indians, and women need no amplification here. According to Stephens (1970) the profession of guidance should do everything in its power to break down such barriers. But this zeal for activism in social reform still leaves individual needs unmet. More freedom is a worthy goal; but in the meantime choices are still to be made under existing constraints. A first step in vocational guidance for people whose horizons have been limited may therefore be to help them discover opportunities for choice that unaided they might not have seen. In general, these opportunities occur at common choice-points when most people are expected to make quite definite decisions, leading to some immediate action. These choice-points also prompt people to anticipate distant choices, although usually with the recognition that long-range plans may remain quite tentative and general. (That choices for the somewhat distant future tend to be unstable has been thoroughly demonstrated—see, for example, Flanagan and Cooley, 1966, Nichols and Astin, 1966; that they very often should be unstable, because of changes in conditions, in values, and in knowledge and understanding, has previously been argued—see Katz, 1963.)

Reinterpreting the 1937 Definition

Defining content as opportunities for choice does not stray far from the definition of vocational guidance by NVGA (1937), which uses the words "choose an occupation, prepare for it, enter upon the progress in it [p. 772]." A new statement can preserve some sense of professional continuity by starting with a reinterpretation of the language of the 1937 "principles and practices." Official documents written by committees tend to encompass various points of view. As a rule, doctrine changes gradually. Since the new orthodoxy is seldom diametrically opposed to the old, the new can generally be found latent in the old—perhaps adumbrated by a subordinate clause, a qualifying phrase, an afterthought. Skilled exegesis maintains the currency of dogma by stretching old words to cover changing circumstances. It allows an entire professional group to move cohesively, even while individual members shift their positions in relation to the center.

For example, if the 1937 definition is taken literally, "prepare . . . , enter . . . and progress" are coordinate with "choose." This construction indicates that the content of vocational guidance incorporates not just options for choice, but the actual preparation itself (as in vocational education, for example). On the other hand, Myers (1941) has defended effectively the interpretation that vocational guidance includes choosing or planning the preparation but does not include the preparation itself. In a similar vein, vocational guidance may be said to deal with the choices to be made among different ways of entering an occupation and among different ways of progressing in it. If this is the case, the language of the 1937 definition may be redundant; but it refers to the same content as our initial approximation. Choice remains the dominant motif.

The definition by NVGA (1937) also explicitly incorporates "educational guidance"—since "preparation for an occupation involves decisions in the choice of studies, choice of curricula, and the choice of schools and colleges [p. 772]."

A few object to this use of the term "vocational guidance" as too comprehensive. They believe it should not subsume educational decisions, which involve other considerations than choice of or preparation for an occupation. They maintain that although educational decisions often overlap vocational decisions, education is not just preparation for an occupation. It has intrinsic importance. It is closely concerned with certain areas of human development—intellectual, ethical, social—that may be more important than vocational development. They would prefer, therefore, to keep educational guidance distinct from vocational guidance—and certainly not subordinate to it. They would retain both "guidances," however, and even add others.

Much more numerous are those who object that the term vocational guidance is too restrictive, that it purports to partition the individual's vocational choices and vocational development from the total range of life choices he makes and from his total development as an individual. They would prefer that all "guidances" be merged, perhaps in the term "career guidance."

Career Guidance and Decision-making Skill

The term career guidance suggests that the individual's major choices—of education, of occupation, of leisure activities—are but manifestations of the choice of a way of life, or a life style. It also suggests some sense of continuity, a pattern or a theme, running through the course of the various choices an individual makes during his life. Thus, it implies both horizontal and vertical dimensions. Exponents of this point of view are likely to cite Super's (1953) notable definition of the process of vocational de- self-concept [p. 190]." Indeed, some have preferred to eliminate all reference to content of choices and indicate that guidance is concerned exclusively with the process of decision making.

Efforts to develop decision-making skill are, of course, not to be scorned. Still, the existence of such a skill as an independent entity that can be generalized and transferred from one situation or context to another has not been established. Decision making does not take place in a vacuum. One of the elements the decision maker deals with is information. Indeed, decision making may "be regarded as a strategy for acquiring and processing information. . . . The person . . . either does not know what information he needs, does not have what information he wants, or cannot use what information he has (Katz, 1963, p. 25)." Ways of defining, getting, and using information may vary considerably from one kind of content to another. A man concerned with choosing a wife is likely to find that ascertaining what he should know about a certain population of girls and getting that information involve dimensions, actions, and procedures palpably different from those he uses in choosing an occupation.

As Broudy, Smith, and Burnett (1964) point out, in developing decision-making skill not all problems are equally useful for pedagogical purposes: in dealing with complex and multidimensional problems, one of the first steps is to make a judgment about what sort of data and what sort of knowledge are relevant. Thus, "molar problem-solving requires the transfer of both content and operations. . . . The requisite cognitive frames cannot be picked up incidentally to the ordinary routines of living [pp. 234–235]."

However, if decision-making skills can be developed in any context—with any content—the vocational domain has much to recommend it as a universal training ground: acceptance, experience, and relevance across a wide range of ages.

Choices and Self-concept

Thus, while vocational development is a continuous process, it is not just a process, devoid of content. The nature of the choices which the individual perceives and to which he responds provides the terms in which his self-concept is expressed. A substantial proportion of these choices may be regarded as manifestations of a vocational self-concept, which Super (1963) has defined as "the constellation of self attributes considered by the individual to be vocationally relevant, whether or not they have been translated into a vocational preference [p. 20]."

If self-attributes are vocationally relevant, we may assume that the individual relates them to choices that he perceives as vocational. These vocational choices are rarely isolated; one leads to another, forming a sequence. This sequence depends partly on the outcome of each choice. Having chosen, the individual performs well or poorly, enjoys satisfaction or suffers discontent. The effects of such outcomes usually appear in the content of subsequent choices: lack of success and satisfaction is likely to lead to changes in plans. Each single choice, therefore, bears some relationship both to antecedent and to subsequent choices.

Tiedeman (1961) has described this relationship as a "means-ends chain." We may reason that, since man both remembers and imagines, he can evaluate past performance and predict future performance. These evaluations and predictions represent his self-appraisals; a number of such self-appraisals may be integrated into his self-concept. At the same time, decisions and plans express his self-concept. Self-concept is thus engaged in a reciprocal role with decision making: the concept of self shapes the individual's choices and is shaped by them. If we accept Tiedeman's analogy of choices as a means-ends chain, we may extend the metaphor to suggest that, as the chain lengthens, the individual tends to become increasingly the captive of the chain. His freedom of maneuver is progressively restricted by the succession of choices he has made. He may still choose freely among available options, but the options themselves appear to have been circumscribed. Careers do not follow a fixed course. They wobble. They offer many opportunities for change. Yet we repeatedly find in them a certain sense of continuity and harmony—continuity of themes over time, harmony among manifestations at any point in time. This is the continuity provided by the self-concept of the decision maker.

Work and Career

Unquestionably, then, career guidance is an enticing term. Certainly, the connotation of career in suggesting the total range of life choices is much more encompassing than that of vocation—even if the latter includes education as well as occupation. It has often been asserted, however, that in our society occupation seems to be the dominant feature of career. Careers are differentiated largely in terms of occupations. The Lynds (1937) have called a person's job "the watershed down which the rest of one's life tends to flow [p. 7]."

Nevertheless, it may be that the importance of occupation in career is changing; certainly its importance may vary greatly from one person to another. We have become increasingly aware of the full sweep of the range of attitudes toward occupation—from dedication to alienation. It may be that one of the most significant career choices a person makes today is to determine just this: the importance of occupation in his own career. Then the content of vocational guidance would include not only such traditional occupational information as the requirements, conditions, and rewards of various occupations, but—on a more fundamental level—the variety of attitudes toward work itself. A primary choice is the extent to which an individual wants an occupation to fill his career.

For this kind of decision, the term "career guidance" has some advantages. It suggests a degree of neutrality that may be appropriate for a world in which the nature and meaning of work are changing rapidly and perhaps unpredictably. Even now, many people must count not on a lifetime vocation, but on "serial" occupations—changing not just jobs but kinds of work. If each occupation is to reflect their self-concepts, can they maintain a steady view of their self-images through such an occupational kaleidoscope? Will they not fall prey to "identity crises"? How well do most current occupations—even steady ones—provide the gratifications necessary to fill a career? Wilensky (1964) has found the general level of job satisfaction—particularly among industrial workers—to be low: "the typical American man is lightly committed to his work [p. 149]." Dubin (1956) concluded that "for almost three out of every four industrial workers studied, work and the workplace *are not* central life interests [p. 131]." This indifferent and uncommitted attitude is now often regarded largely as a function of the separation between the worker and the product, the monotony of many kinds of work, the decreased economic need for human labor, and the frequent changes in occupation required by changes in the economy and in technology. These phenomena have been invoked often enough to become a familiar refrain. But does alienation from work necessarily imply alienation from society? Must all men "fulfill themselves" vocationally? Must work always, in the language of the statement by NVGA (1937), "represent the active expression of the individual's whole personality [p. 772]"?

If this were ever true, the argument seems to lose face validity in the tendency for working hours to consume a decreasing proportion of man's total lifetime. Consider trends toward shorter work weeks and longer vacations. Consider the increased duration of education at the youthful end of the span. Consider the pension plans that encourage early retirement. Consider also the likelihood of further increases in life expectancy that may stretch the retirement years. All these tendencies add up to the suggestion that many people need not—and indeed cannot—depend on vocations for total fulfillment. More and more satisfactions can be left to family and community activities, to leisure and avocations. Therefore, the term "vocational adjustment," which figures so prominently in the 1937 NVGA statement, may have to give way to "career adjustment." One function of career adjustment may be to strike an appropriate balance between vocational and non-vocational activities as sources of gratification.

Vocation and Work

But is alienation or a noncommittal attitude toward work entirely a recent phenomenon? Have our perceptions perhaps been clouded by the reformist spirit of the vocational guidance movement? Does the word vocation itself somehow prejudge the case? Does it tend to preserve an obsolescent ideal? Does it imply that occupation can and should be the central life interest for all men? Does it, perhaps, baited with egalitarian sentiment, lead us into an etymological trap?

In Shakespeare's *Henry IV, Part I,* Falstaff playfully springs this trap: "Why, Hal, 'tis my vocation, Hal; 'tis no sin for a man to labor in his vocation [I, ii]." The paradox in Falstaff's oily rationalization swings on two hinges. First, we regard the "vocation" to which Falstaff has dedicated his talents—"purse-taking"—as a sinful pursuit. Second, we recognize the early meaning of "vocation" as a calling to the service of God (usually in some activity of a spiritual nature), as well as the meaning—more common today—of occupation, profession, or work.

Falstaff capitalizes on the transition from the dominance of the old meaning to the dominance of the current usage: if man is called to his work, and the call comes from God, clearly " 'tis no sin" for man to heed the call. The early meaning has never quite been obliterated from the modern lexicon. It is not just youths who enter training for the priesthood who must be attuned to hear, recognize, and respond to the "call." Youthful commitment or dedication to any culturally approved life work resonates to the same vibrations. And, indeed, Falstaff attacks the notion that only one set of values must prevail for all: individuals may even be "called" to occupations that are denied universal approbation. This notion of a calling, however, is reserved—as was the religious "vocation"—for a somewhat select group: it implies fitness to serve. For those who are not attuned, are not fit, are not selected, there is no "vocation." Instead, there is "work."

The distinction between vocation and work, which has been progressively blurred during modern times, now seems to be re-emerging. Perhaps a brief—and necessarily oversimplified—historical rundown will clarify the distinction and its implications for guidance.

Persistent Problems of Commitment and Adjustment to Work

The Ethic of Work

In the antiquity of Western civilization, there seems to have been no mention of work choice or work guidance. Work had long been regarded as a curse. To the ancient Greeks and Romans, work was at best a necessary evil. Pope's translation of the *Iliad* contains this couplet: "To labor is the lot of man below; And when Jove gave us life, he gave us woe."

The ancient peoples saw no dignity in menial tasks. Slaves worked. Men and women who could not avoid the necessity worked. Aside from soldiery, achievements deemed worthwhile by the Greeks required leisure. Their most notable contributions—in art, drama, philosophy, politics, and so forth—were the products of a leisure class supported by slave labor. The modern notion that the dramatist or philosopher or athlete works at his profession would have been incomprehensible to the Greeks, whose most competent "old pros" never lost their amateur status.

In the days of the Caesars, the practical Romans had managed to translate their distaste for work into a 6-hour work day, and about half the days of the year were designated as holidays. The early Hebrews, too, "conceived of work as dismal drudgery," but accepted it as "an expiation." As Wilensky (1964) points out, "Rabbinical literature held that no labor, however lowly, is as offensive as idleness [p. 126]." Still, neither they nor the early Christians saw work as partaking of "vocation." The Christians came to differentiate "work" from "vocation," but did not differentiate one kind of work from another.

It was not until the Renaissance and the Reformation that work came to be identified as a major way of serving God. Luther emphasized the equal spiritual value of all kinds of work and regarded excellence of performance as a high duty. According to Weber's (1930) famous treatise, the "Protestant Ethic" assisted in the rise of capitalism by giving powerful religious approval to hard work, worldly achievement, and high profits.

Regardless of the validity of Weber's thesis, it is clear that the prevailing attitude toward work had undergone a change (at least among intellectuals). It had taken on a connotation of religious endorsement in the spirit of the Italian proverb, "Working at your calling is half praying." The merchant, the farmer, the craftsman, all served God well by doing their work well. The differentiation, then, was between successful work (work that God prospered) and unsuccessful work. Even the industrial revolution, which stretched so many workers on the rack of the machine, did not dampen the glorification of work. To the hard-working Carlyle, whose own energies and productivity seldom flagged, man's heroic stature was not diminished by the kind of work he did—as long as he worked: "All work," he wrote in *Past and Present,* "even cotton-spinning, is noble; work is alone noble."

Gradually there had emerged, from the concept of work as a spiritual calling, the concept of work as a secular calling. Work was extolled not just for the glory of God, but for the self-fulfillment of man. Thus, Carlyle, again in *Past and Present*, wrote what we may call a secular benediction: "Blessed is he who has found his work; let him ask no other blessedness. He has a work, a life-purpose; he has found it, and will follow it." Note how close this is to the early formulations of the vocational guidance movement. To *find* one's work implies knowledge of ways in which individuals vary and work varies, and some fit of one's own characteristics to the distinctive characteristics of an occupation. The nineteenth century social reformist, Ruskin, kept one foot on the spiritual dock as he too stepped into the secular boat: "God intends no man to live in the world without work; but it seems to me no less evident that He intends every man to be happy in his work."

Thus, Carlyle and Ruskin were concerned not just with success but with happiness. A similar concern for individual satisfaction and fulfillment, along with a humanitarian and reform spirit, is found in the origins of the vocational guidance movement. (But note that the vocational guidance movement, while making obeisance to the importance of individual goals and purposes, has never deprecated the importance of success.) For this concept of self-fulfillment in work was entirely compatible with the ambitions of achievement-oriented, upward-striving America around the turn of the century. The opportunity to rise economically, to earn a better living, helped to glorify hard work. Where barriers to economic and social mobility were relatively high (for example in the South, for whites as well as blacks), work continued to be regarded as debasing and ignominious. But the Horatio Alger ideal prevailed elsewhere. Man's worth was assessed in terms of his productivity. Of course, many failed to rise, even though they were hard working and conscientious. But the ideal of work as a means for upward mobility was substantiated often enough to remain credible and acceptable. It may be said to have formed a major tenet of the American ethic.

Furthermore, as the pressures of humanitarianism and reform—to say nothing of the labor movement—began to improve the lot of the working classes, there began to materialize in some measure the promise that hard work and productivity would be rewarded not only by a laborer's rise *through* the strata of classes, but also or alternatively by his rise *with* the laboring class. Success—or productivity—in work was expected to raise the level of economic rewards for *all* classes to the extent that all persons would feel pride of accomplishment and satisfaction.

Satisfaction and Success

It came to be assumed that, since satisfaction was largely a function of success, an individual would find his greatest satisfaction in the work that he could perform most successfully. This suggested the crucial importance of choice of work. While all work grew increasingly acceptable, vocation came to mean the kind of work a man could do best. The trait-and-factor theory that dominated vocational guidance at least until the mid-century mark derived its logic quite directly from these premises. The appropriate content of vocational guidance according to this theory was the observation and classification of aptitudes on the one hand, and of occupational requirements on the other. (The *process* was primarily to match the variables in these two domains for best fit, and to advise the individual in such a way as to induce him to choose the option that gave him the greatest chance for success.)

This theory, that man should choose the work at which he will be most successful, survived the depression of the 1930s but began to be supplanted during the postwar boom. The difficulties of getting a job at all during the depression years put increased stress on identifying abilities that had a market value. What a man could do was of no interest in its own right save as it related to requirements for success on the job. Thus, the Minnesota Employment Stabilization Research Institute, established in 1931, studied psychological factors in employment and unemployment and tried to develop systematic methods for fitting people to jobs. "Security" was the watchword, and school courses entitled "vocations" placed special emphasis on "preparing for and entering" a job. Success was then construed to represent getting a job and holding it.

The shake-up of World War II, although retarding the careers of many young people, broadened the horizons and stimulated the ambitions of others. It jarred many loose from their hometowns and from their preconceptions. Veterans Administration subsidies offered men who had been in military service opportunities for exploration of more ambitious and daring vocational goals than they would otherwise have considered. Federally supported vocational guidance programs in the Veterans Administration and in State Employment Services brought such opportunities for upward and outward mobility to the attention of larger populations. Since the wartime youths had already tolerated a certain amount of career interruption and travel, they were receptive to information about training and education, and to the attractions of a geographically broad labor market. Thus, educational and occupational information became less parochial. A plethora of national guides to colleges—and other institutions—were published, and publication of the first *Occupational Outlook Handbook* (United States Department of Labor, 1949) gave greater access to nation-wide labor market forecasts. The forecasts for high-level occupations looked good. The manpower needs of the war had drained off the pipelines for the professions at the early college level. The reviving consumer goods industries all needed skilled talent.

With the promise that the economy would support lofty aspirations, the cautiousness of the depression years gave way to a venturesome spirit. Men whose lives had been spared in the war were no longer content merely to earn a living. They were confident they could meet the demands of occupations that promised high fulfillment of ambitions. They were not obsessed with requirements, which they felt they could take in stride, but with rewards. They sought more than economic rewards. The depression was gone. A minimum level of subsistence was taken for granted. After the regimentation, monotony, and rigidity of army discipline, they wanted to enhance their self-esteem in an occupation that used their talents—they wanted status, autonomy, a chance to use initiative.

The Instrumentality of Occupations

Thus, they craved information that went beyond the bare-bones facts of salaries and other economic benefits. They were concerned with the distinctive ways in which various occupations would implement their concepts of self, would fit their aspirations and values, would provide satisfaction for their psychosocial needs.

This type of information was scarcely available in the extant publications, which tended to confine descriptions to the tasks involved in an occupation (job analysis) and to the requirements for entry, training, financial returns, and so on. These were matters of interest, but were insufficient. Samler (1961) has drawn particular attention to the gap between the information that appeared in such publications as the *Dictionary of Occupational Titles*, the *Occupational Outlook Handbook*, and many commercial *Briefs* and *Monographs*—all oriented exclusively to "Economic Man"—and the information that was of great concern to "Psychological Man." An approach toward developing the latter type of information has been suggested by Hughes (1958) in his identification of common "themes" in various occupations. As Overs' abstracts (1964) of sociological studies show, the literature of occupational sociology contains a number of penetrating studies on such psychosocial constructs as role, status, appraisal of self-worth, and so on. But this kind of material has not been sufficiently extended or organized for use in vocational guidance.

Consequently, data for analyzing and classifying occupations according to such dimensions have not been readily accessible to guidance practitioners and their clients. Instead, the single dimension of economic reward has continued to dominate in the available materials. Yet some of this differentiation by level of economic reward, although no less perceptible, may now be less salient. As the "people's capitalism" has continued to raise the economic rewards of most occupations, economic distinctions between high-level vocations and other employment have tended to decline in utility. In terms of material recompense and creature comforts, distinctions between white-collar workers and blue-collar workers have become blurred, and distinctions between different occupational levels have become less impressive than they were. Semiskilled workers have been able to afford automobiles, houses, television sets, and virtually all the other highly visible consumer products available to people in the highest level occupations.

In fact, during the affluent 1950s, these extrinsic similarities in the payoff of work at different levels may have contributed somewhat to the threat of shortages in high-level occupations. Many youths seemed content to aspire to intermediate and lower levels, even though they had enough ability to succeed in more demanding work. (Of course, it may well be that the relatively small size of the population cohorts reaching college age during this period was the primary cause of vacancies in colleges and prospective shortages in such rapidly expanding occupations as engineering, mathematics, and the sciences.) This problem became highly publicized after the success of Sputnik, which triggered programs for action. Thus, it became a matter of national policy (as reflected in the National Defense Education Act) to identify high-ability secondary school students and encourage them to continue their formal education.

Consequently, the content of vocational guidance during the middle and late 1950s reflected the national purpose: it emphasized financial aid and other opportunities for higher education, the rewards of high-level occupations, and the many openings for the future in such positions.

Unemployment and Guidance

Then the emphasis shifted again. A moderate economic recession, an increase in the labor supply (as the babies produced by the booming birth rates of the postwar 1940s reached working age), the effects of fast-moving automation and other technological developments in eliminating many unskilled and semiskilled jobs, and the growing pressure of the civil rights movement, all combined to focus public attention on unemployment—particularly "structural" unemployment, which reflected the ill fit between jobs that were unfilled and people who were seeking work. For even as the economy rebounded to record highs in the middle 1960s and total employment rose, unemployment—especially long-term unemployment—did not show a corresponding decrease.

Closer scrutiny of the unemployed during that period disclosed that unskilled workers, who made up about 5 percent of the total labor force, were accounting for 15 to 20 percent of the long-term unemployed (Wolfbein, 1964). Semiskilled workers, who made up about 18 percent of the total labor force, accounted for about 30 percent of the long-term unemployed. While the total unemployment rate was around 4 percent of the total labor force, the unemployment rate for teen-age boys remained over 12 percent. Among high school dropouts, the unemployment rate was around 25 percent. What Conant (1961) called the "social dynamite" of young unemployed dropouts in congested slums was later detonated in several cities.

Vocational training programs for segments of these long-term unemployed populations were established, and knowledge of such programs became an important bit of content for vocational guidance. But many programs of rather specific vocational training foundered on the trainees' lack of basic education. These educational deficits are not easily made up. School-like instruction is spurned by the dropouts—this is what they have already dropped out of. Therefore, the Office of Economic Opportunity established Job Corps programs that emphasized combinations of vocational training and basic education, offered at residential centers (to break the continuing influence of depressed environments). But even these specially tailored programs often failed. They were widely believed to have run afoul of the attitudes of the trainees, which were described as a disorientation toward work—an unwillingness or inability to accept the discipline of work. This kind of discipline used to be absorbed almost unconsciously in early and middle school years by middle-class pupils, to be transformed into some commitment to education and vocation. It includes adherence to time schedules, meeting standards of performance, accepting correction and evaluation, and cooperating with others.

These attitudes of self-discipline have been taken to represent an early stage in the development of vocational maturity. As much as the three R's of education, they have provided the foundations on which successful vocational education could build. Vocational guidance, too, in its focus on choice of occupations or kind of education, has taken for granted the early mastery of this stage in vocational development. But for the uncommitted youths, whose vocational development may have been severely retarded, there is a prior choice to consider—whether they want to opt for work at all. There seems to be evidence that nonwork has become a way of life for some—at least in the sense that they display neither hope nor desire to prepare for and hold a "regular job." Thus, the content of vocational guidance must include also—for these groups—the characteristics of nonwork as well as of work; for the choice between these alternatives is even more basic than later branchings. Must vocational guidance then include information relevant for assisting the individual to choose, prepare for, enter, and progress in nonwork? Must it embrace the values of nonwork pithily expressed in the reversed aphorism, "Work is the curse of the drinking classes"? Or should it be assumed that vocational guidance must reflect the middle-class values favoring work over nonwork—that society really permits no "choice" between work and nonwork (except for the wealthy)?

The pejorative terms used to describe nonworkers ("defectives," who cannot work; "delinquents," who have turned against work and toward socially unacceptable substitutes for work; "drifters," "beatniks," "hippies," and "playboys," who have withdrawn from work) suggest that the culture has taken a stand against nonwork. As we have indicated, during the 1960s the "War on Poverty" devoted much of its energies to a war on nonwork. Even though this attack on poverty proved inefficient, work has been regarded as so important for morale (of taxpayers and government officials as well as of the unemployed) that proposals for changes in welfare regulations and for other income maintenance programs have invariably emphasized incentives to work. An occasional voice speaking for a reverse income tax has been interpreted to reflect an increasing tolerance of nonwork, an acceptance of an economy in which the need for human labor will have diminished. But this view seems to be a narrow one—probably restricted to extrapolations of shrinking manpower needs in goods-producing industries. The need for manpower to perform services is virtually unlimited. These services do not have to be circular, as in the fabled village where people supported themselves by doing each other's laundry. They can meet great social needs: for example, one of the most significant findings of the first summer of Project Head Start—which provided young children with kindergarten and preschool experiences—was the effectiveness of using large numbers of teacher aides, particularly unemployed teen-age boys (Dobbin, 1965).

These adventitious job assignments are hardly vocations; yet the opportunity they offer for exploration and examination of work values and for change in self-concept seems to warrant considering such options as part of the content of vocational guidance.

During the 1960s an even fiercer attack on the middle-class values favoring work over nonwork came from within. Numbers of the children of the middle-aged middle-class rejected their parents' commitment to work and began to drop out at a rate that caused alarm and bewilderment in their elders. More recently, many of the dropouts have been unable or unwilling to sustain their withdrawal from work. Without necessarily abandoning the counter culture, they have tended to return to some form of work. They report, in a number of cases, that work—even work to which they feel no strong commitment—restores a balance to their lives that they were missing. One wonders whether the total deletion of regular work from an individual's life space may not upset the delicate ecology of human happiness; such otherwise desirable elements as relaxation, leisure, and freedom become too gross and insupportable. This has been the experience often reported by retirees, whose withdrawal from work suffers from no lack of social approval. Unquestionably, vocational guidance has more difficulty in coping with the choice of options from the realm of nonwork than from the more familiar domain of work.

Serial Careers

Vocational guidance must also make provision for another unstable career pattern—the "serial career." One of the dominant characteristics of work in modern America has been change. As occupations become obsolete and training becomes inappropriate for new occupations, most workers cannot count on careers in a single occupation. They must count on serial careers. For example, recently, engineers in aerospace industries, long the darlings of the economy, suddenly found their jobs wiped out. It is expected that many will be retrained for urban planning and other social needs, although at this writing no large-scale retraining programs have yet materialized.

Wilensky (1961) emphasizes the "chaos" in modern labor markets, and concludes that "Most men . . . never experience the joys of a life plan because most work situations do not afford the necessary stable progression over the worklife [p. 523]." His study of the "middle mass" of workers in the Detroit area—a relatively secure and prosperous group, in terms of salaries and possessions—indicated that "only 30 percent can by any stretch of the imagination be said to act out half or more of their work histories in an orderly career [p. 526]."

Retraining may be needed frequently during such serial careers, as new occupations open up and obsolete occupations are phased out. An example of this need has appeared in the dramatic shift of employment from goods-producing industries to services-producing industries. As early as 1950, a majority of workers were in the latter category; and by 1960 service workers exceeded goods-producing workers by almost 50 percent (Wolfbein, 1964). Vocational education may, therefore, be concerned more and more with developing abilities and attitudes that will give young people about to enter the labor market maximum versatility and flexibility. Criticisms of specialized vocational education have long been rampant. A recent study (Eninger, 1965) indicated that two-thirds to three-quarters of recent graduates in vocational curricula (in vocational schools or in comprehensive high schools) did not enter the trade for which they had received training. It seems clear that only a small proportion of the secondary school population can profit by early commitment to prolonged vocational education that prepares only for a specific trade or provides a narrow range of skills—and even for them, the profit may be short lived.

Clearly, then, the content of vocational guidance must include in its lore some provision for the nature of change in occupations. There may be positive values in change itself. The question was raised earlier of "identity crises" that might arise in the course of serial careers: if each successive occupation is to reflect a person's self-concept, can he maintain a steady view of his self-image through such an occupational kaleidoscope? A partial answer may be that individual characteristics that facilitate change—for example, adaptability, flexibility, versatility—may be important components of a person's self-image. Readiness to tackle a variety of tasks is surely not foreign to man. Primitive man had to be versatile. Every person was likely to do every kind of work that was then extant. There was little specialization. The modern man may again expect to do many kinds of work. One difference lies in the timing: modern man may have to work at one highly specialized task for several years before he changes (after a period of retraining or reeducation) to another highly specialized task. Primitive man changed frequently, from hour to hour or day to day. Then, too, primitive or even preindustrial man could identify his work clearly with the product. He was close enough to the product so that he could derive gratification and reinforcement from the visible, tangible, usable outcome of his labor. Modern man, while often denied this consummation, can still find other satisfactions in work. These may include the sociability of the work milieu, the opportunity to make friends and organize recreational activities. But such extrinsic benefits seem to fit rather awkwardly into the old concept of vocation, which implies commitment to a calling, to the work activity itself and its product—not to the concomitants of the work setting.

Vocation and Self-fulfillment

The preceding survey of changing conditions of work and changing attitudes toward work leads to a question basic to the content of vocational guidance: has the concept of vocation itself, which developed in its modern sense from the Renaissance to the twentieth century, failed to attain relevance for all in our society? Does the very use of the word vocation misrepresent the nature of the choices that many people have made?

Up to this point, such words as vocation, occupation, employment, labor, and work have been used rather loosely, often interchangeably. Perhaps, however, the different connotations of some of these words can be exploited to define more clearly the kinds of choices that are made in respect to careers. The choices involve not just different kinds or classes of activity, but also—perhaps primarily—the attitudes of the choosers. This is not to deny that the thing chosen and the mode of choosing are closely interrelated. It is to suggest, however, that attitudes may vary considerably for given conditions of work—as will be elaborated later.

It has been emphasized that vocation implies a complete and wholehearted dedication, usually requires a long-term commitment, and fills the vessel of career nearest to the brim. Because of this high level of requirements, expectations, and rewards, the term vocation is often associated with professional and managerial levels—Level I and, perhaps to some extent, Level II in Roe's (1956) classification system. The professions are characterized by long periods of preparation, delayed entry, ethical standards, bodies of theoretical knowledge, a high degree of autonomy, concern with vital areas of human activity—characteristics which seem particularly compatible with the concept of vocation. Like managerial responsibilities for decisions and for supervision of others, these characteristics make rigorous demands: long hours, nervous tension, severe pressures. In return, the person who chooses a vocation has a sense of the importance of what he is doing, glories in his responsibility for it, finds his accomplishments intrinsically rewarding. The hardships he undergoes for his vocation are not self-denials; on the contrary, he "finds himself" in his vocation. Although vocation and profession may often be associated, vocation is not confined to the professions, nor does everyone who elects a profession choose it as a "vocation" in this sense. Still, the professions and managerial positions in our culture impose the greatest demands for commitment and seem to possess the greatest power to reward it. Since the call for high-level manpower is likely to continue strong over the long term, an increasing proportion of the population should be able to find outlets for vocational expression. For example, the number of professional and technical workers grew by over 50 percent in the decade 1960–1970, representing an increase from 11 percent of all employed persons in 1960 to

14 percent in 1970 (United States Bureau of the Census, 1970, p. 225). But barriers to entry are still steep, the demand for services continues to rise, and the proportion of the population in the main working ages for professional occupations, 30–59, is expected to remain stable until 1980. So members of these groups can count on no more leisure in the future than they have now.

Occupation and Flexibility

Less consuming, less demanding, and less fully rewarding is occupation. What one occupies, he does not necessarily possess; nor does it possess him. He holds it for a while—longer or shorter—and it has some hold on him—stronger or weaker, but he does not give it (or it does not command) single-minded commitment and fidelity.

Occupation may be associated most frequently with the lower level professionals, the semi-professionals, the technologists, the administrators, and the skilled—Roe's Levels II, III, and IV—although time-serving members of the "higher level" professions also qualify. Occupations make substantial demands: they require differentiated training and application, and absorb energies and attention, but are likely to offer less autonomy, less stability, and less self-fulfillment. They provide the satisfactions of mastery and a sense of competence, of "function pleasure" and intrinsic interest. They demand less initial investment in training. According to the prophets of "cybernation," however (e.g., Michael, 1966), the non-professionals may have to change their type of job several times in a working career: "Conventional expectations about settling down to a lifetime job, or of doing the same thing all of one's working life, will more and more evolve into expectations that what one does, and when one will need to learn another job, will depend on a rapidly changing technology over which the individual has little or no control [p. 44]." Their total time spent in education and retraining, by installments, may therefore rival the educational investments of professionals. Typical of the changes which send people from one occupation to another are those which have already been seen in the shifts from goods-producing to services-producing and from blue-collar to white-collar occupations. These trends are projected to continue to 1980 (United States Department of Labor, 1970–71). The steady upward shift during the 1960s in average years of schooling completed is expected to continue during the 1970s. Thus there will be a higher proportion of the population with the basic education required for entry into these occupations, or required for short-term training (and retraining) prior to entry. Particularly noteworthy is the rapid growth in two-year colleges, with an estimated 2,400,000 students enrolled in 1,070 institutions as of fall 1970 (*Junior College Journal*, 1971). The Carnegie Commission on Higher Education expects two-year college enrollments to reach 4,000,000 by 1980. These institutions seem particularly well adapted to offer the comprehensive programs for continuing education and reeducation that may be needed for rapidly changing occupations. Therefore, the supply of workers for "occupation" is likely to be plentiful, even for the increasing demand.

Employment and Leisure

Employment describes the next step down in degree of commitment. It suggests less differentiation and education than occupation. People who are "employed" are busy and paid. They can be identified most readily in the production jobs that have survived mechanization and automation. But as automation becomes more sophisticated and extensive, these workers may be virtually interchangeable from one job to another. While machines have replaced the slave labor of antiquity, men are still needed in some capacity to monitor the machines. No matter how far automation takes over these monitoring functions, a perpetual motion machine has not yet been invented. Somewhere, at some time, there is—if not literally then figuratively—a button to be pushed by a person. Employment, *per se,* requires little commitment, offers few intrinsic rewards. It requires some attention and some time, but demands no distinctive skill. The employed person does not live to work, but works to live. His work contributes in some way to society, he knows, but the connections between work and product are usually difficult to see. The rewards tend to be all extrinsic. Employment fills only a small portion of the vessel of career. There are time and energy for other things—for hobbies, for leisure, for avocations. This detachment or alienation from work may tend to encourage a hedonistic trade-off: employment represents an exchange of time at work for the wherewithal to pursue intrinsically rewarding activities in the time away from work. Conditions of work are defined in terms of hours, pay, comfort, and fringe benefits. Improvement in these does not depend on individual excellence or vigor on the job, but is the virtually automatic bounty of technological advances and union power—what was called in the General Motors labor contract of 1948 "the annual improvement factor." The employed person, then, finds little intrinsic satisfaction or ego-involvement in his job. He is likely to adhere to Omar Khayyám's dictum to "take the cash and let the credit go."

However, we must beware of making this case too strong, partaking of the intellectual snobbery of Mencken, who said, "A man who gets his board and lodging on this ball in an ignominious way is inevitably an ignominious man." What the employed person does may require little differentiation among human beings, but to be human is to be already very much differentiated from other species. We must recognize that satisfaction does not always vary directly with further differentiation. Often, efforts to improve the common lot successively restrict the area left each person for individual expression. For example, the housewife who serves meals of canned or frozen foods may sacrifice the intrinsic rewards of cooking. But if she takes no joy in cooking, her family may prefer the standardized meals, and she has more time and energy for other activities that can offer her more potent rewards.

Employment is by no means always an involuntary status for those who can do no better. Since the late 1960s there has been some tendency for youths of high ability, who have attended selective colleges, to seek out employment that is unchallenging. For example, according to a news report (Reinhold, 1971), many recent graduates of Harvard were taking jobs as taxi drivers, warehousemen, bookstore clerks, and the like. One may speculate that they feel such jobs provide the necessary remuneration (enough to buy a "stereo and wheels"), without encroaching on the identities, avocational activities, and life style they cherish. Employment, they believe, gives them more freedom to follow their "calling" than would vocation or occupation.

The beauty of employment is that if large numbers of people can perform the necessary function, the time required of each on the job will not be great. Moore and Hedges (1971) document the spectacular gains in leisure achieved during the first half of this century. They point out that, although these gains decelerated somewhat during the 1950s and 1960s, the average American worker "gained about 50 hours a year in time free of work" during the decade from 1960 to 1970 [p. 6]. This gain resulted both from reductions in the normal work week and from increases in holiday and vacation time. The Bureau of Labor Statistics projects productivity to continue to increase during the 1970s at a rate of about 3.1 percent annually (the average over the last two decades). While part of this gain will undoubtedly be reflected in increased income, a substantial proportion is expected to result in further increases in leisure. Indeed, a number of unions have given considerable emphasis to reductions in working hours. The continuing reduction in farm employment and increased employment in service industries will also tend to lower the average work week. Moore and Hedges (1971) also cite reductions in work life attributable to earlier retirements as social security benefits and pension plans are improved. Furthermore, the advent of the four-day week (Poor, 1970) and similar trends (such as shifting mid-week holidays to Mondays) promise to free larger numbers of people for bigger blocks of leisure. Such blocks of leisure have greater utility for pursuing avocational interests than the same amount of free time spread more thinly.

Avocation, incidentally, permits an ideal relationship between the domains of possible activities and the patterns of human variability. It eliminates the need for compromise between what the individual wants to do and what society will pay him to do. He can choose an avocation without reference to manpower needs or the labor market. As long as employment provides him with livelihood and leisure, he can find self-fulfillment in other sectors of his life.

Here, then, is a happy circumstance for vocational guidance. Vocations and occupations, which provide little leisure but tend to offer intrinsic rewards in keeping with the degree of commitment and investment required, are likely to take an increasing proportion of the work force. Employment, which may be a bore, can be spread thin, leaving ample time for avocations.

Level of Work and Fulfillment

This bald statement makes desirable here a repeated word of caution against equating vocation, occupation, and employment exclusively with level. Although these terms are readily associated with level, and can be easily interpreted in conjunction with level, the crucial element is not the level, or the conditions of work, but the attitude of the individual toward it—what we have called the extent of his commitment to his work, the degree of fulfillment he finds in it, its power to fill his career. That this attitude may vary across workers within any level is obvious, yet an illustration or two may help to emphasize the point. There is, of course, that old stand-by, the upper-class youth who enters the family law firm simply because it is expected of him. For him, the profession of law may be only "employment." Perhaps more interesting is Koningsberger's (1966) observation of Chinese factory workers:

> To most of the factory workers, who are newly trained men and women, any machine is still a minor miracle, and to be in control of a lathe gives its operator an immense thrill of importance and power, for he feels he has a share in the success of the machine, the factory, and the People's Republic [p. 120].

Koningsberger goes on to say that these workers are content despite a 48-hour work week. For them, factory work is a "vocation." Does this suggest that in the spirit of Carlyle, Ruskin, and pioneers of the vocational guidance movement, all work may yet "call" people? In this vein, Levenstein (see Chapter 4, this volume) suggests that social responsibility may provide a sense of commitment and fulfillment for men at work in an age of automation:

> As economic incentives diminish in intensity, psychic needs will come to the fore. As individual material needs are met with increasing ease, social responsibility will have to become a more persuasive motivating factor [p. 143].

Levenstein, however, does not tell us how to accomplish this. Under certain conditions, social responsibility can be a very powerful motivating force. But it is by no means certain that such conditions will exist or that this attitude will prevail. Levenstein indicates that it should prevail, that making it prevail is perhaps an appropriate purpose of vocational guidance. If so, we might attempt to recapture the essence of vocation in a "call" to the service of one's country, or of mankind. An example is the patriotic call to military service in wartime. This induces men to enlist—but it may fall short of helping them to maintain a sense of commitment and fulfillment while peeling potatoes on KP. (Indeed, plans to establish a volunteer army have been foreshadowed by curtailing the housekeeping chores of soldiers at some army camps.)

In this connection, it may be interesting to note that much current disenchantment with technology can be found among staid middle-class people who have become quite dependent on it. Their disillusionment is not philosophical, but practical. They complain that nothing works any more, because no one cares any more. They are resigned to frequent breakdowns of the products and services they use in their daily lives. They see neglect and lack of commitment pervasive at all levels—physicians, medical technologists, and hospital orderlies; engineers, draftsmen, and inspectors; architects, plumbers, and laborers. But such low levels of commitment seem less likely to survive long periods of preparation for the higher level vocations and occupations. In short, then, while we dutifully note that a person's attitude toward his work—not the level of the work itself—is the main determinant, we realistically recognize that the probabilities are greatest for finding vocation in high-level work, occupation in the middle and upper-middle range, and employment at the lower-middle and low levels.

The Mission of Vocational Guidance: A Reformulation

Vocational Guidance or Career Guidance?

The distinctions between vocation, occupation, and employment represent three substantially different types of career, and the choice of one another is a crucial part of the content of vocational guidance. If the term vocational were used literally, the content of vocational guidance would refer to the choices to be made by those who have branched into the area labeled vocation; occupational guidance and employment guidance would cover the other areas; and career guidance would be the comprehensive term including choices between and within the areas of vocation, occupation, employment, avocation, and nonwork. There is much to commend this use of career to refer to the totality of life style, including both horizontal and vertical dimensions. Thus, career would incorporate the possible patterns of choice at any given point in time—education, work, community service, affiliations, hobbies, and so on, in various mixes. It would also include choices along a time line: how do options at any point in time relate to options in the near, intermediate, and distant future?

Although "career guidance" is gaining currency and, indeed, is used in the title of this book, a mild objection must be raised against this change in nomenclature. One can with more impunity tamper with ideas than with titles. Vocational guidance has given its name to a professional organization that has achieved widespread recognition and acceptance. It has roots in history. The part of discretion, therefore, seems to be to retain the name and change the concept. This, in fact, is what has been happening over the years, at a particularly accelerated rate since 1950. As long as the connotation does not mislead, it seems preferable to go on using vocational guidance as a (perhaps somewhat elegant) synecdoche for what we might otherwise want to call career guidance.

Choices and Values

Before rebraiding the terminology unraveled in this discussion, each strand will be used to wrap up a little more securely some parts of the vast content of vocational guidance.

First, the basic choice between vocation, occupation, employment, and nonwork is essentially a choice between arrays of values, or value systems. A previous definition (Katz, 1957, 1963) identifies values in this sense as characteristic expressions and culturally influenced manifestations of needs. Values are distinct from needs in that they are usually described teleologically, in terms of the goal or satisfaction that is sought rather than the motivating drive. They are distinct from interests in that they refer to the worth of outcomes and results of an activity rather than to the "function pleasure" derived from performing the activity. Thus, altruism and high income are (often conflicting) occupational values. *How* one likes to help people or make money—by talking to groups or repairing machinery, or solving mathematical problems—expresses occupational interests.

Some of the confusion between values and interests may be dispelled by recognizing that intrinsic activity interest is itself a value. For example, when Ginzberg, Ginsburg, Axelrad, and Herma (1951) talk about the "interest stage" in early adolescence, they are saying that interests are highly valued at this age: that is, it is a typical early adolescent value to choose activities for their intrinsic interest or function pleasure. Some values thus seem to vary systematically with age: for example, the 12-year-old boy who shows no concern for personal appearance or popularity with girls can be expected to reveal a different value in later adolescence. In this instance, one value can supersede its antithesis with very little stress. No irrevocable commitment to the future has been made on the basis of the earlier attitude. On the other hand, a change from valuing "adventure" highly to valuing "security" highly—or a shift from "immediate gratification" to "tolerance of delay"—while also somewhat predictable during growth from adolescence to adulthood, may be accompanied by problems in reconsidering choices previously made and patching up preparatory activities already engaged in.

Values are frequently introcepted from family, peer groups, and other cultural influences. Much about the genesis and development of values, or even about the major dimensions of the values domain, is yet unknown. Nevertheless, an illustrative list such as the following, supported by various studies, may help clarify the concept of values as it applies to vocations: money-income, power-authority, stability-security, adventure-excitement-change-variety, autonomy, knowledge-new ideas, altruistic service, prestige-fame-recognition, leisure time, and intrinsic activity interest. One cannot claim that such a list is complete for all purposes or that it represents ten independent dimensions. That the names represent different levels of complexity and abstraction (e.g., money-income and autonomy), however, does not necessarily betray any fuzziness in the constructs. For just such complex lists have proven useful: eighth- and ninth-grade students have been able to grasp the concept of values, with the help of a similar list, and to apply this concept to their own planning (Shimberg & Katz, 1962; Gribbons, 1960). Furthermore, college freshmen and other high school graduates have construed this domain of values as quite distinct from the domains of aptitude and interest (Norris & Katz, 1970).

Goals and Instrumentalities

Exploration and examination of individual value systems are, then, early steps in the basic choice between vocation, occupation, employment, and nonwork. Equally important is knowlege of the fit between any individual value system and the rewards and satisfactions typically available within each of the major options—vocation, occupation, employment, and nonwork. The individual's value system specifies the nature of the gratifications and rewards he seeks. What he also needs to know is where he can encounter these gratifications and rewards. Thus, while the primary content area of vocational guidance is the choice of goals, the secondary content area is information about the means for attaining those goals. This does not imply that there are two distinct stages—that we choose goals first, and then means. Choices from these two content areas are intermixed over time, and indeed often interact. Cause-effect can flow in either direction. For example, a high school student who has made a vocational choice—perhaps, tentatively, engineering or physical science—elects Algebra II. Or, conversely, the student may elect Algebra II (on the basis of previous performance and experience with mathematics, or on an exploratory basis, or perhaps simply because it is there)—and the outcome of this choice leads him to entertain a self-concept that includes probable college attendance at intermediate range and, among other long-range options, the possibility of a vocation in engineering or physical science. Thus, "primary" and "secondary" do not refer to time, but to the size and scope of the choices. The "primary" choice may lead to "secondary" choices, or it may be induced by them—or, what is more likely, "primary" and "secondary" choices may interact in a complex way.

Shaping Work to People

We must recognize also that there is not necessarily a perfect fit between the domain of values and the satisfactions offered by all possible options. (This is one reason for the need for compromise in choice.) Only the naïveté of a Candide would expect to find perfect compatibility between what a person wants and the opportunities for gratification that our society offers, whether in vocation, occupation, employment, nonwork, leisure, avocation, or any combination of these. Thus, knowing what one wants is not quite the same as deciding which among an array of available options (or combinations of options) suits one best. That is why the content of vocational guidance must include not only individual values but information about options.

When man fills any work role, he is not merely passive; he tends to shape it to his wants. In fact, insofar as man's work was invented by man, it must be related not only to his capabilities but to his predilections. From the earliest times, out of the manifold ways in which man might have used the earth's resources for his sustenance, he has tended to choose and retain some, to ignore and reject others. If he is to continue to exercise human influence on the nature of work in a society where automation seems to have picked up an almost inhuman momentum of its own, he must not abrogate concern for his own values. When a person can find no work that seems to offer him an opportunity for success and satisfaction, we tend to think that the person is inadequate. This condition may also, or instead, reflect an inadequacy of the society. We expect a person to compromise his values in terms of the options available—that is, to take on a less-than-ideal kind of work. At the same time, we recognize that society may often have to compromise too, accepting a less-than-ideal worker, allowing him (to some extent) to shape his work after his own image.

A strenuously developing economy, emphasizing maximum efficiency and productivity, is not likely to initiate such a compromise. But what of a mature and affluent economy, with a surplus labor force? If we assume that work *per se* is important—is better than nonwork—can not such a society create vocations and occupations that emphasize individual values even at the expense of economic values? There is some precedent for this. During depression days, many federal projects—e.g., in theater, art, and writing—found capable people and paid them to work in the field of their capability, provided them with an opportunity for success, self-fulfillment, and satisfaction, and derived from the bargain socially useful products.

We can make everyday observations of ways in which people use what leeway they have to shape the nature of their work, not necessarily in keeping with the vectors of social and economic forces. Campbell (1966) illustrates this point in a slightly different context:

> Large numbers of men in our society continue to want to farm; yet we have no use for them. Psychotherapists continue to practice in the face of highly inconclusive results as to their effectiveness. Pharmacists . . . have leaned their occupations more toward the retailer than toward the scientist . . . whence their training comes. Morticians . . . have molded an occupation more oriented toward sales activities than toward either the biological sciences which is part of their training or the social service area which is part of their desired public image [p. 856].

One may take issue with the second, third, and fourth examples, which seem to reflect economic forces. Still, the notion is an intriguing one, warranting further examination. It is mentioned here as relevant to the emphasis on the prime importance of individual values as part of the content of vocational guidance. Thus, of all the choices an individual makes, his choice of values is the most crucial.

Strength of Return

Since discrepancies between one's values and the satisfactions offered by available options may require a compromise, another important element in the content of vocational guidance is information about the kinds of rewards and satisfactions typically found in each option. These satisfactions may vary somewhat across individuals who have chosen any one option, but usually this variability is less than the variability across options. For example, a youth who is trying to decide between such options as teaching and law can ordinarily expect systematic differences in the rewards inherent in these alternatives; similarly differentiated expectations might hold when the options represent school subjects, colleges, vocation vs. employment, or any other array. The differentiation is not only of kind, but also of amount or degree. That is, although two vocations may show similar profiles in the rank order of satisfactions they tend to offer (for example, relatively high stability-security, relatively low adventure-excitement-change), there may be characteristic differences in magnitude (for example, teaching may typically offer more stability-security than law). Since any choice requires an investment (in time, in money, in restriction of future opportunities, or whatever), it may even be possible to relate the magnitude of the satisfactions typically expected to the magnitude of the investment. This relationship may be dubbed the anticipated "strength of return." These concepts require further development in a description of *process.* They are introduced here to suggest that there is much essential material to be added to that portion of the content of vocational guidance called "occupational information." Such material would allow the individual to assess the instrumentality of each occupation, its relative capability of providing those satisfactions that are weighted as most desirable according to his value system.

Predicting Entry and Success

Existing educational and occupational information typically stresses the requirements for entry (as into colleges, professional schools, apprenticeships, occupations, and so on). Some of these requirements are expressed as aptitudes or abilities (for example, scores on the Scholastic Aptitude Test or the General Aptitude Test Battery), although other requirements are sometimes mentioned (for example, being the son of a union member). Since the discrepancies between abilities or other individual characteristics and requirements may reduce probabilities of entry, or of success, realism of choice may also call for compromise. This is the compromise most commonly referred to in the literature, the compromise that narrows the discrepancy between what an individual wants and what he has a reasonable chance of getting. How this can be accomplished is again a matter for discussion of process. Here it is necessary to mention only the lag between prediction data that could be obtained for most options and what is actually available. Hills' work in Georgia (Hills, Franz, & Emory, 1959), papers by Cooley (1964, 1966), and a pilot project in Indiana secondary schools and colleges (Educational Testing Service, 1965) point the way toward developments that will flesh out this portion of the content of vocational guidance. More recently, Novick (1970) has described the contribution to prediction for guidance that may be obtained from a Bayesian approach.

A "Curriculum" for Vocational Guidance

It will be valuable to recapitulate what the content of vocational guidance—the choices that our society permits among career options—should include. Perhaps, like curriculum developers, this content we can express in terms of attitudes, understandings, knowledge, and skills.

A "curriculum" for vocational guidance should start with the individual's understanding and acceptance of his own responsibility for making career choices, supplemented by knowledge of appropriate sources of assistance.

It should include an understanding of the sequential nature of choices—the relationship of a choice at any given point in time to antecedent and subsequent choices. This includes skill in reality testing—in using the outcomes of early choices in the confirmation or revision of hypotheses about self.

It should include knowledge of options in the domain of human values. This knowledge should be accompanied by an attitude of willingness to explore values, to subject them to scrutiny and probing, so that an individual's explicit value system represents examined values.

It should also include recognition of predictable changes in value systems. Values are not immutable. People change, and conditions change. These changes interact, and what a person once wanted he may no longer prize. (Remember Goethe's warning to be careful what you want when you are young, because when you are older you are likely to get it. And Shaw's aphorism to the effect that the only thing worse than not getting what you want is getting it.)

It should include awareness of the full array of conditions of work and attitudes toward work. A classification has been proposed that exploits the somewhat different connotations of vocation, occupation, and employment, emphasizing not only the extent to which each fills the vessel of career but also such qualitative differences as, respectively, commitment and intrinsic reward; change, flexibility, and versatility; hedonism and leisure. The category of nonwork, too, has been considered, and the question has been raised whether this may be taken as a legitimate alternative.

It should include some grasp of the rewards and satisfactions characteristic of each specific option at each choice-point so that the individual can determine the fit of these characteristics to his own values as he perceives them at that time. It must not ignore man's capability for shaping an option according to his own values.

It should include awareness of the cost and consequences of each decision—that is, the nature of the investment made, what is being risked, or lost, or foreclosed, by choosing a given option.

It should include knowledge and understanding of probabilities of entry and success in each option considered at any choice-point.

Here, let us add that it should also include information about ways and means of proceeding. Ours is a complicated world, often needlessly complicated. In such enterprises as applying for a college scholarship or getting a job, there is no one agency to which an individual can go for complete instructions or processing. Even in working out ways and means, there are choices to be made, priorities to be considered. Choices must be made among different resources for information and among various agencies that offer help. Perhaps eventually some kind of "clearinghouse" operation will be established. For example, Lester (1966) has urged a revamping of the governmental Employment Service system to obtain a more comprehensive job-exchange and a freer flow of job information. These and other modifications should not only help the labor market to function more effectively, but simplify the demands now made on the individual's know-how, initiative, and "connections." The Department of Labor is currently trying out, in a few regions, use of computers to maintain classified lists of jobs and of people seeking work. Computer-based college locator services are also in operation, and clearinghouse operations have been proposed for college admissions and financial aid awards. In principle, these seem to be quite feasible. Such exchange or clearinghouse operations would not restrict freedom of choice, but would enhance it by making all options more accessible to all individuals. They would not manage manpower, but would disseminate information. Unless or until such operations are established, however, free and full access to information of this kind cannot be taken for granted. The content of vocational guidance must, therefore, include provision for obtaining the most elementary and pedestrian kind of practical information and for developing skill in its use.

What remains for a consideration of the content of vocational guidance is also borrowed from the field of curriculum development. It is the need for a detailed exposition of objectives, scope, and sequence. While objectives and scope have already been touched upon, sequence or timing seems to require more attention. What specific attitudes, understandings, knowledge, and skills constitute vocational maturity at various ages? How should they be ordered? Thus, what content should the elementary school child be dealing with? the junior high school pupil? the high school, college, or graduate student? the school dropout at any of these levels? the beginning apprentice? the journeyman? the young worker? the mature adult? the unemployed of various ages? the handicapped? the man in his 60s approaching retirement? the married woman?

Ginzberg et al. (1951), Super (1957), Miller and Form (1951), Havighurst (1964), Tiedeman and O'Hara (1963), and others have outlined stages in career development. Super's Career Pattern Study (Super & Overstreet, 1960) and other longitudinal studies (e.g., Gribbons & Lohnes, 1968; Crites, 1969) have suggested and tested hypotheses pertaining to the course of career development, to the definition of vocational maturity at various stages, and—by extension—to the appropriate content of vocational guidance. But we still do not have a full "curriculum" for vocational guidance. Since career extends, as has been suggested, along both horizontal and vertical dimensions, objectives and content need to be specified for each cell in the matrix. Work on some cells has been done, and much more is now going on. A classic contribution was Super and Overstreet's (1960) investigation of indices of vocational maturity of ninth-grade boys, and the Career Pattern Study has continued to track its population into adulthood. Katz (1957) developed curriculum materials for eighth and ninth graders, working from premises very similar in many respects to Super and Overstreet's conclusions, but with special emphasis on values. The rationale underlying these materials is explicated in a monograph (Katz, 1963) which also considers appropriate content for another cell in the matrix: college choices made by 11th or 12th graders. Martinson (1959) and Borow & Lindsey (1959) developed materials for vocational guidance of college students. Lifton (1960) has developed materials for grades three to six. Hansen (1970) has described a number of current programs, including several computer-assisted ones, at various levels.

These and other recent and current projects have tended to deal with the questions about objectives, scope, and sequence that are crucial for developing a curriculum in vocational guidance. Similar questions have also both plagued and stimulated developers of curricula in the traditional school-subject disciplines. For example, what logic determines sequence? Is there a sequence inherent in the structure of the subject itself? Is one operation or function prerequisite for another? Is there a sequence that is "right" genetically—a "readiness" determined by age? Or should the individual be trusted to determine his own appropriate sequence by following his own interests, according to the gospel of progressive education?

If the structure of the subject is to guide us, how shall we look at structure? Are there not many structures to be perceived in most subjects? For example, in the social studies, sequence may be based on chronology, or on geographic proximity, or on certain themes or issues that cut across time and place. To some extent, these questions can be answered empirically: if we can agree on criteria for evaluating outcomes (Katz, 1966a), different structures can be tested experimentally. Agreement on criteria probably requires professional sponsorship of a "blue-ribbon" working committee which can express its consensus in terms of specific behaviors that represent progressive mastery of the content of vocational guidance and that can be observed. Appropriate observations could then be systematized into measurements, and the measurements used for evaluation of alternative structures and procedures. There is a model for this kind of interlocking development and evaluation in the operations of the curriculum builders in many areas of education—modern languages, natural and physical sciences, social sciences, mathematics, and so on. Perhaps a serious drawback to "curriculum development" in vocational guidance has been the lack of good standardized instruments for measuring outcomes in relation to objectives.

This continuing curriculum analogy seems most appropriate for vocational guidance in a school setting, but the out-of-school individual may also require comprehensive services. A good array of measures would be extremely useful in helping him to find out where he is in his vocational development; like good placement tests they would enable him to choose the "treatment" for which he is ready.

Good criterion instruments would also enable us to put dogmas about genetically determined sequences to an empirical test. So-called "genetic" formulations have failed to measure the impact of instruction on the perceived order of phenomena. For example, Ginzberg et al. (1951) declared that substages in vocational development were genetically determined, with interests, abilities, and values successively dominant at ages 11–12, 12–14, and 15–16, respectively. However, these stages may just as well be regarded as culturally determined. The 11–14-year-old boys in their sample who showed little awareness of values may simply not have been exposed to appropriate stimuli and experiences. The genetic readiness to develop such awareness may have been present, waiting to be evoked by encounters with the environment that more generally occur in our culture by ages 15–16. But there is no necessity for the vocational guidance program to wait until then for awareness of values to develop. In fact, there are compelling reasons not to wait—mainly the importance of the choices made earlier (Katz, 1963). Indeed, it has been demonstrated (Gribbons, 1960; Shimberg & Katz, 1962) that relatively brief periods of instruction can move the "values" stage up to ages 12–14. In short, then, the existing evidence for genetic determinants does not seem firm enough to depend on. Although it may be reasonable to assume that genetic factors must be taken into account in determining sequence, it is not yet clear just what they are and what influence they exert. Certainly, the timing of choices in our culture is late enough to avoid any serious impediment from genetic factors. Therefore, an open-minded empirical approach seems justified. Sequences can be developed according to plausible theories of structure, and put to the pragmatic test: do they work as hypothesized in accomplishing the objectives that will have been specified to represent progressive mastery of the content of vocational guidance?

The Relevance of Vocational Guidance for Youth in the 1970s

To talk of the timing of choices in our culture reminds us that the content of vocational guidance we have considered here is strongly culture bound. Much of it is based on accumulated experience—such as information about the choices to be made, about the instrumentality of various occupations, about the probabilities of entry and success in various options. Indeed, even the dimensionality and definitions of individual values are derived from the culture. The compromises involved in choices can be seen as a transaction between the individual and the culture. In short, vocational guidance is concerned with helping the individual to see the culture in himself and to see himself in the culture. It induces him to ask first, "Where have my values come from?" Then he is expected to cope with the question, "Where are they taking me?"

But some proportion of youth now reject the culture vehemently and deny the relevance of its accumulated experience for their career decisions. They see little worth in many of the vocations to which their elders have given whole-hearted commitment. They associate these vocations with an establishment that has fostered war, pollution, inequity, and a "plastic" civilization. They pride themselves on resistance to that establishment or withdrawal from it, and regard themselves as part of a counter culture. They want no part of their talents used to conduct war in Indo-China, to build the SST, to construct new highways, to explore space. Some of them have been more willing to accept a "calling" to clear urban slums, to educate the illiterate, to end racial discrimination, to eliminate hunger, to organize war resistance, to improve health, to clean up air and water, to protect consumers; they have accepted activist roles either within the system or—claiming that the social or political order prevents them from acting effectively toward such goals—in opposition to it. Others have been "called" to a simpler way of life, less dependent on technology and bureaucracy; rejecting what is "plastic," they have turned to handicrafts and to organic agriculture, often in communes. Still others have been "called" to contemplation and mysticism. Finally, there are some who have withdrawn to the special awareness they feel they can obtain only from sensitivity-heightening or hallucinogenic drugs.

Is the content of vocational guidance relevant to youths who identify with one or more of these elements in the counter culture? The options offered by the counter culture, we must reply, are part of the content of vocational guidance. They are options for choice. The values espoused by one generation are as legitimate for exploration and examination as those embraced by their elders. Indeed, the primacy given to individual values in vocational guidance today is very close to youth's emphasis on "doing your own thing." The content of vocational guidance as defined in this chapter can incorporate a choice between handicrafts and engineering, or between draft resistance and voluntary enlistment. It can countenance the weighting of such values as sensitivity, simplicity, and community as well as money, status, and power. It is open to new interpretations of the instrumentality of various occupations. It does not, however, accept all elements of the counter culture. It makes no allowance for escape from rationality into hallucination. It holds out also against the validity of Tarot cards. With these reservations, the content of vocational guidance defined here should be no less relevant for the mid-1970s than for the decades preceding. Career choices will continue to be made. Many of these choices involve multidimensional and complex options. We cannot expect individuals to acquire relevant knowledge and adequate understanding of the options incidentally. Instead, all options that youth wants to consider rationally should be included in the content of vocational guidance. Then, with all possible help in mastering the knowledge, concepts, and competencies he needs for informed and rational decision making, each individual will be free to make his own career decisions.

REFERENCES

Borow, H., & Lindsey, R. V. *Vocational planning for college students.* Englewood Cliffs, N. J.: Prentice-Hall, 1959.

Brewer, J. M. *History of vocational guidance.* New York: Harper, 1942.

Broudy, H. S., Smith, B. O., & Burnett, J. R. *Democracy and excellence in American secondary education.* New York: Rand McNally, 1964.

Campbell, D. P. The Minnesota vocational interest inventory. *Personnel and Guidance Journal*, 1966, **44,** 854–858.

Conant, J. B. *Slums and suburbs.* New York: McGraw-Hill, 1961.

Cooley, W. W. A computer-measurement system for guidance. *Harvard Educational Review*, 1964, **34,** 558–572.

Cooley, W. W. Redefining career plan groups. In J. C. Flanagan &

W. W. Cooley, *Project TALENT one-year follow-up studies.* Cooperative Research Project No. 2333. Pittsburgh: University of Pittsburgh, 1966. 205–224.

Crites, J. O. *The maturity of vocational attitudes in adolescence.* Iowa City: University of Iowa, 1969.

Dobbin, J. *Observations of project head start: A report on 335 project head start centers.* Princeton: The Institute for Educational Development, 1965.

Dubin, R. Industrial workers' worlds: A study of the "central life interests" of industrial workers. *Social Problems,* 1956, **3,** 131–142.

Educational Testing Service. *Manual of freshman class profiles for Indiana colleges.* Princeton, N. J.: Educational Testing Service, 1965.

Eninger, M. W. *The process and product of T & I high school level vocational education in the United States.* Pittsburgh: American Institutes for Research, 1965.

Flanagan, J. C., & Cooley, W. W. *Project TALENT one-year follow-up studies.* Cooperative Research Project No. 2333. Pittsburgh: University of Pittsburgh, 1966.

Ginzberg, E., Ginsburg, S. W., Axelrad, S., & Herma, J. L. *Occupational choice: An approach to a general theory.* New York: Columbia University Press, 1951.

Gribbons, W. D. Evaluation of an eighth-grade group guidance program. *Personnel and Guidance Journal,* 1960, **38,** 740–745.

Gribbons, W. D. Changes in readiness for vocational planning from the 8th grade to the 10th grade. *Personnel and Guidance Journal,* 1964, **42,** 908–913.

Gribbons, W. D., & Lohnes, P. R. *Emerging careers.* New York: Teachers College Press, Columbia University, 1968.

Hansen, L. *Career guidance practices in school and community.* Washington: National Vocational Guidance Association, 1970.

Havighurst, R. J. Youth in exploration and man emergent. In H. Borow (Ed.), *Man in a world at work.* Boston: Houghton Mifflin, 1964.

Hills, J., Franz, G., & Emory, L. *Counselor's guide to Georgia colleges.* Atlanta: University System of Georgia, 1959.

Hofstadter, R. *The age of reform.* New York: Vintage Books, 1955.

Hughes, E. C. *Men and their work.* Glencoe, Ill.: Free Press, 1958.

Junior College Journal, Feb. 1971, **41,** 60.

Katz, M. *You: Today and tomorrow.* (1st ed.) Princeton, N. J.: Cooperative Test Division, Educational Testing Service, 1957.

Katz, M. *Decisions and values: A rationale for secondary school guidance.* New York: College Entrance Examination Board, 1963.

Katz, M. Criteria for evaluation. In Ann Martin (Ed.), *Occupational information and vocational guidance for non-college youth.* Pittsburgh: University of Pittsburgh, 1966. (a)

Katz, M. A model of guidance for career decision-making. *Vocational Guidance Quarterly*, 1966, **15,** 2–10. (b)

Katz, M. Counseling—secondary school. In R. Ebel & V. Noll (Eds.), *Encyclopedia of educational research.* (4th ed.), 1969. (a)

Katz, M. Theoretical foundations of guidance. *Review of Educational Research*, 1969, **39,** 127–140. (b)

Katz, M. Can computers make guidance decisions for students? *College Board Review*, Summer 1969, **12,** 13–17. (c)

Koningsberger, H. China notes. *New Yorker*, 1966, **42**(9), 57–125.

Lester, R. *Manpower planning in a free society.* Princeton, N. J.: Princeton University Press, 1966.

Lifton, W. M. *What could I be?* Chicago: Science Research Associates, 1960.

Lynd, R. S., & Lynd, H. M. *Middletown in transition: A study in cultural conflicts.* New York: Harcourt, Brace, 1937.

Martinson, W. D. *Educational and vocational planning.* Chicago: Scott, Foresman, 1959.

Michael, D. M. The plausible future: Some trends, some questions, and some answers. In *A report of the invitational conference on implementing career development theory and research through the curriculum.* Sponsored by the National Vocational Guidance Association, Airlie House: Warrenton, Virginia, May 1–4, 1966.

Miller, D. C., & Form, W. H. *Industrial sociology: The sociology of industrial organizations.* New York: Harper and Row, 1951.

Moore, G. H., & Hedges, J. N. Trends in labor and leisure. *Monthly Labor Review*, February 1971, **94,** 3–11.

Myers, G. E. *Principles and techniques of vocational guidance.* New York: McGraw-Hill, 1941.

National Vocational Guidance Association. The principles and practices of educational and vocational guidance. *Occupations*, 1937, **15,** 772–778.

Nichols, R., & Astin, A. Progress of the Merit Scholars: An 8-year follow-up. *Personnel and Guidance Journal*, 1966, **44,** 673–681.

Norris, L., & Katz, M. *The measurement of academic interests.* New York: College Entrance Examination Board, RDR 70–71, No. 5, 1970.

Novick, M. R., & Jackson, P. H. Bayesian guidance technology. *Review of Educational Research*, October 1970, **40** (4), 459–494.

Overs, R. P. (Compiler) *Abstracts of sociological literature on occupations.* Cleveland: Research Department, Vocational Guidance and Rehabilitation Services, 1964. (Mimeographed)

Poor, R. (Ed.). *Four days, forty hours.* Cambridge, Mass.: Bursk and Poor, 1970.

Reinhold, R. "Recent graduates of Harvard found taking manual jobs." New York *Times*, March 3, 1971, p. 45.

Rockwell, P. J., & Rothney, J. W. M. Some social ideas of pioneers in the guidance movement. *Personnel and Guidance Journal*, 1961, **40,** 349–354.

Roe, A. *The psychology of occupations.* New York: Wiley, 1956.

Samler, J. Psychosocial aspects of work: A critique of occupational information. *Personnel and Guidance Journal*, 1961, **39,** 458–465.

Shimberg, B., & Katz, M. Evaluation of a guidance text. *Personnel and Guidance Journal*, 1962, **41,** 126–132.

Stephens, W. R. *Social reform and the origins of vocational guidance.* Washington, D.C.: National Vocational Guidance Association, 1970.

Super, D. E. A theory of vocational development. *American Psychologist*, 1953, **8,** 185–190.

Super, D. E. *The psychology of careers.* New York: Harper, 1957.

Super, D. E. Toward making self-concept theory operational. In D. E. Super, R. Starishevsky, N. Matlin, & J. P. Jordaan, *Career development: Self-concept theory.* New York: College Entrance Examination Board, 1963.

Super, D. E., & Overstreet, P. L. *The vocational maturity of ninth-grade boys.* New York: Bureau of Publications, Teachers College, Columbia University, 1960.

Tiedeman, D. V., & O'Hara, R. P. *Career development: Choice and adjustment.* New York: College Entrance Examination Board, 1963.

United States Bureau of the Census. *Statistical Abstract of the United States.* Washington, D.C.: Government Printing Office, 1970.

United States Department of Labor, Bureau of Labor Statistics. *Occupational outlook handbook.* (1st ed.) Washington, D.C.: Government Printing Office, 1949.

United States Department of Labor, Bureau of Labor Statistics. *Occupational outlook handbook.* 1970–71 Edition. Washington, D.C.: Government Printing Office, 1970.

Weber, M. *The Protestant ethic and the spirit of capitalism.* New York: Scribner's, 1930.

Wilensky, H. L. Orderly careers and social participation: The impact of work history on social integration in the middle mass. *American Sociological Review*, 1961, **26**, 521–539.

Wilensky, H. L. Varieties of work experience. In H. Borow (Ed.), *Man in a world at work.* Boston: Houghton Mifflin, 1964.

Wolfbein, S. L. Labor trends, manpower, and automation. In H. Borow (Ed.), *Man in a world at work.* Boston: Houghton Mifflin, 1964.

4

work and its meaning in an age of affluence

AARON LEVENSTEIN
Bernard M. Baruch College,
City University of New York

What effects has the era of industrial technology, with its mass production, interchangeable parts, specialization of labor, and fragmented occupations had upon work as human experience? In this chapter, Aaron Levenstein tells us that society has purchased industrialization and the resultant rise in material productivity at a fearsome personal price to the individual. While his concern is chiefly with the diminished meanings of work for those who labor in manufacture, those in other occupational settings may be affected as well.

Adult man's psychological identity, Levenstein asserts, has long derived mainly from his occupation and from the bond with society which his work affords. The traditional intrinsic rewards of work, however, are no longer available to many. It is difficult for workers who lack a proprietary or creative attachment to their jobs to achieve ego involvement. Industrial efficiency, which was exalted in the early scientific management approach of Frederick Winslow Taylor and given later impetus by the emergence of automation, focuses upon the *system* of production and subordinates the role of the worker within the system. Too frequently, man labors at tasks which are piecemeal, fashioned by others, remote from the finished product, and incapable of gratifying his most human needs. He is left in psychological conflict with his work and alienated from it. Moreover, feelings of alienation are likely to grow with the further impact of automation. As occupations become less central in man's life, the potential function of leisure-time experience in allowing effective expression to his personal and social motives assumes critical significance.

Can we, then, construct a social order in which nonwork activities supplant productive labor as the source of self-esteem and a feeling of purposeful achievement? Levenstein thinks not. His pessimism is anchored in the belief that men and women who devote their working lives to jobs which are devoid of personal meaning and which thwart important psychological motives cannot but fail to feel the adverse effects upon their behavior outside the work role. Given the depersonalizing experience which is an organic part of so many jobs in a technologically sophisticated society, they must not expect leisure alone to function as the restorer of personal worth and as a sufficient source of self-fulfillment. Who we are and what we are, contends Levenstein, are too intimately interwoven with our work for that.

Is there a possible means of escape from the dilemma? Levenstein proposes one, but he does not claim that its achievement is easy, nor can the reader feel confident that we know how to bring about the massive transformation in work values which Levenstein's solution appears to require. He pleads for a strengthening of the individual's valuing of his work by enabling him to see its broader social purpose, indeed, by convincing him of the importance of that work to the very survival of society, and by having both society and the individual subsequently act on that belief. A profound communal commitment to work is called for.

It is education, particularly by means of instruction in the humanities, which Levenstein believes can perhaps best nourish the individual's awareness of his oneness with mankind and his sense of societal purpose through work. It may be true that typical man can no longer be intimately involved with the product of his labor from inception to completion. But he can learn to appreciate the contribution his economic effort makes to an ongoing civilization. While his work may be partial and fragmented, man himself, concludes Levenstein, "can belong to the whole."

H. B.

Sigmund Freud has said that work is man's link to reality. What happens to that link in an age of affluence when old incentives cease to be adequate? What happens when the nature of work itself is revolutionized by the new technology of automation which has untold psychological consequences? If the application of cybernetics lives up to its highest potential—namely, the production of a cornucopia of products with a minimum expenditure of human labor—man will witness a new day of affluence undreamed of in human history.

Two elements in the current scene seem to be significant in an examination of work and its meaning for man: first, that traditional incentives toward work are being rendered obsolete by the technology of abundance and, second, that a reorientation toward reality is made necessary by the new conditions.

Most employers are already aware that the work attitudes of the latter half of the twentieth century are far different from those that prevailed at the beginning of the century. The flow of goods made possible in the United States by technology has diminished the incentive power of hunger—the original propulsion toward work. The new industrial revolution is making it unnecessary for man to labor in routine jobs. In the face of plenty, society could not allow men to go hungry, even though it might tolerate poverty and malnutrition, a state of affairs in which men are permitted to be wretched but not to die of starvation. The welfare state—with its relief, its governmental social security, its minimum wage regulations, its privately established health, welfare and pension gaining—has blunted the cutting edge of hunger as a weapon to force men to work.

The new technology, with its promise of even greater abundance to come, has already led serious-minded economists to speak of a national guarantee of at least a minimum standard of living. Even conservative economists are talking about a "negative income tax" under which those who file returns showing less than a given income—say, $3,000 a year—will be entitled to a subsidy from the federal government. It is a measure of the revolutionary sweep of recent times that a conservative economist like Dr. Milton Friedman, one of Mr. Goldwater's advisors in the 1964 presidential campaign, advanced this idea, while a liberal economist like Leon Keyserling opposed it on the ground that it would impair the incentives needed to maintain full production. Technology will decide the question. But however it comes out—whatever economic devices are used—the prospect of abundance seems reasonable enough.

Besides the question of how society can guarantee to all its citizens equal access to abundance, the question arises of what happens to man, his attitudes, his understanding of and relationship to work when this abundance is realized. For some time now, man's outlook has shifted in a direction that is unique to the twentieth century. His way of life is oriented toward leisure; life is no longer centered on work. Once the function of leisure time was to refresh the individual—hence the origin of the term recreation—so that man could recreate the resources needed to return to his tasks; today the major function of work is to make possible leisure time. The nature of tasks has changed as a result of the division of labor, and goods and services are more the product of the machine than of human effort. Pride in craftsmanship, emotional involvement in the task itself, the proprietary feeling of the artisan, these are rapidly fading away and will disappear entirely for millions of workers as automation advances. Man's need for achievement may be satisfied less and less by his work; it may be fed increasingly by his leisure-time activities.

The Specter of Industrialization

Religion once provided an urgent motivation to work. Men believed that their daily occupations were meaningful enough to fulfill their lives. Whether they symbolized the meaningfulness of occupation by a hagiology which identified the craftsman with a specific saint, or whether they expressed it by the concept of "a stewardship of talents" as did the Puritans, or whether they linked their work and worship as did the Hebrews by using the same term *avodah* to represent both, they did indeed find in their economic activities an identification with life's basic meaning.

But this spiritual motivation began to change as society moved into the period of industrialization. Frederick Winslow Taylor (1912), who promoted the concept of specialization and paved the way for the development of mass production industries, expressed the posture of a world beginning to take shape just at the turn of the century. He said:

> In my judgment, the best possible measure of the height of the scale of civilization to which any people has risen is productivity.

> This is the way you measure civilization—the capacity of a people to produce goods. Now then, how do you produce goods? The most efficient way of producing goods is through the basic principle of industrialization, the utilization of interchangeable parts in the mass production process [p. 1471].

The consequences of this development for the individual were correctly discerned and enunciated by Taylor (1911). He declared accurately that "in the past the man has been first; in the future the system must be first [p. 7]." The basic premise was that man increasingly would be secondary to the system. Taylor (1907) recognized the dilemma this presents, and he tried with rather ingenious semantics to suggest a humanistic value that would emerge from it. His words were: "Let me say that we are now but on the threshold of the coming era of true cooperation [p. 57]." He used the word cooperation, an affirmative term with happy connotations, while saying that "the time is fast going by for the great personal or individual achievement of any one man, standing alone and without the help of those around him [p. 57]." By now the time for individual achievement has gone by, and the organization of production today is based upon a concept which management itself articulates as team operation in which no man is indispensable and every man is submerged to the system.

Among the first to foresee the human consequences of technological advance was the young Karl Marx (to be distinguished from the older, materialist Karl Marx), a nineteenth century idealist, who perceived as one of the principal products of the first industrial revolution man's "alienation from his work." Marx spoke of alienation as the feeling of not being at home in a world where one is forced to work at tasks which are partial, incomplete, and external to the individual; tasks which, in fact, are not the design of the worker himself, but of others. Later, he undertook to explain why this comes about, attributing the cause to capitalism, a particular type of economic structure.

We now see that the etiological premise of Marxism has proved to be wrong historically. The only form of industrialization known to Marx was capitalism, and it was capitalism that he viewed as the cause of alienation. The truth is that alienation is inherent in industrialization, regardless of its economic form. It makes no difference whether a country has industrialized on the basis of a free economy, a totalitarian planned economy, a social democratic economy, or a mixed economy. Whenever there is involvement in industrialization—the production of goods through the concept of interchangeable parts, mass production under which the individual worker produces only a component which is then fitted together with other components —alienation takes place, and the economic form does not make any difference whatsoever.

As a matter of fact, the Marxist philosophers of our own day are becoming aware of this. Some years ago, the New York *Times* (1966) carried a report of papers read at a conference on Marxian philosophy. A central theme was that the phenomenon of alienation is not confined to the Western world, that it characterizes youth in Soviet Russia and the other communist countries of the world. Even in China, communism's most intense disciple, the leadership finds a very wide gulf between itself and youth.

A leading Yugoslav Marxist, Gajo Petrovic (1967), declared frankly at the conference "that the problem of the alienation of economic life cannot be solved by the abolition of private property. The transformation of private property into state property, be it capitalist or socialist state property, does not introduce an essential change in the situation of the working man, the producer [p. 153]." Regardless of what type of state is established or what forms of ownership prevail over the instruments of production, invariably the individual confronts a world in which his work has been rendered meaningless because it is partial and fragmented.

The paradox of this problem is that no other efficient system for producing goods is known. If a high standard of living is to be maintained, if the needs of an exploding population are to be met, society has no choice but to rely on advanced technology. Wherever a culture seeks to provide for a large expanding population—in India, China, all of the emerging countries—it is compelled to move toward industrialization. As Milovan Djilas (1957), once Tito's right-hand man, pointed out in *The New*

Class, the key question of our age is what form of economic and political structure is most capable of producing an industrial society rapidly. This is the central issue that must be resolved by the underdeveloped countries whose populations are doomed unless they can industrialize.

New Perspectives Are Needed

There is nothing in the chronicle of twentieth century events to suggest that work is soon to disappear from the life of man. Nothing that has happened yet in automation indicates that the time will come when perpetual motion machines will make it unnecessary for men to concern themselves with the problem of production. Nature will still require of man that he earn his keep, even though it will no longer snap the whip like Pharaoh's overseers supervising the pyramid builders. The twentieth century view of work, in an automated society, is as different from the nineteenth century's attitude as the latter was different from the slave's attitude in Pharaoh's day. But work, however reconstituted in an age of automation, will not disappear from human history. Society must still be concerned about the problem of incentives. In the presence of affluence, the old incentives will no longer work, or will work less effectively. Substitutes will have to be found for those that disappear; those that survive will have to be supplemented or will have to receive a new infusion of vitality.

At this juncture it is difficult to see what the new incentives will be—as difficult as it was for early nineteenth century man to anticipate the kind of economic incentives that would eventually emerge from the industrial revolution and that today can be read in any standard union contract, with all its so-called "fringes." There is still a desire, of course, to move up on the economic scale, to receive a higher income each year, to enjoy more and better goods and services, to move up from a Chevrolet to a Buick.

The annual rise in our standard of living, however, is almost automatic. But it derives not from the increased expenditure of energy by the individual in the course of his working time, nor from hard-won gains in personal skill; it comes from the increased yield that technology creates. The merit increase has been supplanted by the length-of-service increase, to use the language of the personnel administrator. Or to use another personnel term, the employee is reaping the benefits of an automatic progression policy in the nation's system of wage and salary administration. The annual increment is no longer confined to civil service and to education; it is generally accepted in industry. Every employer goes to the bargaining table today with the foreknowledge that he must give his employees some improvement over the terms in the preceding contract, without regard for improved performance in return.

Our social policy is based on the premise that both management and labor are entitled to share the benefits of a rapidly advancing technology. This policy was first formally articulated in the "annual improvement factor" which Alfred P. Sloan wrote into the General Motors contract of 1948: "The annual improvement factor provided herein recognizes that a continuing improvement in the standard of living of employees depends upon technological progress, better tools, methods, processes and equipment, and a cooperative attitude on the part of all parties in such progress. It further recognizes that to produce more with the same amount of human effort is a sound economic and social objective."

Of course it is a sound economic and social objective. But such an automatic progression policy introduces a startling new element in the problem of motivating men in their jobs. Once increased reward depended on personal effort—perhaps harder work, perhaps upgrading one's skill, perhaps ingratiating one's self with the supervisor, perhaps playing office politics—but nevertheless personal effort. Today increased reward depends primarily on impersonal factors—the increased efficiency and output made possible by technology, by better marketing methods, or by the growth of the company due to the general national prosperity. All the employee is asked to do is not to rock the boat.

Though this may be economically rewarding, it can hardly be psychologically rewarding for the worker. The ancient seers warned that man cannot live by bread alone, and their modern counterparts, the omniscient psychologists, tell us that in addition to bread man must have self-esteem and status, a sense of worth, a feeling of purposefulness in what he is doing. In the past the targets of personal purpose were well defined: for the Puritan in early America, purpose and meaning were found in clearing a patch of land in the forest; thus one made a home for himself and his family, and at the same time carried out that "stewardship of talents" which was the religious obligation of all men (Tawney, 1926). But the religious link has long since been broken by the secular society that industrialization has created. And now this new secular society must find an ethos through which personal effort and human involvement can still be instrumental in satisfying psychological needs and providing mental—and if you will, spiritual—health. For regardless of what automated production can do for man's physical well being—indeed because of what automation achieves for him in material affluence—man faces more keenly than ever the problem of purposeful effort.

Out of this malaise, it is possible to discern the general direction for the formulation of new incentives. As economic incentives diminish in intensity, psychic needs will come to the fore. As individual material needs are met with increasing ease, social responsibility will have to become a more persuasive motivating factor. The growth of population which required the increased efficiency in our production methods that only automation could achieve has multiplied the complexity of social organization. *The new incentives will have to derive from man's realization that he stands in a new relationship to society.*

It seems likely that this awareness can come only out of a deepening social crisis. The function of crisis in history is not only to end the old, but to begin the new. Crisis is both the undertaker of the past and the midwife of the future. Without it there would be no incentive to erase the evil in our man-made institutions or to extend the good. A social crisis is merely a situation in which the accumulated errors of the past and the advent of new conditions compel us to alter our established ways.

Specifically, the current crisis involves the problems of transition in moving from the first into the second industrial revolution. The transition into the technological revolution, of course, will be made. The lasting problem is what will happen to man when he has found his new place in the automated structure, for technological advance constitutes a social assault on individual identity. Alienation is bound to increase as the full impact of automation is felt. More and more, the production worker whose hand produced the goods is being replaced—in production as well as in the office—by the white-collar worker who does not handle materials but pieces of paper. The distance between the worker and his product is therefore widened, and the sense of personal contribution to the product is further undermined. Machine-intelligence is substituted for human skill. The greater portion of those employed share none of the glory of the programmer; even the highly skilled among the employees serve as maintenance men rather than direct producers. If the vessel of working time is to be filled with something of value to the individual, new concepts of meaningfulness will have to be evolved from this social crisis.

The problem, of course, is not new, but the circumstances in which it must be solved are new and therefore difficult. Nor is the problem confined to working time; it is found in all the processes of time utilization, whether a man is concerned with earning a living, functioning in a political framework, or engaging in leisure (Levenstein, 1967). There are some who suggest that there can be acceptance of self separate from identification with work. They say that a person will find freedom only outside of the work scene; there he can allow his individuality, his unique personality, to flower. This may be true, but one must pause to question seriously whether the individual can be subjected for hours to tasks that are inherently meaningless because they are incomplete, or because they represent the production of goods in which the person has no proprietary interest, without his behavior outside of the work situation being affected accordingly. Who we are and what we are bears a very close relationship to what we do to earn our living and achieve the kind of status possible in an industrial society. The problem can be resolved only in terms that go deep into the character of human individuality and that define the structure of the whole human value system.

The most significant aspect of the technological revolution of the past two or three decades is not what technology has done to the production and distribution of goods, but what it is doing, and what it is capable of doing, to the human being himself.

Even in the world of automation the human being is still present—to provide the programming, to supervise the machine when necessary, to provide maintenance, or simply to push the buttons. And as long as the human being is on the scene, he must be taken into account. The machines may be able to operate for quite a while even if the employee goes out on strike, as some unions like the Communications Workers have discovered, and the strike as a labor technique may ultimately become obsolete. But the situation is made more serious when the worker has no recourse. Society cannot afford a frustrated, devitalized population, consisting of citizens who spend their working time in a state of alienation and who carry it over into their leisure time.

A Larger Purpose

What is required now is a restoration of the individual's personal involvement in the tasks he performs, but with a new understanding of their nature, for a man no longer works only for himself. Indeed, the primitive needs of the individual in an industrial society can so easily be satisfied that no appeal on that level can call forth his effort or excite his dedication. More sophisticated needs are operative, and they go beyond the individual. They relate to the survival of society, without which ultimately the individual is lost. In our American society, the only reason that can justify greater individual exertion is the need of society itself. Just as the family—a larger unit than the individual—could spur men to greater individual effort, so now the awareness of the larger community will have to motivate men and women in their shops and offices. The knowledge that their participation in economic life produces results that ripple out to the far corners of the globe should provide the new incentives needed to compensate for those that have been weakened or rendered obsolete.

So far there has been a reluctance to spell this out. Steeped in a tradition of so-called individualism, man has insisted that economic activity must be inspired by individual—that is to say, narrowly selfish—interest. He does not acknowledge that individual fulfillment comes primarily in community, and he does not yet believe that the larger the community the greater the opportunity for fulfillment. Man has not known how to contend with the problem of size because he has permitted it to bring about depersonalization. The challenge is to enlarge individuality by learning to live in a larger sphere of activity.

Within the community the individual plays an important role because of the very complexity and interdependence resulting from increased numbers and from the technology of affluence that has accompanied size. Now all can suffer at the hands of one. The mind stumbles in the presence of the awful fact that one individual in a plane can push the button that will release the nuclear holocaust. One man in an automated oil refinery, by malice or by simple neglect, can bring the whole process to a halt. Fantastically expensive controls are needed so that other men, and subtly fashioned equipment and processes, may guard against such an event. A few thousand workers in a metropolis of 8 million can stop the transportation system from operating today; tomorrow, another few thousand can with equal efficiency shut down the office buildings and bring commerce to a halt by refusing to deliver heating fuel; the day after, the sanitation employees can refuse to work and suffocate the city in its own garbage.

The more of us there are, the more we are dependent on each other. Men survive as a society only because in at least this compartment of their minds they understand that the polity depends on each man exercising responsibility. Stuart Chase (1948) recounts that William James, long before this interdependence had become as tight as it is now, wrote:

> A social organism is what it is because each member proceeds to his own duty with a trust that other members will simultaneously do theirs. A government, an army, a commercial system, a ship, a college, an athletic team, all exist on this condition without which not only is nothing achieved, but nothing is even attempted [p. 62].

Today, the changing nature of work calls for a redefinition of man's relationship to society and its instrument, the state. The outstanding characteristic of the way work is performed in our day is the requirement of organization. In the Stone Age, man was close to his raw materials and could survive without complex rules and regulations. As man moved into the ages of metal, commerce had to be developed to bring the raw materials across great distances; specialization began because skills that were not universal had to be brought into play—the skill of the smith and the art of the designer. A new relationship was born among men, resulting from the interdependence that specialization created. Isaiah described this hard economic fact in prophetic terms when he said: "They helped every one his neighbor; and every one said to his brother, 'Be of good courage.' So the carpenter encouraged the goldsmith, and he that smootheth with the hammer him that smite the anvil, saying, 'It is ready for the soldering.' And he fastened it with nails, that it should not be moved." Specialization had taken place. Each would not only have to do his own task, but help his neighbor carry out his.

Man's alienation from himself, a reflection of his alienation from the society in which his self must exist, is promoted today by the ideology of a business system that clings to the individualism of a pioneer community long since replaced by an integrated community. Man's individualism must be redefined to recognize the importance to his selfhood of the encouragement that the goldsmith received from the carpenter, however remote each craft may have seemed from the other. This is a task of the first order for education.

Education in an Age of Affluence

It would be imprudent to suggest that any one institution alone will resolve the crisis created by the progressive industrialization of society, but education is in a strategic position to help foster in the individual a sense of purpose in the work he does. To undertake this task, teachers will have to work toward developing a new value, one based on the understanding that all work, even that which may be fragmented, is meaningful because it contributes to a social end. The critical need is to convey to the worker, or student as potential worker, that those who advance the growth of society by the tasks they perform at work are carrying out a significant social purpose, one that links them directly to the roots of contemporary society.

This is no easy thing to do. Unhappily, in recent years the arenas of education in which this should be accomplished have been increasingly slighted. What is it that makes a man capable of understanding his relationship to society? Not science, not vocational education in its present form, not technology; it is the humanities that make it possible for man to understand that he is linked to a long line of human beings who have gone before. It is the nature and duty of history to make man understand that he is part of an enduring human race that has lived over the centuries, indeed over millennia. The function of the classical languages, infrequently taught in our schools today, was to give a sense of oneness with the Latins, the Romans, and the wellsprings of our own culture. These studies represent areas of knowledge that develop the sense of mutual human involvement and it is only from this concept that work truly becomes meaningful. Yet, these are the very areas that tend to be submerged in this present period of human history. They are neglected because of man's involvement with a technology that provides affluence and abundance. Looking at higher education, one must be concerned by the appalling retreat from the liberal arts, the failure to provide the funds liberal arts schools need, because society now favors the sciences. For it is the liberal arts that are capable of providing an understanding of the wide-ranging character of modern society essential for a pursuit of self and identity in relation to work.

As society moves forward to tomorrow, meaning and purpose in living will be found only if education and the culture are capable of persuading men that they are not isolated islands but truly a part of the mainland of society. Brought up to believe that work is primarily an instrument for protection against personal deprivation or a means of self-aggrandizement, this generation and the generations immediately ahead must come to look upon work as the link between themselves and the most important fact of reality, namely, the larger social group—that is to say, the nation and indeed the world.

In the swirling process of social change, society is responsible for both economic and psychological stability. The most persuasive force that can make the individual accept this reality is the very crisis of affluence in which he finds himself. Unless man contributes to a world-wide stockpile of abundance, unless he can harness technology to the needs of the spirit, the lights of civilization will go out. A new balance must be struck between the insular interests of the individual and his ties with the mainland of society. He can never return to the days of the artisan who started a task and found satisfaction in the completed work of his hands. He is destined, henceforth, to make only a part, perhaps only a small part, but he himself can belong to the whole.

REFERENCES

Chase, S. *The proper study of mankind.* New York: Harper, 1948.

Djilas, M. *The new class.* New York: Praeger, 1957.

Levenstein, A. Technological change, work and human values. *Social Science*, 1967, **42,** 67–79.

New York *Times.* Marxist attacks state ownership. April 27, 1966.

Petrovic, G. *Marx in the mid-twentieth century.* Garden City, New York: Anchor Books, Doubleday, 1967.

Tawney, R. H. *Religion and the rise of capitalism.* New York: Harcourt, Brace, 1926.

Taylor, F. W. On the art of cutting metals. *Transactions of the American Society of Mechanical Engineers*, 1907, **28,** 57.

Taylor, F. W. *Hearings before special committee of the House of Representatives to investigate the Taylor and other systems of shop management under authority of House Resolution* 90. Vol. III, 1912, p. 1471.

Taylor, F. W. *The principles of scientific management.* New York: Harper, 1911.

5

work and the productive personality

GARDNER MURPHY
Emeritus, Menninger Foundation

What lessons for the humane and effective career development of young people are to be discovered by examining the child's imaginative play and his exposure to the adult world about him? In Chapter 5, Gardner Murphy probes this theme and relates the work potentialities of the child to the concepts of productivity and progressive mastery. In doing so, he develops compelling arguments for the proposition that the child at play and at school may be father to the man at work.

Attitudes about work and toward self as remote worker-to-be take root early. Growing children are influenced by diverse images of work, both positive and negative. In the sex-typing of children, boys and girls learn what is acceptable social behavior partly in terms of work roles although, traditionally, it has been boys more than girls whose worth has been judged and whose behavior therefore has been shaped in terms of work. Notions about the effective life as predicated on preparation and planning for successful work is hardly a genetic phenomenon but, rather, must be cultivated over time in the social development of the child. Lower-class children, who lack contact with upwardly mobile, work-oriented adult role models, do not typically exhibit the sense of planfulness and the elevated occupational aspiration level that we have come to associate with children from middle-class homes.

If work is to contribute to psychological growth and well-being,

Murphy believes we must find means to make it intrinsically rewarding, that is, self-fulfilling. We cannot accomplish this if the economic product of work is its sole justification or if a common, inflexible criterion of quality is set for all. The social rewards of work, Murphy contends, must be so arranged as to flow from the individual's productivity *relative to his capacity.* Such ideas, of course, run sharply counter to currently acceptable political and economic definitions of competence, but Murphy would far rather see productivity tied to the capacity of the person to be progressively released in the utilization of his potentials.

To develop productive personalities, we must individualize the conception of work and teach people to value it most when it is really their own. There are significant implications here for the occupational socialization of the child. The feeling world of the child engaged in exploring his marvelous environment is, after all, not so different from that of parents fortunate enough to have self-fulfilling work. He can be taught to understand, then, that his joy in his own normal activities bears a resemblance to the satisfactions adults may experience in their jobs. This message can be concretely conveyed by exposing the child to effective role models in school, to teachers whose behavior convincingly signalizes genuine love of their own work, and by building a curriculum which dignifies both the general concept of work and the specific products of the child's work. Imbedded in this curriculum must be the idea that a constructive society is one in which the mutual support members give one another is effectuated through cooperative work.

Can realistic views of work and work-like experience, then, be transmitted exclusively by ingenious academic example? Murphy thinks not. He favors schools "in which the child is introduced early to real industrial operations which he begins to carry out with energy and with understanding of the articulation of work and symbolic skills." In broad feature, what Murphy recommends seems strikingly harmonious with the United States Office of Education's notions of career education.

Helping the child develop into a productive personality is best seen in relation to providing opportunities for progressive mastery. The work-relevant experiences he meets must be sequenced, arranged from simple to complex to conform to his ever enlarging capacity to confront and profit from problem-solving activities. Moreover, to be psychologically meaningful, they must be experiences that satisfy the developing child in terms of his own standards. This picture is, however, more a hope than the reality. "Somebody, somewhere," laments Murphy, "failed to make school work function as real work . . ."

H. B.

The newborn child does much more than respond reflexly to fresh stimulation. To be awake means to be active, seeking and holding the things that act upon eyes, ears, and skin, resisting, grasping, and pushing against the environment. With the package which we call life there is *activity*; and changes ensue in the perpetual pull and push of child and environment.

Potentialities for activity become rapidly differentiated. Many a philosopher has undertaken to define the difference between work and play. But in the beginnings, the reaching, the manipulation, the drawing of objects to the mouth, and soon the protesting cry or joyful smile or laugh can be conceived either as work or as play. It is out of this matrix of continuous activity that learning begins, learning as growth goes on, and new potentialities become evident. Some of these activities are valued by the grown-up world as leading to good results, and if there is much effort and a considerable productivity in consequence, we call this "work" and are proud of it. Indeed, we make it a major part of life.

There is, for Freud (1962), a fundamental question of personal adequacy conceived in terms of adequacy in love and in work. Work fulfills one's identity, as Erikson (1968, pp. 122–125) has taught us. Carlyle (1843) tells us: "Blessed is the man who has found his work." Work is a large part of life, an aspect of life which can bring fulfillment as deeply as can the joy in love or esthetic appreciation, or the delight in use of any and all of the equipment that makes us human beings. Work cannot be separated off as a tougher or more difficult part of life, a part that has no intrinsic value of its own, but has to be paid or rewarded to take on meaning. On the contrary, work can be defined as the exercise of potentialities, and the effortful, laborious aspects of work can be regarded as merely those which catch the eye of individuals who are sorry for the worker or of those who wish to punish or reward him. Work is basic biology. It is structured because activity of an ordered and disciplined sort not only gets more done, but is intrinsically more fulfilling. It is the fulfilling aspect, not the punishment aspect, that should be emphasized.

In contrast to this biological view of play and work there is a legitimate sociocultural view of work and of work potentials. At different times and places men applaud or abhor physical labor. They may give honorable status to all work, or on the contrary, they may make some types of work degrading and others noble, or they may even regard all work as below human dignity, denying the leisure to enjoy the arts or to think philosophically as a fulfillment toward which a working class cannot aspire.

Earlier Attitudes Toward Work

An especially brilliant analysis of the varying sociocultural modes of evaluation of work appears in the contributions of Max Weber (1930) and R. H. Tawney (1926). Weber pointed out that since the Protestant Reformation, there has been a clear, well-defined tendency of Protestantism to emphasize the importance of work as a device for assuaging the guilt which miserable sinners experience through their intrinsic worthlessness; as man works, God may grant him prosperity, and the fact that he is prospering removes the fact that he might be among the eternally damned, for it is through the success of his works that he apprehends his status among God's elect. Tawney developed the theme that it was among a special group of workers, the middle-class shopkeepers and merchants, that Protestantism arose, rather than among the land owners and the warriors. The rise of capitalism depended, in part, upon the sense of worth in the act of working. One was everywhere reminded of the parable of the talents: he who hid his talent in the ground had no worth; he who could multiply what his Lord had given him found favor in his Lord's eyes.

Already a paradox becomes evident in the Protestant ethic. We know, for example, that unskilled and poorly rewarded work—such as that found in the labor of the small farmer, fisherman, or mariner—was valued less than the work of the merchant; on the other hand, somehow the conception of work in general was achieving a certain nobility. The very era in which individual competition was elevating the successful merchant among his fellows was the era in which Robert Burns was writing: "A man's a man for a' that." There are multiple and conflicting levels of worth assigned to work in the Western tradition, and the plot thickens as very complex systems of ideals about the worth of various kinds of work get built into the American tradition.

Much, of course, has remained of the older tradition which declared that work was inherently symbolic of a low level of human value. The classical expression of this gentle, cynical, and subtle analysis is Veblen's "Theory of the Leisure Class." Historically minded as it is, Veblen's work (1934) recalls that in the age of the warrior some members of the warring classes may not only be free of all ordinary work, but may settle into complacency as those worthy to enjoy leisure. Those who have grubby work to do are without honor; those who have won the means of subsistence through their own or their ancestors' predatory activity have been able to order society in such a fashion as to look down, pityingly or scornfully, at those who work. There is still a considerable touch of the Veblen motif in life today, especially when it takes the form of ostentatious demonstration that man does not need to work. (One may remember the tapering fingernails of the ancient Chinese which showed plainly that one could not work, or the bound feet preventing one from walking, or similar decorative touches which purported to show that one could not really work no matter how much one might aspire to do so.)

In the Athenian democracy, free workers had a status expressing their skill, but it was to the warrior that the main glory went. Most of the population were slaves, infrequently able to buy their way, through their work, to the category of the free. Men of superior power and position regarded work as beneath them. As James Harvey Robinson pointed out, there was no possibility that science would be discovered at such a time and place, since puttering around with things, shaping and remaking them, or even devising instruments to look more closely at them, was beneath the thought of a free man. It was only after the decline of the great city states that the Greek spirit of inquiry, having thrown off this fear of labor, considered the works of Archimedes and the Alexandrian astronomers.

Also in Rome, and much of the Western history that followed Rome, work was of low status. However, it must be remembered that in the monasteries, medicine, astronomy, architecture, and many of the nobler crafts were developed; the monks were often the leaders with the peasants as the followers in the prosecution of these labors. A guide through Mont St. Michel explained, as his eyes swept the land beyond the shoals and beaches, "The monks were the architects, the peasants the workers; without this kind of slavery the work could not have been done." The medieval guild system was, of course, a cultivation even a glorification of skilled work. The commercial revolution turned many land owners and many artisans into merchant capitalists with the big rewards going to the shrewd entrepreneur; the accelerated pace of the industrial revolution in the nineteenth century enabled thousands of high-level craftsmen to become entrepreneurs, an example being Josiah Wedgwood, the potter, father-in-law of Charles Darwin, to whom we owe the preservation of many of the magnificent Greek ceramic models.

Work as a Source of Conflict and Value

From each change in the definition of work came a new kind of personality, specifically a new ego, a new definition of what it takes to work well, what it takes to make a valuable product. Superior skill means superior status, and in a money economy, superior income and economic power. With increasing sensitivity on the part of the maker of fine things comes also increasing appreciation on the part of the consumer. The guildsman appreciates and buys the superior work of another guildsman in a related field. Spiraling values of increasing respect for certain kinds of work therefore appear, until a mass production era, again by destroying skill and the worth of skill, debases both the handicraft and him who makes it.

This trend reinforces the feeling, already noted, that productive work has ethical and even religious value. The Puritans, having tended at first to be afraid of beauty as the work of the devil, found beauty coming in at the back door in the form of beautiful works, as in the new translations of the Bible and the new poems and hymns of the seventeenth and eighteenth centuries; and through an appreciation of textiles and jewelry as fine self-adornment became legitimate; and the little white Protestant Church, repudiating the grandeurs of Gothic architecture, became in time an exquisite representation of simple, sound, good taste which required good builders, good carpenters, and later on, good bricklayers, good iron-mongers to carry to success. It seems that the ego of the builder and of a worshipper was striving to become worthy of the presence of God. Just as one wears his Sunday best, his "Sunday-go-to-meeting" clothes because anything less would be an indignity to God, so labor expressive of good taste, sense of proportion, and even charm and delicate refinement began to ennoble all but the crudest and least skilled aspects of work.

Wherever the barriers to movement from one class to another were firm, as was the case for example in the rural South for many whites and for Negro slaves, work could be debasing; but wherever such barriers were softened, as in the commercial and industrial development of East and Midwest, a kind of work could often be found which lifted status and self-respect almost instantly. In one lifetime a man could pass from a very humble to a very respected position through buying and selling, but often also through the skills which are representative of the professions. The ego dynamics of all such men were structured in terms of the worth of productive work, not simply in terms of family or landed possessions. To be without work was often equivalent to being without honor.

But look at these paradoxes to which man seems to have been committing himself! Work is proof, one may suppose, that one has no great possessions, no great power, no great tradition behind one. One works because one must. "In the sweat of thy face shalt thou eat bread." The harder, dirtier, and longer the work, the more it tends to mean dishonor. At the very same time, and in the very same human community, work has been a symbol of successful discovery of a way of being productive, success in training for the task, success in carrying it out, and success in the recognized worth of the product in the eyes of other men for whom it has use. The conflict is inherent, not accidental, and the children who grow up in our society are touched by these varied aspects of work. We are a part of all that we have met. The Greek and Roman, the medieval, the Renaissance, the commercial and industrial eras all have left their residues, their definite sedimentary deposits in our minds and hearts.

The conflict is worse for boys than for girls although the girls are touched by all these same forces; much of the work of girls and women is still not called work, but is described in very mixed and complicated language having to do with homemaking, care and protection of the young, and participation in community activities, especially religious and educational activities. The descriptive units of work are hard to define. One finds it difficult to measure homemaking and the protection and guidance of children in terms of the dollars and cents for the hours and minutes which are characteristically assigned to masculine labors, and of course, the comparisons between women in terms of their success in these responsibilities are very much more difficult to assess. In the past, pride and shame with respect to fulfillment, or failure to fulfill one's task as a woman, depended to a large degree upon involuntary matters like good looks, health, charm, patience, subtlety or intuition in perception; the very language of work seemed inappropriate. It is likely that conflict over the possession of attributes such as these can be as painful as conflict about failure to obtain what a man regards as honorable and rewarding work.

To stick to current English usage, and our ordinary ideas about work, there is no doubt that these particular stresses are acute as masculinity becomes defined. That is to say, the differentiation of tasks, duties, and modes of self-fulfillment in terms of sex will mean that during those years when children are learning sex identity, learning what it is that boys appropriately do, and that girls appropriately do, one develops an ego that is oriented around quite different conceptions of one's relation to work, and consequently quite different conflicts and stresses regarding success in work, pride or humiliation in the kind of work that one's father does, and eagerness or apathy regarding the work patterns for which one finds oneself being prepared. Studies of the attitudes of middle-class and working-class children toward their future vocations reveal that the conception that there is a *real choice* among types and grades of work and a real possibility of preparing, through patience and devotion, for an especially high level of work is characteristic of middle-class children who see these ideas and ideals in their own parents. It is not simply that the working-class child is less likely to have a model at home or across the street which he can emulate with delight, but also that he simply does not value life primarily in terms of work status. He reveres men who are strong, skilled, quick, courageous. He is sensitive to past and present heroes with whom a tough or even violent capacity for a rugged solution of a threatening situation means far more than the steady locomotion toward a remote and honored goal. In other words, it is not just that the working-class child has less chance to make an ideal center for adult life; he is not likely to organize his values in such a way that they prominently face him day in and day out, year in and year out, as he moves into an adult role. In Lois Murphy's studies (1962) of children in Kansas—children who were studied from their early years to their present age of 16—there was abundant confirmatory evidence of the point made countless times before, namely that many very able children simply do not think of going to college or of holding any position higher than that of their fathers at a semiskilled or unskilled level even when the opportunities exist, and even where an occasional persistent and energetic parent may encourage such an effort. One may agree that often the lack of planfulness on the part of the working-class child is due to the lack of models, but even when the models are conspicuously and constantly held up they do not necessarily work; and the reason, crudely and simply stated, is that the ego often is not there. The conception of life as built around successful work is one that has to be built in by steady indoctrination over a long period, and if this indoctrination is not available, this conception of life will ordinarily fail to appear.

It is apparent that there is conflict in attitudes toward work, particularly in the mixed pattern of ideas in the middle-class world in which work is sometimes ennobling, sometimes debasing. In present day American culture, these conflicting attitudes are reflected in three half-conscious notions about work and what work can do to the person who works. First, work may be seen from the point of view of the maker, *homo faber,* the man or woman who creates. In this sense the person is defined in terms of what he or she makes or can make. This is a production definition from the beginning, but it represents only one part of man's total conception of the productive worker. Second, work is defined in terms of consumer qualities. What good is there in what the person does? What kind of utilities and satisfactions can he derive from the work? Here the focus is no longer upon the worker but upon the work of his hands. And third, in a competitive society, work is seen as a competitive striving for position, type or form of work, and the worker as outdoing someone else, achieving more or higher quality work. The worker takes on the quality of a victor against other workers. The weighting given these three definitions of work in our society is probably not very sound biologically. It seems clear that the strain and stress effect of a competitive motive is emphasized, rather than the deeper and more abiding satisfactions that just come from making and from receiving the direct fruits of one's toil. If man is to find ego-fulfillment and a generalized level of enjoyment and satisfaction from work, a more equitable balance must be achieved in giving consideration to his readiness to make, his readiness to profit from the work done, and his readiness to take part in the competitive prestige-winning types of activities.

The Concept of Productivity

Let us look more closely at the word *productive,* and at the conception of productive work. What is it really that makes one kind of work productive, and another merely something to be gotten through, a sort of fifty cents an hour babysitting or minding the store when neither the children nor the store have any great meaning for us. Productivity lies in three things: (*a*) the intrinsic value of the thing produced; (*b*) its enduring quality, the length of time the product will continue to have meaning; and (*c*) the originality, newness, pioneering value of the product as something which is not found growing on every tree, but contributes a new idea for the community of the race.

In a new society such as ours, there has been great emphasis upon productive work as contrasted with work in general. To split rails was good if it meant new arable farmland; to fly a kite was good if it brought down electricity for new industrial tasks. A number of studies made of the attitudes of children and youth toward work of different types place engineering and professional skills usually at or near the top, semiskilled industrial operations in the middle, and just heavy, raw, unskilled or repetitive tasks at the bottom. The pattern seems to be just about the same throughout Western society, and although some of the early studies in the Soviet Union found children responding in terms of the great dignity of lower level work tasks, it appears that both the monetary and the prestige rewards in their industrial society are very similar to those in ours. In fact there is much to suggest that industrial man is pretty much the same kind of animal wherever he has time to work through the inevitable ego transformations that have already been mentioned.

Earlier the distinction was made between work as honor and work as a penalty, either a penalty for wrong-doing or a penalty for simply being unfavored, ungifted, left out. The problem in distinguishing between work as honor and work as penalty takes on a new form when, with industrial development and especially with automation, there is less and less left to be done at the crudest work level. Not only the great unemployment problem, but the great problem of the debasement of work and of the human dignity that goes with it, lies in the fact that there are more and more people available to do tasks calling for fewer and fewer people; not only the unskilled, but even the semiskilled are found to be replaceable. As a Detroit engineer explained, when the middle-speed computers came into the city in connection with the automotive industry, the city was able to absorb the change, but when the high-speed computers came in, men went out of work by the thousands, and no permanent machinery for absorbing such excesses of workers, such supernumerary toiling hands, has been devised. The very thing that a worker may be proud of at his semiskilled task is something which sheer mechanical operations can do better than bone, muscle, and sinew operations.

It has, of course, often been pleaded that the "service occupations" can more than keep pace with the outmoded manual operations, that there will be more hostesses, receptionists, and entertainers as there are fewer dishwashers, bolt sorters, or textile operatives. This would be a very hard point to try to prove by extrapolating from known trends. In the meantime, automation is particularly damaging to the work aspirations of the lowest economic levels encompassing much of the Negro population. These are the groups among whom steady work ideals have been least clear and meaningful. The self-image for them is just not a work image; it is an image organized around many other things than work itself. Although work may be hard, it is not regular, and though its economic reward when present may seem considerable, its prestige and status rewards are not incorporated into the center of the self-image where they control the activities during the time when one is preparing oneself for work.

The profound impact being made by two recent studies of work can be viewed in these terms: namely, John Gardner's studies (1961) of "excellence" and Robert White's studies (1959) of "competence." These are vivid and compelling descriptions of the joys and values of effective effort toward personally and socially valued goals. It is possible, Gardner argues, to achieve excellence in a democratic society. Though the word *excel* may mean to be preeminent, it is possible to derive delight from the quality of work done, and derive honor from competitive success without humiliating others and without limiting the opportunity of others to achieve their own form and style of excellence. White develops the theme that there is an intrinsic need to use the equipment, the potentials that we have, almost as in the "instinct of workmanship" of Thorstein Veblen, Hartmann's "conflict-free ego spheres," and the epistemic curiosity of D. E. Berlyne (1960). There is an intrinsic human delight in using high order equipment, just as there is in using the simple anatomy and physiology with which we are born. We love to think; we love to work with our heads. After several decades of experimentation with animals on the assumption that they had to be motivated through their visceral needs, given a pellet or dish of bran mash for each "right" response, scientists have discovered with a great bang in recent years that they will solve problems for the fun of it, and often leave the food dish piled high to one side while they outwit this baffling problem that must be solved. This was not generally assumed to be characteristic of man until it had been shown in monkeys and even in rats, but the autonomous delight in using one's brain has become respectable again as a research problem.

This could even be related to the technological revolution that we have been considering; it might even prove to be possible to get sustained research done on the curiosity motive, the motive of thinking for the fun of thinking. Now that thought has become so fundamental, so central among the industrial needs, as various raw materials shrink in volume, and various baffling problems of getting along together on this planet bewilder and stagger us, we may find that brains rather than blood represent fundamental motives, including those related to the act of working. It is easy to sympathize with Karl Buhler's ideas on function pleasure and to believe that this new excitement, the love of intellectual work, is a variant upon the basic function pleasure idea, the idea that whatever man has, just being human is in itself intrinsically a source of motivation. Instead of extrinsic rewards for what he does—pellets of food or the nod of social approval—he will find it possible to make work itself intrinsically rewarding, and this is the area where most of the solutions to our problems lie.

In our kind of society, work at a dignified level can become an ego center, and in fact, it usually does; and intrinsic satisfactions as well as extrinsic rewards for thinking as such can become more central—not that they should or must necessarily become the center. But to upgrade the value of intellectual work is one of the great problems of education. It is not very much like the ideas held up to disdain in Aldous Huxley's *Brave New World* (1932) or the ideas set up in Plato's *Republic* (1950) in which people are born to and trained to different levels, with vast gulfs separating one level from another. This is not a plea for an eternal disjunctive relation between types of work. On the contrary, it is a plea for general recognition of the dignity of work, the frank admission that intellectual work is worth more and definitely needs greater compensations than have been given to it, and the implied conclusion that everyone needs to be rewarded for whatever intellectual competence he has so that he gets both the intrinsic and the extrinsic satisfactions that go with rewarding work.

Flexible Standards for Evaluating Performance

The ideal, "to each according to his needs; from each according to his ability," though not absolutely fulfillable, is still a working possibility from which it would follow directly that social rewards would be arranged in terms of the productivity of the individual relative to his capacity, and that variations in his productivity, from year to year or from phase to phase in his growth, could be given various degrees of social reward. In other words, the individual could pass from a lower to a higher level of productivity by virtue of the rewards given commensurate with production. This would mean, to some degree, measuring a person according to his own standard rather than pitting the weak against the strong with inevitable relative defeat all along the line.

This would push us in the direction of the concept of "working to capacity," and that would inevitably follow if external rewards were the only ones involved. Fortunately, the balance is corrected, as there are also the intrinsic satisfactions from work. What may be underachieving from the teacher's or community's point of view may be a period of finding one's way, groping in the dark, releasing inner potentials, or the sheer need to wait until a growth spurt chimes in with the external pressures of the time.

But how can productivity of these many types be evaluated on one scale, one common dimension? It is not only that society has been making many measuring scales in terms of prestige, power, money, special privileges, exemption from threats and difficulties, but that the inner ego organization itself is manifold and complex. I may, at the same time, respect myself for the fine work I am doing and be aware that it is not really as fine as it appears, for my standards are flexible and capable of changing.

All that has been said so far implies the achievement of static standards which become a straight-jacket if they are rigidly constructed. Ideals like excellence, complacency, good work well done, are marvelous when they are flexible and leave growing room for new kinds of values. There will certainly be conflict between different norms, and there will certainly be multi-level styles of evaluation. There will not only be different social classes and different cultural groups, but even within the individual, there will be different kinds of appeals to good work, different ways of accepting these appeals, and different kinds of satisfaction from different kinds of work. A person can be organized around his work, and most people in our society are likely to be organized in this way. There is much to plead, however, for a certain diversity, or as William James said, "pluralism" in work norms and work styles. Along with the disciplined musicianship of a highly creative violinist can come his shy and furtive efforts to learn the cello too, or even the flute, or to try his hand at conducting, or even at composition. Too rigid a definition of himself as the best violinist in his home city may prevent his eager response to other challenges, his readiness to do some things that he is not particularly good at doing, his capacity to do things because of their very appeal and their intrinsic promise, and not just because they represent the highest level of skill which he has mastered.

This whole conception of work, as involving spontaneity and the fulfillment of one's functions, is ultimately in sharp contradiction to a competitive definition of excellence or of competence. Educators pay a considerable price for the way in which they use the competition motive, overplaying this motive and underplaying the enormous inherent satisfactions, the ego-fulfillments, which are there from the beginning. If the child at three or five or eight has already enjoyed his sensory, his motor, his cognitive equipment, and he feels that this "being me" is good, why is it then that work has to be ladled out to him in terms of maybe winning some prestige that somebody else won't have? In the last analysis productivity has nothing to do with competition, and to pit people against one another on the basis of their competitive powers is to do grave injustice to the intrinsic delights which work can offer.

But what kinds of standards other than the competitive are possible? There are functional standards which go right to the heart of the person. These are the satisfactions a man feels from functioning as he is organized to work, either through his intrinsic hereditary gifts, or through the elaborated forms which these hereditary gifts take through the long and arduous and disciplined learning process. Work fulfillment involves the progressive capacity to be more and more released in the utilization of potentials.

Developing Productive Personalities

There is a constant stream of explicit and implicit messages to the little child about work and its value. Often he is told how his parents worked hard doing chores, meaningful tasks, and he gathers that there is prestige and sometimes material rewards for these tasks. But many of the tasks which used to be done, like mowing the lawn and caring for the furnace, may be meaningless to the apartment house dweller in an urban industrial period in which the whole concept of chores to be done has shrunk to the vanishing point. All the more burden therefore is shifted to the work that is supposed to be done in school. Here on the one hand, there is a great deal said about hard work and discipline, and on the other hand, about making things easy. Not only are textbooks frequently represented as painless sources of information, but the child becomes aware that the grownup's world too is being shortcut all the time. He sees the advertisements of this or that "made easy," and big gains for little labor. No wonder he is confused. The trouble is that work as an abstraction is represented as both good and bad. Of course, there is no solution until a more refined analysis of the concept is worked out.

Specifically work may mean almost anything from senseless butting one's head against a meaningless task to solving a delicate and beautiful problem with a delicate and beautiful solution. The concept of work itself as a source of prestige has to compete with the status accorded successful aggression, skill whether involving work or not, intelligence and charm which are often represented as falling from heaven whether they do so or not.

Where does work come in as a source of gratification and as a source of reward? Might it not be possible for those who direct the child's education to individualize the conception of work, holding forth work as suitable for oneself and one's own gratification and fulfillment, something of which one may be proud if it is really one's work? Even in the working-class child, as we call him, there is nothing to make work personal. One "picks up" a job. One does a "lick" of work. One gets paid for it. One then passes on to the real fun which is defined in nonwork terms.

Would it not be possible to go still further and build upon the inherent delight in whatever is normal activity of the child, enriching it at the same time by conveying that this is also adult activity for the most part and in most respects? Could those who hold the child's attention teach very concretely in terms of the satisfactions which parents, teachers, and big brothers and sisters have in their work? Is the system amenable to the kind of manipulation which will enable the child to be exposed to that teacher who really loves his or her work? Often the teacher complains of the number of hours of work in such a way as to suggest that invariably the more work there is, the more burden it is. This measurement of work in crude physical terms, though sometimes understandable, is going to make it extraordinarily difficult for the boy or girl to conceive of work as intrinsically gratifying. It is suggested that it may be possible for thoughtful teachers to lead their charges even beyond personal fulfillment to a consideration of what is really worthwhile socially. Work is no longer just fulfillment through local and specific tasks but fulfillment in a patterned reciprocal system of activities in the school in which the boy and girl begin to realize they are becoming whole people, outgrowing the limitations of early childhood and becoming through identification and participation adequate to carry through.

Questions then arise as to the school atmosphere, the attitude of the individual teacher who means the most to the child, and the boys and girls in grades ahead, or older brothers and sisters in the family who can play a very large part in dignifying work. Several recent meetings of curriculum builders have struggled with this problem of the way in which work attitudes, and more broadly, all attitudes of personal worth and achievement, are represented by the curriculum. One conference, brilliantly guided by Robert Havighurst and Ralph Tyler, was labeled "Ego Strength and the Curriculum." The conferees extemporized and exchanged with one another ideas about how the curriculum can actually build a strong ego, an ego adequate to life's demands. It was universally recognized that it was not the subject matter, or even the organization of the courses with reference to one another and their place at various age levels, that made the major contribution to mental health, but rather the way in which the curriculum was individualized to give the maximum of satisfaction and the maximum of power to the growing mental and emotional capacity of boy and girl. One may conceptualize productivity in terms of steps taken toward an ultimate goal, also in terms of the new feelings which arise as coordinated and disciplined activity is carried out and given immediate expression.

This means much more than having a series of test scores or profiles or even factor loading information about the various components involved. It means a quasi-clinical type of understanding where a developmental sequence is really comprehended. And this will require careful selection of teachers, not just in terms of their grades or the impression they make on people or the term papers they write, but with consideration of the warmth, quality, and subtlety of their interpersonal relationships and their capacity to understand boy and girl, to take them in a broad integrated sense and see where fulfillment is possible for them.

One can push this concept of productivity quite far in an individualistic direction but then must pause and consider, of course, the interdependence of the satisfactions of all. Work fulfillment in a democracy can only come when the work is for the good of the group, not just momentary personal gain, and only if the work is done by a *group.* It may be the relatively simple task of all pulling together as in pulling a hawser or in a tug-of-war. It may be at a slightly higher level as the oars are pulled together in the boat race; higher still as coordinated interchanges occur in basketball or baseball; higher still when individualized skills are articulated into an intricate symbolic sphere as in professional tasks involving, let us say, the consultation of physicians or of educators, one with another, for a complex total objective in which each can give what he or she has to offer. This is work that is really fulfilling in our group life. It has to be individually fulfilling, but then it branches over into a type of fulfillment which depends upon high level coordination, and this becomes ego fulfilling in the deepest social sense. The curriculum builder has to begin by dignifying each specific piece of work, and then the concept of work in general, and then the conception of an ego to be fulfilled, then the conception of the mutual support of one another, an ego building process which articulated and cooperative work can provide. This, in turn, has to be viewed in terms of a time dimension so that the school and curriculum planner can see clearly the probable effect upon ego-fulfillment and not just upon units chalked up in supposed preparation for further chalking up of further record, giving credit supposedly toward life itself. The curriculum builder can invest each work and each work plan as a whole with a quality of joy in mastery and of individual ego-fulfillment, all ordered from the simple to complex level as the nervous system and the body as a whole become differentiated and integrated through the years.

But there is danger here of a real "make-work fallacy" no less insidious than the make-work fallacy of the economist. The work must satisfy the boys and girls in terms of *their* standards. It must really be work in a sense of the term which carries meaning and dignity. It is possible to differentiate among three ways of trying to fulfill the requirements that life should be rich in work.

First, boys and girls may carry out tasks involving discipline for its own sake. The inevitable result will be that the boy and girl learn that concepts of honor and dignity are applied by the teacher just as easily to things which have no worth in themselves as to things which have great worth, and dignity can become an empty word. In a city equipped with efficient and inexpensive cleaning devices of all sorts it would be appropriate to try to instill respect for disciplined work by having the child's elbow grease used in a period of "clean up" in which he will inevitably learn that hard work and elbow grease are turning out a product *not* worthy of modern standards. This example is reminiscent of nurses in training in certain hospitals of yesteryear who spent six months as hospital slaves, service which counted as six months toward their three years of training to be graduate nurses, and made the hiring even of inexpensive labor unnecessary. This hollow sham could fortunately be seen through, but new variations still appear.

A second example is getting boys and girls to do work in the name of kindness, to prepare things for people for whom the task done is supposedly useful, but who in point of fact have quite different needs—for example, the beautiful paper baskets made by kindergartners and first graders to take as a gift to Aunt Susie across the street. Affection and the generous impulse toward Aunt Susie might well begin by inquiring what Aunt Susie would really like to have and could really use.

The third level is to introduce the child to small editions of the world of work to which the great adult world is devoted. There has been quite a battle, for example, in Gandhi's modern India concerning the issue known there as "basic education." In villages remote from the cities, it has been possible for tiny children to learn about the spinning and carding of cotton and to carry out in order the various processes that lead to making the adult and child clothing that is required. "What!" asks the horrified skeptic, "Is this a rationalization for continued child labor?" The point has been, however, that in the Indian village where purchase of industrially processed textiles comes hard, it is possible to help the primitive economy of the village family, to introduce the child to the reality of adult economic operations, and to give him a sense of dignified participation in the work world to which all belong. Here confusion can arise the minute that this activity is continued blindly despite the availability of modern textiles and the adequacy of a mode of distribution from the cities in which they are made. Basic education of Gandhian type can be enormously supporting under certain conditions but has proved to be stultifying when applied without vision. The pro and the anti arguments in the field of self-sufficiency have become a burden to the flesh. Work that is really work in the broad sense of production for human needs, gratifications, and fulfillments can never be equated with unnecessary labor pursued on the conviction that it is good for people to have it hard, and that working is just one of the hard things of life. We all know of schools in our country, and there are similar schools in Western Europe and the Soviet Union, in which the child is introduced early to real industrial operations which he begins to carry out with energy and with understanding of the articulation of work and symbolic skills. Work is given a social context, and the child acquires a deeper understanding of its meaning.

Another quagmire of confusion has appeared in connection with the idea of alternating between work and study or theory and practice. It is the alternation of work and rest, as stated earlier, that has given a creative and even a prophetic quality to some of the most heroic workers, inventors, and creators of ancient and of modern societies. In every case the creative work has really been *work* that at the same time was creative, and the rest was in itself a kind of work, a rebuilding for the sake of higher order creativity which is to follow. If the rest from work is "boondoggling," or if it is pursuit of high level scholarly activities which are somehow conceived to be *not* work, or if it is of a basically different type from the "real work" in an industrial or commercial or artistic or teaching situation, the rift has been perpetuated between work intrinsically satisfying because it involves the whole person and work which is sheerly laborious, effortful output of energy not clearly understood or articulated with theoretical knowledge. Some kinds of work-study alternation seem to be effective; others in which a rift is maintained or a series of starts and stops occurs, both in the work sphere and in the study sphere, drive home to the student that somehow the planners of his education achieved no real integration. Often seen in the ordinary lecture-laboratory combinations in high school and college is the tragedy of fine comprehension of the lecture combined with blind and stupid carrying out of laboratory exercises which are conceived by the brighter student to be a sheer waste of time; and on the other hand a boring lecture felt to be unnecessary by those who have studied the textbooks or who have grasped the principles evident in the laboratory experiments. The work schedule can be split in terms of days and hours or even content to be learned, but the mind of the learner cannot be split, and he will see through the artificial character of any separation that is created. If work does not include work for the mind, it is not fully human work.

Opportunities for Progressive Mastery

In the preceding pages it has been suggested that there is a certain amount of pressure and effort involved in all real work. This may be a slow, smoldering fire, or a series of conflagrations. At least, for most, there needs to be an occasional real conflagration. There needs to be pressure either supplied by the imaginative delight of the worker who is really participating as a person in the work, or the momentary torch flame carried from a teacher or a coworker group which lights and relights the uneven flame. Sometimes this is referred to as the value of *pacing*. Floyd Allport has reminded us that it takes much more energy to keep ahead in a foot race or a bicycle race than to follow at a constant distance, because the leader must supply all his own fuel from inside while the eyes of the followers are drawing in energies, buds of stimulation, from watching the legs and swaying forms of those who move on ahead. We need to be paced.

This is related in turn to what students of the arts have called the principle of "progressive mastery." Henry T. Moore presented his subjects with simple chords like major thirds and minor thirds over and over again, but he also presented them with more complex relationships like diminished sevenths. After a very large amount of practice in listening, it turned out that for most observers the good, old, solid major thirds and minor thirds had become boring, whereas the more complex interval relationships like the diminished sevenths had become more interesting and gratifying. There was work to do, and when the work of integrating the tones had been very thoroughly carried out and the chords were self-evident wholes, there was nothing more to do. Progressive mastery is a process by which satisfaction is derived from consolidating one's gains and setting for one's self still higher, more complex goals. As Helmholtz showed, the use of more and more complex tonal relationships has been evident from Greek music right through the medieval and baroque periods to the present. The "cacophonies" of the late nineteenth century and the twentieth century are becoming satisfying and, indeed, necessary to him whose ear—that is, whose brain—has become stretched by more and more experience in coping with the difficult. Work must be ordered in terms of effort which means, in turn, that it must be ordered in terms of levels of complexity, higher levels of integration. Children and youth will differ greatly with respect to what is simple or complex at any given level in their growth, and unless we have the budget and the trained teachers to carry out a highly individualized type of education in the arts and crafts, we shall have to use a rich variety of materials so that there will always be something relatively easy, but also much that is complex and difficult for each person in the group.

Children also differ from one another, as do adults, in the personal habit of making work challenging or making it easy. We may here use the classical methods of Lewin's pupil, Hoppe, who gave people difficult tasks and asked them immediately upon the completion of each task, "How well will you do on the next one?" In simple, easily scored problems, many people set an aspiration level far higher than they can actually achieve. They keep the gap, like the gap of carrot and stick, so great that they are always pushing toward the unattainable. Others set the aspiration level low, and when they have just made a score, their prediction as to what they will do on the next effort is scarcely higher than that which they already know they can do. The individual habits of working and of setting for oneself the standard to be met next are again among the variables to be built into any ordered plan for a curriculum sequence. It follows, however, from all of this that there is no natural "law of least action" by which people spontaneously and "naturally" try to get out of work. They try to get out of boring situations, and they try to get out of the kind of laborious stress which strains sense organs and muscles and bewilders the perceiving and thinking mind. There is, as modern studies of activation level show, a middle region involving plenty of opportunity for effort, but never involving breakdown types of stress.

Here lies the answer to the question of the shortening of the work day and the work week. The work of a 35-hour week in a rather highly paced, repetitive clerical position requires (for personal growth) that challenge and opportunity for creative work of another sort be maintained during the leisure hours. The contraction of work in terms of hours at the same time that it is contracted in terms of interest can lead only to a spongy and eroded personality unless something else takes up the slack.

It is generally assumed that to combine the intrinsic interest, zest, and challenge with the work itself rather than with the leisure hours is the better procedure; but automation makes this difficult. And if it is impossible to get first best, namely joy in the primary work, it is best to try to get as much joy in secondary work as possible. Incidentally, a literal interpretation of this recommendation would be moonlighting, such as for example occurs in cities where it is a matter of course for hospital aides to take on secondary jobs as taxi drivers, or even secondary hospital jobs to augment the family income. There is almost no relation at all in this circumstance between personal growth needs and personal economic needs, and both the formal educational system and the planners of mass media communication and adult education will have to think of the need for real work rather than the need for potboilers that emerge under these conditions.

Much the same issue has come up in glaring form with regard to the problem of child labor. When our society was battling for child labor laws which would at least prevent 10- and 12-hour days for small children in mines and mills, it could little foresee that there would be fairly adequate and universal child labor laws in a half century. And this generation would face the paradox of children leaving schools in droves in the middle teen-age period not to meet family economic needs, but largely because of sheer boredom. These young people would find themselves in a labor market which is particularly tough on young, new, inexperienced workers, and which is particularly unresourceful in thinking of ways to catch and hold their intellectual interests and skills, and for which the school system neglected to prepare them. If they had experienced gratifying work at the beginner or apprentice level and could have continued to find such activity at a gradually more challenging pace, there would be no need for them to compete for messenger and bowling alley jobs which have become harder and harder to find with automation. Somebody, somewhere, failed to make school work function as real work in the sense in which it has been used in this discussion. Maybe who failed was the whole of society.

Personality fulfillment occurs through work which finds a place for multiple work satisfactions and work fulfillments; which emphasizes dignity in the very process of working and satisfactions arising not only from the products but from the very nature of the self-fulfillment which the work entails. There is a desperate need of more adequate information concerning the way in which work is conceived or imagined by child and adolescent; the kinds of self-images which are being developed in the school and community regarding work of various sorts; the provision of opportunities for progressive mastery in the evolution of work ideas and habits throughout the learning years; and the endless flexible restatement of work goals and ego ideals, level by level, in each confrontation of a new work opportunity.

REFERENCES

Berlyne, D. E. *Conflict, arousal and curiosity.* New York: McGraw-Hill, 1960.

Carlyle, T. *Past and present* (1843). New York: Oxford University Press, n.d. Book III, Chap. 11.

Erikson, E. H. *Identity: Youth and crisis.* New York: W. W. Norton, 1968.

Freud, S. *Civilization and its discontents.* Ed. and trans. James Strachey. New York: W. W. Norton, 1962.

Gardner, J. W. *Excellence.* New York: Harper & Row, 1961.

Huxley, A. *Brave new world.* New York: Harper, 1932.

Murphy, L. B. *The widening world of childhood: The paths toward mastery.* New York: Basic Books, 1962.

Plato. *Dialogues.* New York: Pocket Books, 1950.

Tawney, R. H. *Religion and the rise of capitalism.* New York: Harcourt, Brace, 1926.

Veblen, T. *The theory of the leisure class.* New York: The Modern Library, 1934.

Weber, M. *The Protestant ethic and the spirit of capitalism.* Trans. Talcott Parsons. New York: Charles Scribner's Sons, 1930.

White, R. W. Motivation reconsidered: The concept of competence. *Psychological Review*, 1959, **66,** 297–333.

6

toward effective practice: emerging models and programs

LORRAINE S. HANSEN
University of Minnesota

HENRY BOROW
University of Minnesota

There is a sense in which career guidance may be said to have turned full circle. An attitude of profound concern about the uncertainties and dislocations in the work lives of people, particularly of school-leaving youth, led avant-garde social workers and vocational educators to create a new kind of helping relationship in the early years of the twentieth century. Born in a climate of social urgency and nurtured by humanitarian activists, vocational counseling in its infancy was uncompromisingly pragmatic. Emphasis was placed squarely upon direct assistance to clients in matters of planning and choosing appropriate training and employment goals. But the perspective of time teaches that the ardent hopes and bright promises of the early years outran a primitive and faltering guidance technology. Evidence bearing on the effectiveness of counseling services was hardly impressive.

Attention shifted perceptibly in the 1950s and 1960s to issues of career development and vocational choice theory. New conceptual models of occupational behavior, borrowing freely from the logical formulations and empirical findings of the behavioral sciences, sought both to explain how latent careers evolved and to propose (but usually not to implement) broad strategies for guidance. While these were years in which counseling services were progressively extended to growing numbers of vocational clients, it was not a time for daringly innovative programs. The major thrust of progress lay more in the direction of reconceptualizing and theory building and less in the direction of novel practice. Since the mid-1960s center stage has again been given to the operational facets of the movement. In Chapter 6 Hansen and Borow identify some of the prominent features of newly emerging practices in career guidance and present a diversified series of illustrative programs.

A review of the state of the art discloses no complete break with the past. Present-day stress upon the psychosocial aspects of occupational experience, the proposition that vocational development is best viewed as a major form of personal development, and concerns about the career guidance needs of by-passed populations and the alienated—all were foreshadowed by early pronouncements and events in the history of guidance and counseling. Yet, in their delineation of today's concepts and practices, Hansen and Borow make evident the genuinely significant nature of progress. "The best of current and emerging systems," the authors inform us, "are more broadly conceived, have drawn more heavily upon the behavioral sciences for an understanding of the developmental needs and motives of clients, have more effectively organized the institutional resources in the schools and community agencies where guidance is performed, have access to a diversified and sophisticated instrumentation for the practice of career counseling, utilize more varied and effective communication techniques, employ more and better trained personnel, incorporate mechanisms for the assessment of their effectiveness, and enjoy sounder funding, often by means of federal or state subsidies."

To the foregoing list of assets may be added the multimedia approaches and behavioral counseling techniques discussed in this volume by Super (Chapter 8) and by Krumboltz and Baker (Chapter 7), and, further, the accelerating movement toward the adoption of a systems approach in career guidance, a development which Hansen and Borow illustrate by means of both a state model and a national model.

While most programs cited in this chapter have been operational at one time or another, most have been so recently implemented that they are still best regarded as pilot enterprises or latter-day prototypes. Will their ultimate impact on the vocational maturity of clients justify the optimistic expectations which are now held for them? A decade or two hence, perhaps, another book, which might bear the audacious title *Career Guidance for the Twenty-first Century*, may return the answer.

H. B.

It is tempting to describe recent and evolving conceptions of career guidance as radical departures in the history of the movement. Facile judgments of "revolutionary" and "breakthrough" have been applied to some of the more imaginative models and programs which are currently attracting attention. In the presence of such optimism, it becomes sobering to discover in the statements of formidable pioneers of vocational guidance a remarkable correspondence to propositions and proposals which are accepted today as novel. In his comprehensive and balanced interpretive account of the background and promise of career education, Herr (1972) concludes, ". . . many of the elements which appear to be incorporated in present descriptions of career education have been advocated in one form or another for at least the past century [p. 67]."

Restudying the writings of prescient early leaders like Frank Parsons, Jesse Davis, John Brewer, George Myers, and others produces something akin to the déjà vu phenomenon in the reader. Brewer (1926) argued compellingly that the complexities of modern industrial society produced in adolescents a distorted picture of occupational life, and he argued that "there are social and psychological factors that delineate the specifications of an occupation far more accurately than do observations of the task performed or the places of work [p. 62]." Brewer saw clearly that vocational development (although he did not use that term) was to be properly viewed as a major facet of broader personal development. He urged that the vocational guidance movement draw upon the insights of personality and mental hygiene. Andrew White, first president of Cornell University, standing opposed to those who championed the academic purity and isolation of the campus experience, wrote a vocational guidance volume for students intended to help them choose courses of study which might best equip them for occupational life (Borow, 1966). Myers (1927) advocated a comprehensive system of school vocational guidance services that would extend continuously into the college years, observing that "no other activity of the school has greater need of a centralized, unified program than has vocational guidance [p. 31]." An examination of the archives of the movement and the activities of the National Vocational Guidance Association shows similar concern with a variety of other issues which still command attention today—work as a way of life, curriculum as a setting for career guidance, and the adjustment problems of dropouts, ethnic minorities, rural youth, and the unemployed (Borow, 1971).

Vocational Guidance Today: Credits and Debits

What is different about contemporary career guidance? It may be constructive to view the contrast with the past chiefly in terms of degrees of emphasis and implementation. The counsel of earlier leaders, while often forward looking, was not commonly heeded in practice. The three historic models of guidance for vocational life—occupational information dissemination, vocational training tryouts, and short-term counseling centered on testing and prediction—were truncated and restricted applications of the comprehensive and idealized models which had been envisioned. The best of current and emerging systems, on the other hand, are more broadly conceived, have drawn more heavily upon the behavioral sciences for an understanding of the developmental needs and motives of clients, have more effectively organized the institutional resources in the schools and community agencies where guidance is performed, have access to a diversified and sophisticated instrumentation for the practice of career counseling, utilize more varied and effective communication techniques, employ more and better trained personnel, incorporate mechanisms for the assessment of their effectiveness, and enjoy sounder funding often by means of federal or state subsidies.

The following sections of this chapter enumerate some of the newer aims and devices and present a series of operating programs illustrative of current trends in the practice of career guidance. The developments reported here provide evidence both of the field's rich legacy from the past and of its charting of promising new terrain. We would do well to remind ourselves, however, that current vocational guidance, as typically practiced, is hardly as robust as it could become and that the career planning and work adjustment problems of its clientele far outrun its capacity to reolve them. Among the circumstances which attest to the inadequacy of present-day practice are the following:

a. The time available to school counselors for direct work with students is severely limited.
b. Students often hold a narrow and outmoded conception of career guidance and are ill prepared to benefit from it.
c. Counselors and students characteristically overemphasize the problem of specific choice and undervalue developmental and motivational aspects of planning.
d. Counseling often proceeds on the single-job-for-life assumption rather than upon the premise of a sequence of choices within a career.
e. Testing and test interpretation are overemphasized.
f. Job content (formal duties) of occupations is stressed at the sacrifice of the psychosocial and life style characteristics of occupations.
g. Inadequate linkages exist between counseling and education, training, placement, job adjustment, and follow up.
h. Short-term "crisis counseling" is given disproportionately heavy emphasis in guidance work with high school and college students.
i. Disproportionately heavy emphasis in high school is devoted to counseling the college-bound, with too little emphasis given to the work-bound.
j. Relatively few students cite counselors as having had an important influence upon their career planning.
k. Evaluation studies on the outcomes of career counseling have been few, and those which are available do not provide much support for the effectiveness of counseling. However, better designed studies showing more favorable results are beginning to appear.

Expanded Aims, Bolder Strategies

Pressures for the modernization of career guidance services for a more productive return on effort and costs derive from at least three sources. First, there is the concern and pride of leaders and practitioners within the movement itself who are aware of the deficiencies outlined above, who indeed are in a position to observe the limitations directly through their work, and who seek the means to widen the scope and strengthen the quality of practice. Secondly, there are the apprehensions and rising expectations of the organizations which furnish counseling services—the public agencies faced with the task of finding job training situations and work placements in a tight labor market, and the schools and colleges, troubled by problems of reexamined and reordered objectives, by curriculum reform, and by a less docile, more assertive student clientele. Are the guidance staffs helping these institutions to discharge their obligations by coming to terms with the vocational frustrations and life planning uncertainties of their clients and students? Finally, there is the larger society, and the stern cost benefit criteria which it imposes on counselors and their employing institutions alike. There are disturbing dislocations in the lives of people, youth and adult, the message seems to read. What is the hard performance record of the public agencies and the schools and colleges which are created and sustained to deal with such problems? It is part of the austere temper of the times that current tax dollars in support of new career education and career development projects and programs are allocated less in the spirit of a reward for past services commendably rendered and more in the sense of an urgent directive, with conditions of accountability attached, that the quality of educational, training, and guidance services be sharply improved.

The combined forces of the circumstances noted here have led many in career guidance both to question and modify older, conventional approaches and to generate and experiment with broader objectives and different strategies. Such changes, of course, are not confined to a narrow band of time. They have been taking place continuously as altered social vectors have prescribed, but the pace of change has clearly accelerated and the mandate for progress is stronger.

Movement in career guidance has been occurring along three dimensions: aims and scope; tools and resources; and program conception. The sections which follow take brief excursions in each direction, noting representative examples en route. The categorization of changes presented here is mainly one of convenience and is presented in the interest of an economical mapping of recent and current trends. The aims, instruments, and programs of career guidance do not fall into discrete classes. They hold an interdependent and reciprocal relation to one another, both in their development and in their application.

The Enlarging Image

The human goals of contemporary career guidance do not differ drastically from those enunciated early in the twentieth century. Rather, they are clarifications and extensions of earlier positions. Theorists, researchers, and especially practitioners, while still too often preoccupied with concerns about vocational choice (an almost universal fault among earlier workers in the field), have become increasingly attentive to the social growth aspects of occupational behavior. The summary construct which embraces the developmental emphasis is *vocational maturity,* explicated by Donald Super and his research colleagues in the Career Pattern Study at Teachers College, Columbia University (see Super, Chapter 8; Super, 1957; and also, Super & Overstreet, 1960). Current work centers increasingly on the needs and means to promote occupational awareness and a sense of planfulness in clients rather than on mere choice making. Thus, strategies are likely to focus on the *process* by which educational and vocational choices are evolved rather than on the *act* of choice; upon client understanding of the serial nature of careers; and upon exploratory experiences by which the client can sample occupational life, both vicariously and directly, as he builds a realistic and informed career plan consonant with his aspirations and perceptions of self. Increasingly important in the counseling of youth is the notion that occupational decisions involve not merely a choice between job duties or earnings but between alternative life styles as well.

The widening scope of career guidance pertains to populations served as well as to aims. While some of the reform-minded leaders in the formative years of vocational guidance recognized the potential contributions of counseling to uprooted and economically handicapped groups, the philosophical ideal of egalitarianism through career guidance and training is being more fully implemented today. Research has provided a clearer understanding of the effects of psychosocial deprivation upon task-oriented competence (Himes, 1964; Borow, 1968), and pilot projects in career development are yielding knowledge of useful strategies in coping with the skill development and planning needs of the educationally disadvantaged (Leonard, 1968). The horizons of career guidance are being progressively extended to other special populations as well—to women, to "second career" candidates (midlife candidates for career change), and to the physically, emotionally, and intellectually handicapped.

Finally, expansionism in career guidance must be understood in terms of the growth of broad-scale models. When, in the 1920s, the main arena of guidance shifted from the social work centers to the schools, services were chiefly limited to students in the secondary schools. By contrast, we are now witness to the development of integrated kindergarten-to-twelve schemes, and even schoolwide kindergarten-to-junior/community college programs. Moreover, vocational guidance services are no longer wholly confined to the counselor's office, but are in part being restored to their setting within the school curriculum. Tennyson and Hansen (1971) describe the organization of planned curricular experiences to serve the broader developmental and socialization purposes of career guidance which have been identified above. Mention should be made, too, of the emerging shape of career guidance within the systems approach to education, particularly the model now widely known as career education. The systems concept as it applies to career development and career education will be treated later in the chapter.

Promising Resources and Tools

Earlier we observed that current career guidance practice may differ from its prototypes less in aims than in instrumentation. A considerable repertoire of implementing materials and techniques is now at the disposal of counselors and allied personnel workers, and it appears probable that further testing, refinement, and dissemination of these devices and the acquisition of skill in their use will soon produce discernible impact on the quality of counseling and guidance practice. Descriptions of many such tools and techniques are reported by Hansen (1970), Campbell, Walz, Miller, and Kriger (1972), and Herr (1972).

Multimedia resources for presenting educational and occupational information. Traditional vocational guidance relied very heavily upon print media (books, monographs, occupational briefs), orally transmitted facts about vocational life, on-site observations of workers at their jobs, and training and/or tryouts. While these means of communicating information remain useful, they can now be supplemented by a number of newer media. An information storage and retrieval system known as Vocational Information for Education and Work (VIEW), originally developed in San Diego County schools, uses decks of IBM aperture cards with microfilm inserts, a microfilm reader, and a microfilm printer to supply up-to-date local job and training information to students (Campbell, Walz et al., 1972). VIEW has been adapted for use in other communities. Boocock (1967) developed the *Life Career Game*, a simulation approach to educational and vocational planning and decision making. Both this device, which can be especially useful in motivating planning behavior among academically marginal high school students, and the *Job Experience Kits* are more fully discussed and evaluated by Krumboltz and Baker in Chapter 7. Computers have a considerably larger information storage capacity than VIEW and can, additionally, store and yield on request by the individual student personal data about himself pertinent to his planning. Sophisticated computers can interact with the student on career planning matters and, in so doing, serve as a partial surrogate for the human counselor. In Chapter 8, Super reports in detail on the uses of the computer in career guidance.

Inventories, scales, and occupational exploration techniques. While testing instruments have enjoyed long and extensive use in vocational guidance, current emphasis is shifting to their value in aiding self-exploration and occupational exploration and away from formal assessment and prediction. Today's counselor is more likely to use tests to broaden rather than narrow the range of the career options his client wishes to consider. The *Work Values Inventory* (Super, 1970) and the *Minnesota Importance Questionnaire* (Work Adjustment Project Staff, 1967) help the client examine the values he most seeks to satisfy through work and induce him to reflect about the differing life style characteristics associated with occupations. Instruments like the *Ohio Vocational Interest Survey* (D'Costa et al., 1969), the *Career Planning Program* (Act, 1972), and the *Self-Directed Search* (Holland, 1972; Holland, Hollifield, Nafzieger, & Helms, 1972) all group occupations with common characteristics into job clusters and provide structured guidance experiences by which students can use personal data to explore occupational fields vicariously and form tentative plans. The principal assets of such structured techniques are that they (*a*) offer students a meaningful way to initiate the vocational planning experience, (*b*) strengthen their motives to plan, (*c*) instruct them in the many variables to be considered in arriving at informed decisions, (*d*) provide them with forms for recording and interpreting information relevant to plans and decisions, and (*e*) establish a readiness for subsequent face-to-face counseling.

Scales of vocational maturity, while developed and used thus far chiefly as research instruments, can provide school youth with age-referenced information about their readiness for vocational planning and decision making. The three instruments of this type which have been subjected to considerable research and which are currently available for experimental use with students are the *Vocational Development Inventory* (Crites, 1965), the *Career Development Inventory* (Super & Forrest, 1972), and the *Readiness for Vocational Planning Scales* (Gribbons & Lohnes, 1968).

The Program Concept

Programs entail comprehensive plans within which aims, strategies, resources, tools, and methods are synthesized. They transcend individual techniques and instruments of guidance and, thus, tend to be more adequately conceptualized and more tightly coordinated than the well-intentioned piecemeal efforts of earlier years.

Several authors have recently offered conceptual models for K-12 programs (Herr, 1969, 1971; Gysbers, 1969; Gysbers & Moore, 1971; Osipow, 1969; Townsend, 1969). Most of these models have keyed their sequential career guidance aims and activities to the vocational development tasks which are commonly associated with successive school-grade levels (elementary, junior high school, senior high school, post-high school). While there were earlier attempts at implementing K-12 hypothetical models, Hansen's (1970) search found that most were fragmented and were not part of a systematic school and community-wide effort to facilitate the career development of youth. Within the past several years, however, there has been a remarkable growth both in the number and quality of extended career guidance programs, many stimulated by the vigorous advocacy of career education by the federal government. In some instances, state educational systems have undertaken to develop and establish either statewide career education or career development programs (e.g., Georgia, Florida, Ohio, New Jersey, North Dakota). In addition, many large-city systems have developed intensive programs for inner-city youth, as, for example, Detroit, Chicago, and Rochester, New York. Large suburban areas and some rural communities have also been active in program development. Many of them appear to be reasonably well grounded in career development principles although few have been in existence long enough for their effects on career development to be known. Descriptions of numerous programs of career guidance have been provided by Hansen (1970) and Budke (1971).

Frameworks for Practice: Models and Programs

Ten career guidance programs which were set in operation within the past few years are described below. The identifying program titles and pertinent information about the target populations, settings, objectives, and distinguishing features of the programs are summarized in Table 1. A more detailed account

Table 1
Career Development in Action: Illustrative Programs

Program	Target Population	Locale	Objectives	Principal Features
U.S. Office of Education Career Development Model	All school levels, K–12; urban, suburban, rural	Pilot Schools: Hackensack, N.J.; Mesa, Arizona; Pontiac, Mich.; Jefferson County, Colo.; Atlanta, Ga.; Los Angeles, Cal.	Occupational awareness, orientation, exploration, preparation, placement for all students—graduates and dropouts, college-bound and work-bound	15 occupational clusters Occupational-cluster curriculum structured on 15 occupation clusters and stressing career-related skills and career opportunities and requirements Sequential examination of occupational clusters "Hands-on" experience, field observation, and class instruction Behavioral objectives Additional counselors and paraprofessionals In-service education Placement service

New Jersey Career Development Project	All school levels, K–12; urban	Pilot Schools: Camden; New Brunswick; Rahway	Understanding of self and technology through merging of technical and academic subjects Early self-awareness Occupational orientation and exploration Occupational information and resource utilization Capacity to deal with changing environment Opportunity to discover and use abilities Appreciation of responsibility to become productive member of society	Technology for Children project Introduction to Vocations course Prevocational work-study job placement Programs for potential dropouts Career Resource Center In-service teacher training
North Dakota Exemplary World of Work Project	All school levels, K–12; rural	Pilot Schools: Bismarck, N. Dak.	Development of positive self-concepts Positive attitude toward work	Sequential curriculum built on vocational development tasks Interdisciplinary activities

Table 1 (continued)

Program	Target Population	Locale	Objectives	Principal Features
			Increased student self-awareness	Direct observation of workers
			Increased knowledge of work world	Work experience through cooperative programs
			Reduction of high school and college dropouts	Special attention to needs of minorities
			Increased job-seeking application skills	Post-secondary school summer program in area vocational schools for juniors and seniors to investigate occupational clusters
			Increase in job placement and satisfaction	Guidance services provided to schools without them
			Improved working relationships among state agencies	Teacher efforts integrated around common goal
				Total involvement of teachers and administrators in vocational guidance
				Parent involvement in total process

Developmental Career Guidance Project—Detroit	All school levels, K–12; inner city, minority youth	Detroit urban area	To raise educational and vocational aspirations To broaden perceptual field regarding occupations To help overcome lack of planning To provide better adult role models	Cooperative planning by teachers, consultants, parents, community Involvement of parents and other indigenous personnel as paraprofessional aides Student assistants Variety of activities to get students out in work world Individual and group counseling Extensive in-service training Career as vehicle to building curricular program Close articulation between schools and business community Summer counselor workshops Job Handbook for Students developed by counselors

Table 1 (continued)

Program	Target Population	Locale	Objectives	Principal Features
Project BEACON Rochester, N.Y.	Elementary schools, K–6; Nonwhite youth and others of low socioeconomic background	Rochester, N.Y. elementary schools, including four target schools	To improve and raise educational levels and build children's positive self-concepts through a 7-phase program	Seven emphases in program: Strengthen child's self-image, Early success in language arts, Accent on working with parents, Cultural enrichment, In-service training of teachers, Negro history and culture, Development of new materials Ego-reinforcing activities for students every day Parent participation and involvement Faculty home visits

Career Development Curriculum Guide, Texas Education Agency	Grades K–8	Selected Texas elementary schools	To acquaint elementary students with career development concepts, relating school subjects to careers To build awareness of self and of the occupational world	Careers-of-the-Month Curriculum Guide featuring objectives, learning activities, and resources Materials compiled for 40 career development concepts Single-concept cartoons to stimulate discussion Single-concept cartoons as part of evaluation
Our Working World, Senesh, SRA	Grades 1–6	Elementary schools	To foster an understanding of work as a central focus of elementary school studies To teach the linkage of work with the social sciences	Curriculum materials dealing with child's enlarging world: Families at Work, Neighborhoods at Work, Cities at Work Study of occupations in the context of the social sciences and the humanities

Table 1 (continued)

Program	Target Population	Locale	Objectives	Principal Features
Work Experience/Career Exploration Program (WECEP)	Junior high school students, especially potential dropouts	Pilot Schools: 10 Minneapolis junior high schools and surrounding business community	To reach marginal and poorly motivated junior high students through combined work-study program prior to entrance into labor market To develop positive self-concepts and work attitudes To bridge gap between school and real world of work	Half day in school on academic studies, half day on paid job in cooperating industries Acceptance and treatment of student as a responsible worker Occupational relations class Seminars with teacher-coordinator Use of principles of reinforcement
Wyoming Comprehensive Occupational Education Program (COEP)	All school levels, K–12	Wyoming schools	To develop positive attitudes toward work To build motives for productive citizenship through work To furnish understanding of major job families To encourage students to select tentative career goal by age 16	Standard curriculum provides framework for career guidance activities at elementary level Career development goals arranged sequentially by grade level Career Exploration Program Career Preparation Broad-Skill Program

Vocational Exploration Group (VEG)	Applicable to a wide range of populations, including job-bound high school seniors, employment service applicants, and trainees in job training programs such as MDTA, NYC, and WIN	Chiefly non-school settings, job training sites, community based opportunity centers	Improved job planning attitudes and skills, particularly among disadvantaged clients, school-leaving youth, and others ready to enter the job market Broadened view of employment field Clarification of one's job assets Strengthening of vocational planning motives Increased readiness to make specific training and job decisions	Short-term training in acquisition of job readiness Sequential 5-stage learning process Applicability to disadvantaged clients and out-of-school groups Utilization of latent job knowledge of group members Use of paraprofessionals as group leaders Pyramid model of training Programmed manual for trainers Positive research findings on effects of VEG training

of each of the programs is then presented. The particular examples found here were chosen to represent a variety of locales, populations, aims, and methods. While each program appears to be soundly based, comprehensive, and incorporates imaginative and distinctive features, it should not be assumed that this group necessarily comprises the most effective or promising programs available.

United States Office of Education Career Education Model

Career development, as conceptualized in the USOE, is subsumed by career education, a comprehensive curriculum model centered on occupational life, beginning in first grade or earlier and continuing through the adult years. The program finds its rationale in the pronouncement of then United States Commissioner of Education, Sidney P. Marland, Jr. (1971), who charged that public education has failed to provide adequate career training and who proposed that the entire school program be restructured to make education more relevant by focusing on a career development theme. Hardwick (1971) has argued the USOE position as follows:

> One of the goals toward which the education system must direct itself is the provision for every student to acquire the skills which will allow him to make a livelihood for himself and for his family, no matter at what level of the educational system he leaves. Such skills are not confined to the manipulative skills; they are those by which one can use his capabilities in activities which contribute both to individual fulfillment and society's maintenance and progress [p. 3].

In grades 1 through 12, the sequentially developed USOE model includes structuring of basic subjects around the theme of career opportunities and requirements in the work world. In elementary school, students learn about the wide range of jobs available and their functions and requirements. In junior high school, students examine specific clusters of occupations through "hands-on" experiences, field observation, and classroom instruction. They also receive assistance in selecting an occupational area for further study in senior high school. In the upper secondary years they pursue their selected occupational area and subsequently choose one of three options: (*a*) intensive preparation for immediate job entry upon leaving high school; (*b*) preparation for postsecondary vocational education; or (*c*) preparation for four-year college. The plan allows every student to leave the system with at least entry level job skills and with basic background in academic subjects to go on for further education if desired. Focus is not only on job information and skill development but on attitudes about the economic, personal, and social meanings of work. Counseling and guidance are provided to assist the student in self-exploration and in the development of self-awareness, and placement into an entry-level job or further education is assured every student. Key words are orientation, exploration, preparation, and placement for all.

Fifteen occupational clusters form the matrix within which the curriculum is organized. They are: business and office occupations, marketing and distribution occupations, communications and media occupations, construction occupations, manufacturing occupations, transportation occupations, agri-business and natural resources occupations, marine science occupations, environmental control occupations, public services occupations, health occupations, hospitality and recreation occupations, personal services occupations, fine arts and humanities occupations, consumer and homemaking-related occupations. The USOE model permits existing career-oriented school programs to utilize the many career development curriculum materials already available nationally, with the development of supplemental materials as necessary.

Below are the objectives for each school level of the program:

Grades K–6: To develop in pupils attitudes about the personal and social significance of work.

To develop each pupil's self-awareness.

To develop and expand the occupational awareness and aspirations of the pupils.

To improve overall pupil performance by unifying and focusing basic subjects around a career development theme.

Grades 7–8: To provide experiences for students to assist them in evaluating their interests, abilities, values, and needs as they relate to occupational roles.

To provide students with opportunities for further and more

detailed exploration of selected occupational clusters, leading to a tentative selection of a particular cluster for in-depth exploration at the ninth-grade level.

To improve the performance of students in basic subject areas by making the subject matter more meaningful and relevant through unifying and focusing it around a career development theme.

Grades 9–10: To provide in-depth exploration and training in one occupational cluster leading to entry-level skill in one occupational area and establish a foundation for further progress, leaving open the option to move to other clusters if desired.

To improve the performance of students in basic areas of instruction by making the subject matter more meaningful and relevant through unification and focus upon a career development theme.

To provide guidance and counseling for the purpose of assisting students to select an occupational specialty for eleventh- and twelfth-grade levels with the following options: intensive job preparation, preparation for postsecondary occupational programs, or preparation for a four-year college.

Grades 11–12: To provide every student with intensive preparation in a selected occupational cluster or specific occupation, or with preparation for job entry and/or further education.

To provide guidance and counseling in preparation for employment and/or further education.

To insure placement of all students, upon leaving school, in either a job, a postsecondary occupational education program, or a four-year college program.

To maintain continuous follow-up of all dropouts and graduates and to use the resulting information for program revisions.

The model suggests curriculum development at all levels as the central procedure to restructure the school system. A number of supporting activities would be built in. Basically, the curriculum aspect is seen as (*a*) an occupational-cluster curriculum effort; (*b*) a curriculum refocusing for grades 1–8; and (*c*) an attempt to integrate subject matter with occupational clusters in grades 9–12. The USOE plan proposed the establishment of 15 separate task forces, one for each of the 15 clusters, and each to develop suitable instructional materials and media for the corresponding cluster-core for grades 9–12; an exploratory curriculum for grades 7 and 8; a one-semester exploratory curriculum in each occupational cluster; and guidelines and materials for grades K–6.

In the second component, that of refocusing the curriculum for grades 1–8, the proposal called for the task forces to create a system of behavioral objectives. Subtask forces in the areas of language arts, mathematics, science, and social studies were to be created to select the career development behavioral objectives which might best be achieved in a particular subject-matter field. Appropriate learning interventions were to be chosen or developed next. In the third component, grades 9–12, four subject-area task forces were provided for in the same four areas for the purpose of relating the subjects taught in these grades to the curriculum content identified by the cluster task forces, including the necessary competencies for each occupational cluster.

In the USOE career development model, additional counselors, paraprofessionals, and other personnel are needed to supplement the existing school staff. In-service education must be provided for teachers, counselors, supervisors, and paraprofessionals to orient them to the new concepts and to provide specific training in use of the new instructional materials. It has been further proposed that an advisory council with representatives from management, labor, and government be formed for each of the clusters. Finally, an active placement service needs to be established.

Six school systems were evaluated and selected as sites for the first tryout of the USOE model, starting in the 1971–72 school year. They included Atlanta, Georgia; Mesa, Arizona; Hackensack, New Jersey; Jefferson County, Colorado; Pontiac, Michigan; and Los Angeles, California. Figure 1 depicts the development of the model (Hardwick, 1971).

Figure 1
Suggested Career Education Experiences by Grade Level (USOE Model)

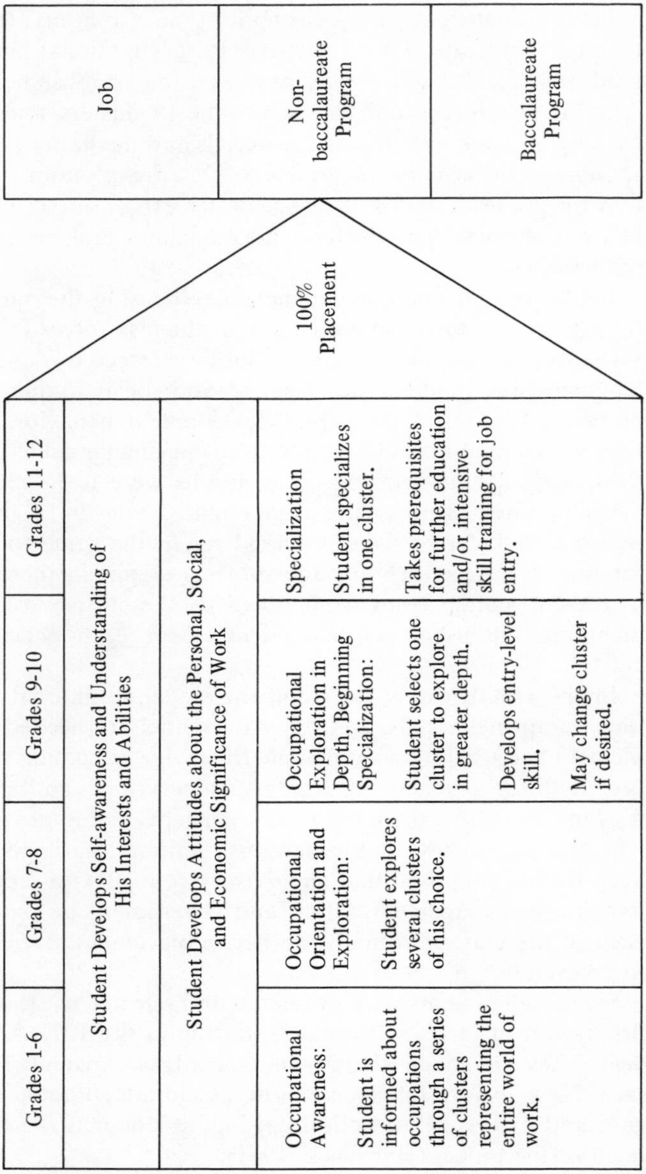

Grades 1-6	Grades 7-8	Grades 9-10	Grades 11-12
Student Develops Self-awareness and Understanding of His Interests and Abilities			
Student Develops Attitudes about the Personal, Social, and Economic Significance of Work			
Occupational Awareness: Student is informed about occupations through a series of clusters representing the entire world of work.	Occupational Orientation and Exploration: Student explores several clusters of his choice.	Occupational Exploration in Depth, Beginning Specialization: Student selects one cluster to explore in greater depth. Develops entry-level skill. May change cluster if desired.	Specialization Student specializes in one cluster. Takes prerequisites for further education and/or intensive skill training for job entry.

100% Placement

Job
Non-baccalaureate Program
Baccalaureate Program

New Jersey Career Development Project

New Jersey is one of the states which has made considerable progress in developing and implementing a K–12 career development program. Acknowledging that the educational problem is actually preschool-to-adult in range, the State Department of Education has moved to initiate the multiphase program which is described below.

The pilot project, funded by the state under the Vocational Education Laws, was launched in January, 1971, in three pilot schools: Camden, New Brunswick, and Rahway. Specified outcomes in student behavior are (*a*) early self-awareness; (*b*) capacity to deal effectively with the changing environment; (*c*) the opportunity to discover and productively use individual abilities; (*d*) increased knowledge of occupational opportunities as an aid in making wiser career decisions; and (*e*) an appreciation of one's personal responsibility to become a productive member of society (Gambino, 1970). One of the main features of the program is the linking of technical activities with academic classroom lessons to foster occupational awareness. Some elements of the project had been in progress on a pilot basis as early as 1965. The major content components at present are: (*a*) Technology for Children; (*b*) Introduction to Vocations; (*c*) Coupled Prevocational Work-Study; (*d*) Job Placement, (*e*) Career Resource Center; (*f*) In-Service Teacher Training.

Technology for Children. This part of the program, designed for children in grades 1 through 6, attempts to bring technical activities and academic lessons together to help children gain a better understanding both of themselves and technology through hands-on experience. Employing a learning-by-doing philosophy, the project has developed a series of "Episodes," activity units in which children become involved in all aspects of a project or topic. All children are given opportunity to participate actively in such episodes as "Establishing a Rubber Stamp Business," experiencing the division of labor in the execution of a job, and planning and executing all parts of the operation through to the finished product. The children in one of the schools printed T-shirts and sweatshirts and sold them in the community. A well-stocked, portable tool chest is available to each classroom, and all children, boys and girls, are taught how to use the tools, with adequate attention to safety. Other episodes include the following:

Language Arts: Discovering Machines, Discovering Modes of Transportation, The Post Office, A TV Production, and Man the Inventor

Mathematics: Shapes, Objects and Things, Time, Motors and Engines, and Aerospace

Science: Materials and Structures, Astronomy, Sound, Exploring Simple Machines, Weather Station

Social Studies: Merchandising, Cookie Business, Mail Service, Weaving and Textiles

The in-service training of teachers constitutes an important part of the project. A film to explain the project to interested teachers and others has been produced.

The expressed goals of the Technology for Children component (called T4C) are to (*a*) aid students by laying the groundwork for self-awareness and assessment of individual abilities and interests; (*b*) supplement the learning of students in fundamental skill areas including mathematics, language arts, science, and social studies; (*c*) expand student learning and appreciation in the areas of technology and the world of work (Dreves, 1970).

Introduction to Vocations. This ninth-grade course, which has been in existence for several years, provides a cycled experience of occupational orientation and exploration designed to increase the occupational awareness of junior high school students and to help them make more realistic career plans. It includes manipulative, classroom, shop, laboratory, and field experiences related to job clusters.

Coupled Prevocational Work-Study. This program, intended for the potential dropout or student who does not respond well to the conventional academic classroom environment, offers summer opportunities for 8th- through 12th-grade students in prevocational experiences. The plan is to connect payment for work accomplished with training in order to attract back to school in the summer those pupils who were unmotivated by the regular year's program. Explicit goals are to (*a*) help keep financially needy students in school; (*b*) assist youth to develop positive attitudes toward work; and (*c*) aid students in their development of individual career plans (Gambino, 1970).

Job Placement Program. The job placement aspect is intended to provide placement for all students and particularly for those who are employment-bound directly from high school. The goals are to assist students in (*a*) gaining work experience by placing them in appropriate part-time employment; (*b*) formulating future plans and decisions by providing appropriate employment experiences; and (*c*) job-seeking activities, especially for those students who have completed their high school education.

The Career Resource Center. A facility will be established in each of the pilot school districts to provide a wide variety of media and materials for both teachers and students. Each center will have an Audio-Visual Media Coordinator and a School-Industry-Cooperation Coordinator. The center team will assume such duties as coordinating the various facets of the model; providing multi-media resources and services to teachers; expediting change, reducing duplication, and promoting efficiency; identifying, developing, and maintaining continuity of individual experiences of students; identifying a knowledge core pertinent to in-service education; and placing the resources of school, industry, and community in full operation.

The New Jersey project attempts to move away from the earlier fragmented efforts to facilitate career development and toward an integrated, comprehensive plan. A recent development has been the selection of Hackensack as one of the test sites for the USOE career education model described earlier. How this pilot program relates to the New Jersey Career Development Project itself is not known at this time.

North Dakota Exemplary World of Work Project

Because North Dakota is a rural agricultural state, its youth have relatively little opportunity to learn about the wide range of opportunities available in the world of industry and business. Many youth leave the state. There are pockets of poverty containing substantial numbers of deprived individuals, including Indians, who need special attention. A study of education in the state revealed that at least 44 percent of the students in grades 9–12 have no counseling services; 80 percent of schools with grades 9 and 10 have no school counselor; only 22 out of each 44 entering as high school freshmen actually graduate; only two regular counselors are employed in the state's elementary schools; occupational guidance is virtually non-existent in the elementary school curriculum; availability and dissemination of occupational information has been inadequate; and the typical North Dakota high school curriculum is alleged to be college oriented (Selland, 1969).

A statewide program of career development, K–12, has been organized through the North Dakota State Board for Vocational Education under funding from the Exemplary Projects Section of the Vocational Education Amendments of 1968. The plan is expected to be completed and disseminated statewide by June, 1973 (North Dakota State Board of Education, 1970).

The North Dakota project calls for a sequential program building on vocational development tasks and implemented throughout the curriculum. It defines career development as every teacher's responsibility. Outcomes expected from the program are:

increased student awareness of self and occupational options
vocationally integrated curriculum, K–12
increased knowledge of world of work through systematic exposures to workers and work settings
reduction in high school and college dropouts
positive attitude toward work and preparation for work
increases in job placement and job satisfaction

integration of educational efforts of all teachers around a common goal

improved working relationships among state agencies and organizations

total involvement of teachers and administrators in vocational guidance (Selland, 1969)

Like the USOE model, the North Dakota elementary school program calls for integration of activity-centered experiences into the existing curriculum to assist in the development of positive self-concepts, appreciation of all vocations, understanding of workers, positive attitudes toward work, and the concept that all work has dignity. The middle school program provides considerable opportunity for broad exploration in a variety of occupational areas and relates this experience to student self-evaluation. The objective is to help junior high school students develop realistic career plans and decisions. Ample provision is made at all levels for direct observation of workers. In the senior high school, grades 10–12, focus is on additional knowledge of occupations and work settings and on the development of skill in job-seeking, job application, and interview activities. Students continue to explore self and preferred life styles, and actual work experiences are planned through cooperative work programs in order to bridge the gap between education and earning a living. At this level there is much focus on guidance.

A unique part of the North Dakota project is an arrangement with postsecondary vocational schools in which juniors and seniors from throughout the state have a chance to investigate occupational clusters directly. They spend one week in "hands-on" activities in each of five broad occupational areas. Intensive summer vocational training is also to be offered through area vocational schools for students who have finished high school or for dropouts who have not had access to vocational education. Five to ten weeks in length, the programs provide job entry skills in such occupations as key punch operator, production typist, cashier checker, and nurse's aide. Supplementary vocational guidance and counseling services are being offered under the project, and parent involvement in the total process is being encouraged (Selland, 1969).

Detroit Developmental Career Guidance Project

A five-year project to improve self-concepts and broaden educational and vocational aspirations of inner-city youth, the Detroit DCGP was among the first projects to conceptualize career development as a K–12 program, particularly one designed to meet the needs of urban minority youth. Directed by George Leonard (1968), the project has several components:

a. Sequential experiences from elementary through senior high school
b. Extensive student contact with business and industry
c. Guidance consultants in project schools to coordinate team efforts
d. Paraprofessionals (mostly parents) utilized for a variety of duties, including home visits
e. Simulated experiences and career games
f. Individual and group counseling
g. In-service training for teachers and project staff
h. Liaison with community agencies
i. Follow-up of students

DCGP, reaching 15,000 students in 10 inner city schools (6 elementary, 3 junior high, 1 senior high), has continually tried to relate the career development program to the home, the peer group, and the classroom. Its broad goals have included heightened achievement motivation and personal destiny control. The notion of career has been used as an organizing concept to build curricular programs and introduce flexibility in the classroom.

Each DCGP school has a guidance team consisting of the guidance consultant, a career community aide, and student assistants who, with the help of teachers, principals, and staff, work with other students and their parents. The several project schools have participated in cooperative planning and development activities. A number of unique approaches have been tried. Special assemblies and programs have been instituted which depart from traditional career day programs. Intimate teacher and parent involvement in career guidance activities is encouraged and wide use of environmental resources is achieved through liaison with community agencies. Each project school has been sponsored by a local company. Among the innovative ideas tried were the School Employment Security Commission in an elementary school where fifth, sixth, and, later, fourth graders applied for actual jobs available in the school building, went through interviews and a selection process, and were evaluated as workers. This was a kind of "learning the rules of the game" experience through simulation of an actual employment setting.

A variety of publications have come out of the project, including *Teaching Self-Understanding* (an elementary teachers' guide), *Career Guidance Manual for Teachers, Handbook for Paraprofessionals, How to Face Future Success* (a job handbook for students compiled by counselors who visited local industry), and a series of career word games for the elementary school developed by Ira Bank.

Several efforts at assessing the effectiveness of the project have been undertaken. They include use of the Student Career Guidance Survey to obtain information on students' leisure activities, occupational information, occupational plans and values, and attitudes toward counselors. A Faculty Attitude Survey was also taken. Evidence is lacking on the effectiveness of the paraprofessionals, consultant-counselor relations, and parent involvement. Among recent findings, based on comparative studies of students both in project and non-project schools, were the following:

a. There has been a significant decrease in the number of dropouts in the project schools.
b. There has been a significant increase in the numbers of project school students going on for further education.
c. A greater number of students in project schools are succeeding in getting jobs one month after high school.
d. Project school students score higher on indices of vocational maturity and on scales of coping behavior (Leonard, 1971).

Results of doctoral dissertations now in progress will provide more data on the effectiveness of the program. Although DCGP students and parents have been extremely enthusiastic, there is a funding problem, and it is not clear at this writing whether the program will continue as a special pilot activity, be absorbed into the regular program, or be dropped. Despite its focus on inner-city youth, DCGP incorporates a number of elements which would seem to be appropriate for school populations in general. It has, accordingly, served as a model for some of the newly emerging programs elsewhere.

Project BEACON—Rochester, New York

Project BEACON represents the efforts of one large city school system to operate a guidance program in close collaboration with the business and industrial resources of the community. As an approach to career development and other aspects of personal development, it is typical of many current elementary school guidance programs.

The project embodies the following seven emphases. The initials of the first six of these form the acronym BEACON.

a. Building the child's self-image
b. Early success in language arts
c. Accent on working with parents
d. Cultural enrichment
e. Orientation—in-service training of teachers
f. Negro history and culture
g. Development of new materials

Like the Detroit Developmental Career Guidance Project described earlier, BEACON focuses on the needs of pupils of low socioeconomic backgrounds and minority group membership. One of its specific goals is to improve aspirations and raise educational levels. BEACON was initiated in 1964 in four target elementary schools, two of which had large nonwhite populations.

The project is largely classroom centered, each teacher incorporating in the classroom a variety of activities under each of the BEACON project goals. A resource teacher is assigned to each school, along with special service personnel. Principal focus is upon the building of each child's self-image through a variety of ego-reinforcing activities. The products of each child's work are frequently displayed, along with his photograph. A "Who Am I?" personal data chart is used each week. Autobiographies are prepared, illustrated with each child's own original drawings.

Special speech and language development kits have been created, and dramatics and role-playing techniques are used extensively. There has also been reliance upon a variety of audiovisual approaches. Linkage was established with a local "Roundabout" television series, and portable cassette recorders were employed to facilitate on-the-spot recordings of interviews and field trip experiences.

BEACON schools have encouraged parent involvement both as visiting consultants during the classroom study of occupations and through volunteer activities. Faculty members engage in home visits regularly during released time. Students were assisted in the making of films, each of which was a personalized "Day in the Life of ——" account of the particular student who took it home for showing to family and friends. The proximity and cooperation of a large photographic company made learning activities such as this one feasible (Stiller, 1968).

Multi-ethnic materials, particularly those dealing with black history, have been introduced and widely used in Project BEACON. Another feature has been the identification and utilization of individuals in the community who might serve as role models for the elementary school children. These have not been well-known persons but local workers who are portrayed in a publication produced by the project. The directory contains a picture of each person, usually taken on his regular job, together with a description of his background, interests, attitudes, and work. Most of these occupational models have included some statement about the job, what they like and dislike about it, and what it does for them. Some of the statements reflect the person's philosophy and attitude toward life.

It is through these types of aims and activities that Project BEACON relates to career development in a broad sense of promoting self-development. Like many of the other elementary school level projects, it starts with the child's awareness of and feelings about himself and connects these perceptions and attitudes with possible educational and vocational roles. To increase the probabilities that such non-traditional approaches to instruction will produce the desired outcomes, it is important that teachers acquire the necessary understandings and skills.

In-service training for teachers and the provision of released time to conduct it have been foundational characteristics of Project BEACON.

Career Development Curriculum Guide—Texas Education Agency

As a follow-up to the Elementary Guide for Career Development, grades 1 through 6, developed by Lee Laws (1970), the Texas Education Agency has produced a curriculum guide for grades 1 through 8. The material identifies 40 career development concepts, behavioral objectives, learning activities, and the resources to be used in teaching them. Based on the precepts and research findings of career development and the characteristics of elementary-school-age children, the Texas guide attempts to relate behavior concepts to academic subjects and to suggest specific ways in which such concepts can be integrated into curriculum. A set of 40 transparencies has also been prepared depicting significant career development concepts (e.g., "All work has dignity"; "All work is interrelated") in cartoon format as a means to stimulating class discussion. The guide also focuses on Careers of the Month as related to specific school subjects.

A discussion manual for the teacher or counselor accompanies the materials. The Texas curriculum materials also include performance-based evaluation techniques and suggest alternate follow-up activities to be used to help children explore work. A unique evaluation technique involves the use of single-concept cartoons to test student understanding of his learning experience. The single concepts taught from grades 1 through 8 provide a fairly comprehensive base for teaching children about principles of career development. Solid evidence is as yet lacking to support the placement of these principles at the grade levels at which they occur in this curriculum; experience may show that some of them should be shifted upward or downward.

An attractive feature of the Career Development Curriculum Guide is the convenient format in which these curriculum materials are packaged. Elementary school teachers would find them comparatively easy to use. The materials have been tried out in selected Texas elementary schools and have also been disseminated to schools in other states (Laws, 1971). Systematic evidence on their effectiveness in helping produce desired social maturation changes in children is lacking at this time.

Our Working World—Senesh, SRA

Lawrence Senesh, an economist, has produced a model of career development and a matching set of materials that focus on work as the central theme of elementary grade studies. These elementary readers and activity volumes were first published in 1967 and are now under revision (Senesh, 1967). Tied closely to the social sciences, the lessons deal with the child's enlarging world, starting with Families at Work, then Neighborhoods at Work, Cities at Work, and so forth. The *Our Working World* series in its revised form will attempt to integrate the social sciences around a career development model. The philosophical aims underlying the Senesh approach appear strikingly harmonious with Levenstein's plea (Chapter 4, this volume) that the valuing of human work be inculcated in school children by means of the humanities.

Although *Our Working World* has a pronounced economic orientation, Senesh has incorporated lessons that stress an appreciation of basic career development concepts in the early years. The *Cities at Work* package for upper elementary levels integrates the concept of work into the history of cities, economics (the city as the marketplace of goods and services as well as ideas), government, urban development, and transportation. Senesh selects certain cities as prototypes—Chicago, New York, Pittsburgh, San Francisco, and smaller cities such as Elkhart, Indiana, to show both the commonalities and the uniqueness of urban communities around the United States. He identifies workers, real human beings who work at the jobs of the city, and intersperses his lessons with human interest stories about people whose lives and work have been affected by changing technology. In *Our Working World,* children are exposed to some of the trauma and problems of readjustment that accompany a move from a rural area to a city. A variety of facts about working life and their place in civilization are woven into human episodes which provide an appealing means for children to gain exposure to concepts such as the division of labor, the humanizing versus depersonalizing aspects of work, economic well-being, work in a mobile society, and job supply and demand. The materials begin with what the child understands best—the family, then move to neighborhood, and subsequently to cities, to nation, and internation in a spiraling pattern which reflects the child's ever-changing capacity to comprehend his expanding world.

In a recent report, Senesh (1971) notes that as the standard of living has risen and the choices of goods, services, and jobs have broadened, occupational frustration, paradoxically, has increased to the extent that it has now become a problem of national proportions. He says, "When students can study the nature and causes of the conflict between human aspirations and the occupational role, they will be better equipped to cope with this problem when they enter the working world." In his career development instructional model, Senesh's approach to the study of occupational life and its frustrations is through the social sciences, looking first at the symptoms of the problem (dropouts, delayed work role, chronic high tension, alienated youth in the ghettos, worker obsolescence, job fallout) and then at the contributions of the different social science disciplines (economics, political science, sociology, anthropology, psychology) to an understanding of various aspects of the problem.

Senesh identifies the central problem to be studied as that of how the social system can be made to insure a match between occupational roles and human aspirations that will lead to maximum individual fulfillment. Figure 2 presents a schematization of his "Fundamental Ideas of Career Development" (Senesh, 1971).

Work Experience/Career Exploration Program (WECEP)

A junior high school program which attempts to reach 14- and 15-year-old potential dropouts through combined work experience and classroom instruction, WECEP has been in operation since 1969 and has served as a model for similar programs in other parts of the country (Muller, 1971). Tried out initially in 10

Figure 2
The Fundamental Ideas of Career Development (Lawrence Senesh)

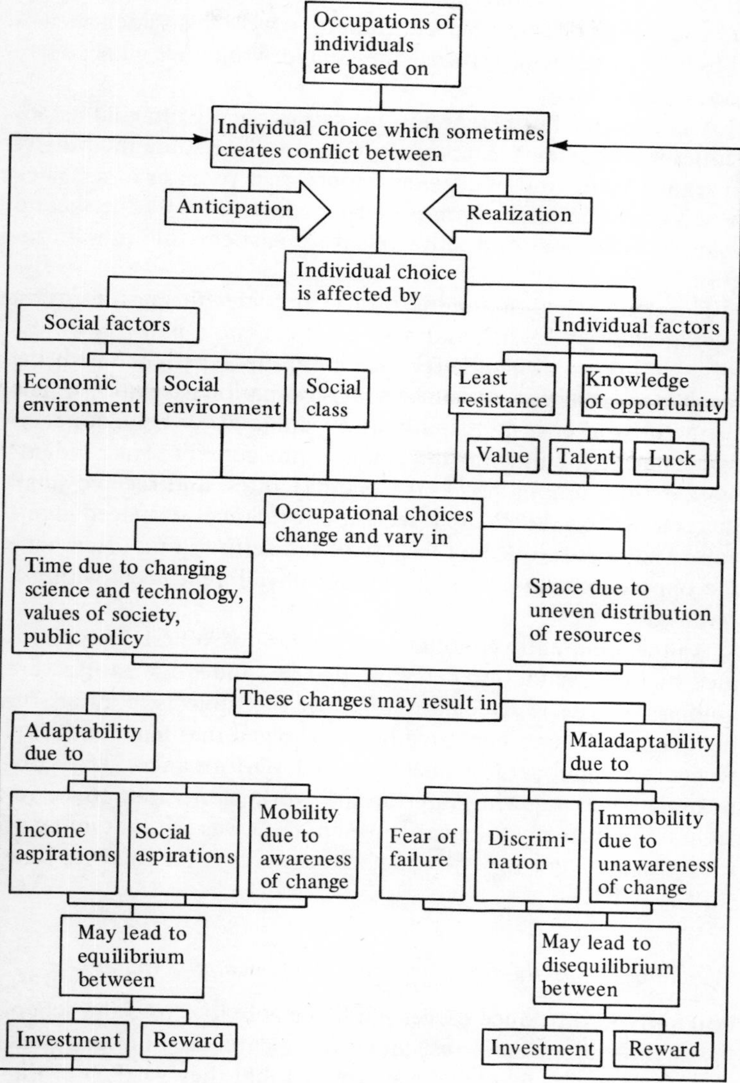

Minneapolis junior high schools, the project identified students who it was felt could most profit from a planned work experience in the early high school years. Teachers, counselors, and other school personnel participated in the student selection process. Effective teacher-coordinators were also identified—those who had demonstrated they could work well with poorly motivated students.

A number of businesses and industries were contacted as potential work settings. Employers agreed to hire students, usually at regular rates, and to provide a conference room or other place which could be used as an on-the-job classroom. By the second year, 80 businesses and industries were participating in the program.

The daily schedule for the project provides for a half day in regular classes (English and mathematics) and a half day on the job, one hour of which is for a small group experience with the teacher-coordinator on matters of occupational relations. The theme of worker responsibility and techniques of behavior reinforcement are built into the small-group activity. The student-workers join unions, work at basic pay rates, and receive small increments for satisfactory work performance at spaced intervals. They take work in a variety of job settings and often have the opportunity to handle a number of different tasks within a given job.

An independently conducted evaluation of WECEP was initiated in 1970. School grades, absenteeism, and work habits were among the criteria selected to appraise the subjects, both as students and workers. Tentative results showed that many students registered significant gains in school performance. They appeared to be acquiring appropriate work habits and to be responding positively to rewards for effort. It was felt that many of the students were experiencing school success for the first time (Muller, 1971).

Wyoming Comprehensive Occupational Education Program

Attempts to introduce career guidance activities into the school curriculum often meet resistance from parents, administrators, and classroom teachers on the grounds that they weaken or displace the academic courses and divert attention from standard scholastic goals. The Wyoming State Department of Education has designed the Comprehensive Occupational Education Program to fit the existing curriculum, particularly at the elementary level (Talagon, 1970). COEP is a K–12 program in which the major themes of career development are sequentially arranged to conform to progressive levels of student maturity in the following manner.

a. K–6—Attitudes Toward the World of Work
b. Grades 7 and 8—Career Orientation Program
c. Grades 9 and 10—Career Exploration Program
d. Grades 11 and 12—Career Preparation Broad-Skill Program

In the elementary grades, the emphasis is upon developing an appreciation of all human work and creating an awareness that useful citizenship is expressed through the occupational role. The units allocated to the seventh and eighth grades attempt to teach how the economy is organized by major fields of work so that students may be better prepared later to explore occupations in relation to their own characteristics and aspirations. The exploratory experiences themselves, occurring in grades 9 and 10, are intended to encourage students to make provisional choices of career goals. The inculcation of diverse job-related skills occurs chiefly in the last two years of high school and is designed to provide the student with flexibility as he considers available employment opportunities and moves closer to choice.

Vocational Exploration Group (VEG)

In an attempt to meet the vocational planning needs of the culturally disadvantaged, participants in government-sponsored opportunity programs, and other individuals seeking successful entry into the labor market, Calvin Daane and his associates (Daane, 1972) at Arizona State University and Studies for Urban Man, Inc. have designed a short-term training experience called Vocational Exploration Group. The program is intended to help clients acquire the motives, work understandings, and job planning strategies necessary to make early and effective decisions on training for work and actual employment. A distinguishing feature of VEG is its assumption that the trainee who participates in the exploration group possesses occupational information that can be discovered, shared with the group, and personalized for the individual members of the group who can then put it to use in their own job decision making. Daane (1972) describes his technique as follows:

> The process evolves from a structured, small-group interaction through a series of sequenced tasks to the man and job issues. The sequence of tasks is designed to develop insight into what jobs are, what they demand, and what they give in return. The process is carried out within a three-to-five-hour time period, and results in immediate action on the part of each member of the group. The practical approach has shown definite advantages for serving large numbers of applicants: it provides motivation to each member of the group and enhances his knowledge of the job market [p. 1].

While Vocational Exploration Group participants in Daane's pilot studies were largely drawn from among public employment service applicants and from sponsored training programs, such as those under the Manpower Defense Training Act and the Neighborhood Youth Corps, the technique is applicable to a wide range of individuals needing short-term vocational planning skills prior to entering the labor market. In one study, secondary school boys and their fathers participated in an exploratory group at the local high school with favorable results. The broad-scale suitability of the method stems in part from its generalized goal of building group understanding of man-job relationships and of helping each individual in each training setting apply the resultant understandings to himself and his particular career planning needs.

The Vocational Exploration Group has been employed mainly in two scheduling formats, the shorter program involving a two-hour session and the extended program involving a sequence of five 45-minute sessions. The contents of VEG are anchored in three substantive issues: job functions (work duties and operations); job demands (worker requirements); and job satisfactions (What does the job offer to meet personal needs?). These topics are dealt with in a multi-step group process distributed over five phases: INCLUSION ACTIVITIES (aimed at reducing fear of job exploration), JOB INVENTORY (clarifies the man-job relations of the individual's preferred occupation by examining the world of work through both the Dictionary of Occupational Titles data-people-things classification and a training-and-education classification), JOB PERSONALIZATION (group sharing of job information), EXPANSION (each group member expands his vocational choice by relating one job to several others), and NEXT STEP (group focus on the specific plan of each member). Visual aids are utilized throughout the experience to facilitate the exploration process.

Findings on the effectiveness of the Vocational Exploration Group technique in improving job planning behavior were provided by a research study of 1,649 subjects drawn from subsidized job training programs, high school training programs, public employment service job applicants, and placement files (Daane, 1972). Subjects were randomly assigned to experimental (VEG) and control groups. "The experimental groups achieved twice as many NEW JOBS and were higher in number for both WORK TRAINING ENTRY and in MOVEMENT FROM WORK TRAINING to jobs. They also gained in degree of EMPLOYABILITY perceptions, REDUCTION in SOCIAL ALIENATION perceptions and decreased DOGMATISM. In each case the gains must be considered pronounced with significance levels generally obtained at the .01 level of confidence or better [p. 35]."

A multiplier effect had been built into VEG through a pyramid model of training. In the process of conducting exploration groups, the group leader works simultaneously as a trainer for new leadership trainees who are given supervised on-site experience in observing, participating in, and leading their respective groups. Daane states that acquiring the skills of a successful VEG leader is not difficult, and he claims that the experiential nature of the program has resulted in the development of many successful leaders who are paraprofessionals. Under a contract from the United States Department of Labor's Manpower Administration, he initiated a project to train personnel in 10 cities to become group leaders skilled in the uses of the methods and instructional resources of the Vocational Exploration Group.

The results of this project were reported to be predominantly favorable (Daane, 1972).

The Systems Approach in Career Guidance

The systems approach to problem solving and effecting change was initially developed in information and communications theory, was later applied experimentally in advanced engineering and management settings, and, more recently, has been proposed in a number of loosely adapted forms as an efficient means to producing change within education. A true systems approach to career development in the schools would call for a large-scale model, with more inputs and greater conceptual complexity than found in the great majority of programs which have been described in this chapter. Although such an approach is not easy to negotiate, it offers greater hope for upgrading the effectiveness of guidance than does the refinement of individual processes, methods, and instruments in counseling. This is a conclusion evidently shared by Campbell (1971), Campbell and Vetter (1971), Herr and Cramer (1972), and others who have proposed new models for career guidance which follow a systems approach.

In essence, the systems approach identifies all significant components of the limited universe in which planned change is to occur, ascertains the relations between components, specifies goals to be reached, converts the goals into operationally defined objectives (behavioral goals), selects those components most important to the objectives, designs from the components the methods yielding the highest probability of reaching the objectives, installs a monitoring (evaluation) procedure, and feeds the results of the monitoring back into the system in order that its efficiency can be continuously reexamined and improved.

The components of a systems approach which is concerned with changing student terminal behavior through school learning is illustrated by Romberg's (1968) model in Figure 3.

Descriptions of two systems approaches to career guidance are presented below. Of these, the Dworkin-Walz model emphasizes the indispensable function of evaluation in an effective systems approach. The Minnesota Career Development Curriculum model stresses the role of in-service education in generating, refining, and installing a career guidance system. In all probability, the most ambitious and comprehensive model of its kind is the systems approach to career education now under development at The Center for Vocational and Technical Education, The Ohio State University (Taylor, Montague, & Michaels, 1972). The Ohio State system incorporates an emerging behavioral model for career guidance (Campbell et al., 1971). Because this work is still in progress, it is not given further description below.

An Evaluation Model for Career Guidance

It is at once surprising and disappointing that a field which, from its beginnings, had been so pragmatic in its outlook, has not tested the product of its services more systematically. However, we have already noted the growing tendency to insist on accountability as a condition of continued support for education, training, and guidance programs, especially new and expanding ones. Most of the pilot programs currently funded by the United States Office of Education and by the various state departments of education make specific provisions for the assessment of outcomes. The same condition holds for virtually all

Figure 3
Romberg's Model of an Instructional System (1968)

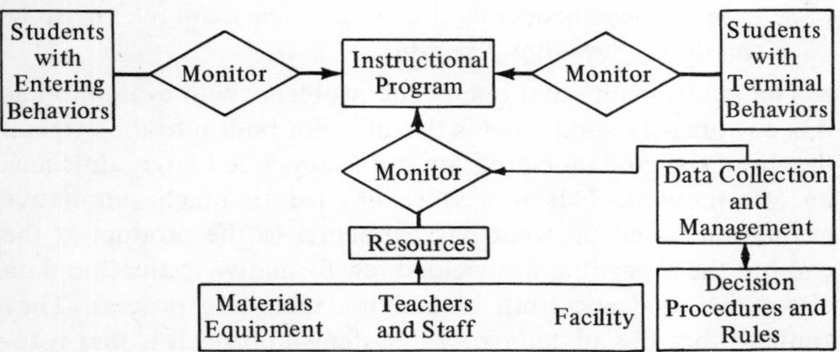

of the illustrative career guidance models and programs presented above.

A number of writers have dealt with concepts and techniques of evaluation as applied to career development (Campbell et al., 1971; Moss, 1968; Wysong, 1971). Perhaps one of the most comprehensive yet concise models is that by Dworkin and Walz (1971). It is included here not because it is an operational program but because it offers a promising framework for more effective practice within the broader context of career development, including the evaluation phase.

The Dworkin and Walz systems model is based on several broad assumptions:

a. Man has a basic need to engage in meaningful goal-directed activity.
b. Society can maintain and develop itself only if individuals engage in meaningful behavior (work) that both maintains and develops society.
c. Career development does not take place at any given point in time.
d. An important goal of the educative process is to assist persons with their career development and adjustment so that they can satisfy their own needs and the needs of society.
e. One goal of education in schools is preparation of individuals who can function in a variety of work roles.
f. The public schools and other agencies should reflect societal conditions at a point in time but must incorporate the concept of change and movement toward the ideal society.
g. Focus of the educative process is on the individual and his needs at different points.
h. Other agencies besides the schools play important roles in career development [pp. 309–310].

The authors note that one of the problems with evaluation as it is customarily conducted is that it is not built into the original design of the guidance program but is appended later, almost as an afterthought. This procedure has led to much summative evaluation based on what has happened to the product at the end but the procedure has yielded few formative evaluation data about the total spectrum of activity, including process. They contend that the advantage of a systems approach is that it focuses on both content and process evaluation, and they suggest that evaluation is "the science of providing information for decision-making." Six cumulative steps, which ideally should be performed in sequence, comprise the basis of their model, as follows:

a. Individual Inputs. If the focus of career guidance is to be harmonized with the needs of populations with which one wishes to work, then it is necessary to identify and describe these needs. This aspect deals with such questions as, "What are the career needs of the population and what needs should be focused on?"

b. Environmental Inputs. There is a need to identify characteristics and needs of the community served, as well as manpower and economic trends of the country as a whole, which may have impact on the local environment. The question posed here is, "What community variables should be taken into consideration?"

c. Objective Inputs. When individual and environmental inputs are identified, the next step is to develop objectives for career guidance programs. These should be stated in behavioral outcome terms rather than as vague, rhetorical generalities and should be ranked in priority. This third stage speaks to the question, "What objectives should be established and in what order of importance?"

d. Setting Inputs. The most feasible setting or settings in which the objectives can be implemented in whole or part should be selected. Implicit is the concern for inter-agency cooperation. One should ask, "Where can what be done best?" and "What is the most desirable setting?"

e. Process Inputs. A variety of methods for reaching the specified objectives must next be identified and developed, both by drawing from promising practices already in operation and by constructing original ones. Such techniques might be derived through literature surveys, consultation with authorities, visits to innovative programs, and one's own creativity. The challenge here is, "Through what methods and techniques can the objectives be best achieved?"

f. Product Input. There is a need to ascertain the degree to which each objective has been achieved in order to provide feedback for planning and decision making. This in turn provides a basis for program redesign and improvement. Step *f*, then, deals with the questions, "How can one assess the degree to which each objective has been achieved?" and "What specific aspects of the career guidance program do we want to modify, eliminate, or leave alone?"

The Dworkin-Walz model also deals with change strategies and the process of introducing new emphases and practices into an educational setting. By failing to give adequate attention to this aspect of program development, many programs encounter misunderstandings, skepticism, and resistance. But the central messages implicit in the Dworkin-Walz model are that sound evaluation is essential to program design, execution, and revision and that the evaluation plan must be inclusive of the population to be served, the community served, the objectives to be realized, the setting in which the evaluation is conducted, the methods to be used, and the product.

Career Development Curriculum Model (CDC)—University of Minnesota

Since 1966, a faculty team has been at work on a career development model titled "A Horizontally and Vertically Coordinated Systems Approach to Facilitating Career Development through Teacher Education and School Curriculum." The project coordinators are Wesley Tennyson, Mary Klaurens, and Lorraine Hansen. While CDC is still under development, a number of its major components are now readily identifiable. These components include:

a. In-service Education. This has consisted primarily of summer workshops for teams of counselors, teachers, administrators, and vocational educators. Workshops have been held since 1967.

b. Curriculum Development. A variety of instructional materials are under construction including Behavioral Objectives for Career Development, K–12; Suggested Teaching-Learning Approaches to Career Development through Curriculum; Learning Opportunities Packages (LOPs) for Senior High

School; Junior High School Learning Packages by Subject; and an Elementary Curriculum Guide, K–6.

c. Preservice Teacher Education. Work has only recently begun on this aspect, but a pilot unit has been taught in the Introductory Course in Secondary Education and a "Module" (Learning Package) has been prepared which introduces secondary level preservice teachers to career development concepts.

d. Pilot Testing of Concepts and Materials. Some of the LOPs (see above) career development concepts are being field tested at Marshall-University High School which is jointly administered by the Minneapolis Board of Education and the University of Minnesota. A grades 7–12 career development program has been initiated at this school. Materials at each level will eventually be field tested in selected other schools.

e. Career Resource Center. A Career Resource Center utilizing volunteers in guidance has been established at Marshall-University High School through the joint sponsorship of the Minneapolis schools, the National Council of Jewish Women, and the University Center for Curriculum Studies.

f. Career Development Laboratory. A laboratory stocked with professional materials for teachers and counselors has been developed.

In-service Education for Career Development. Since 1967 the Departments of Counseling Psychology and Distributive Education at the University of Minnesota have jointly sponsored a series of summer workshops to orient various school personnel to career development concepts and the world of business and industry, and further, to prepare the ground for curriculum development and program plans in the schools of the participants. A typical workshop brought together school counselors and distributive educators in a diversified instructional format which included a course in career development principles, exploratory experiences in industry, small group seminars, and an opportunity to observe and work with a group of high school students enrolled in a work experience program (Tennyson & Meyer, 1967; Tennyson & Klaurens, 1968a).

In 1970, the focus was on secondary school staff teams, each consisting of a counselor, teacher, and administrator. Participants were given a work exploration experience (WEE), integrative seminars on the work experience, and a career development course. A major part of their summer effort was directed toward completing an "Action Plan" to take back to their home school for implementation (Thoni, 1970).

The 1971 summer workshop was designed for teams of elementary school personnel. In addition to their exposure to a career development course and a work exploration experience, the students formed curriculum task groups to write career development materials for primary and intermediate grade levels under the guidance of the teaching staff. During a two-day retreat they were introduced to the career development behavioral objectives which had been developed earlier by the staff, and they used these as a basis for their curriculum work. They modified the objectives and developed learning activities and resources to fit them. They also undertook to relate each learning activity to a specific elementary school subject. The elementary curriculum materials developed by the workshop participants subsequently underwent revision and editing with a view toward eventual dissemination (University of Minnesota, 1971).

Curriculum Development. As is evident from the foregoing discussion, the Minnesota effort involves an interlocking of the curriculum aspect of career development with teacher education. A document tiled *Suggested Teaching-Learning Approaches to Career Development through Curriculum* (Tennyson & Klaurens, 1968a, 1968b) was the result of earlier collaboration between the instructional staff and workshop participants. The career development objectives which had grown out of this work were submitted to a panel of 15 teachers for clarification and reclassification under nine basic dimensions (Tennyson, 1971).

The objectives were submitted to 150 teachers in 10 subject matter areas for clarity rating and relevance to their subject matter. The objectives were then grouped by topic into about 30 categories which serve as the basis for the Learning Opportunities Packages. The Minnesota team has now developed LOPs on the topics Life Style and Work, Rewards and Satisfactions of

Work, Value Identification, Self-Concept Exploration, Significant Others, Social Contribution of Work, and Women and the World of Work. These are self-contained teacher's resource units keyed to the senior high school. Additional LOPs, relating subjects to careers, are being constructed for the junior high schools.

Elementary school materials which were developed in the summer of 1971 were based on behavioral objectives derived from an extensive search by the staff of the literature on vocational development tasks. The current revision consists of 28 vocational development tasks, seven for each level—primary, intermediate, junior high, and senior high—with three to seven performance objectives specified for each. Examples of tasks and objectives for each level are given below (Departments of Counseling Psychology and Distributive Education, 1971):

Primary: Vocational Development Task—Awareness of self
Performance Objective—Describes how he perceives himself as different from those around him

Intermediate: Vocational Development Task—Developing a positive self-concept
Performance Objective—Describes how he and others perceive his strengths

Junior High: Vocational Development Task—Acquiring knowledge of occupations and work settings
Performance Objective—Increases the range of occupations of which he has knowledge and examines their functions and requirements

Senior High: Vocational Development Task—Acquiring knowledge of educational and vocational paths
Performance Objective—Seeks information concerning the content and requirements of educational and training courses that may facilitate occupational goals

The preliminary work on elementary curriculum materials is currently leading to the development of LOPs for the elementary schools. Two 1972 summer workshops at the University of Minnesota focused on career education for the urban disadvantaged, K-to-post-high.

Preservice Teacher Education. It is anticipated that the subject-matter unit on concepts of career development will become an established part of the Introductory Course in Secondary Education. Learning experiences which have proved useful in the summer workshops with in-service teachers will likely be incorporated into the undergraduate teacher preparation curriculum. For example, practice in the identification and clarification of career development objectives and in the construction of Learning Opportunity Packages (LOPs) appears to hold promise for advancing the understanding of prospective teachers about issues in vocational planning and adjustment. As the emerging principles of career education become clearer and gain fuller acceptance, it should be easier to integrate career development units into the curriculum of preservice teacher education. While the application of the Minnesota CDC model to the training of undergraduates has thus far been largely confined to the secondary level, the model is equally relevant to the preparation of undergraduates in programs of elementary education.

Pilot Testing. For a number of years, both established and new career guidance practices have been installed and observed in the demonstration school (formerly University High School and now Marshall-University High School). Earlier efforts included tryouts of the Life Career Game, a Senior Women's Seminar centered on the career potentialities of girls, the team-teaching of ninth-grade careers units, and a simple version of computer-assisted guidance. More recent efforts have focused on the implementation of a serial career development program for grades 7–12. Some of the LOPs have been incorporated into an elective senior high school Psychology of Careers course which was introduced as part of the program. It is planned to involve selected teacher consultants in materials development and to have them try out some of the LOPs in their own schools.

Career Resource Center. A center has been established at Marshall-University High School as the locus for activities concerned with career guidance through curriculum and as a means to enlarging student contact with community and the work world. The Career Resource Center is staffed by trained volunteers who mainly provide services in the educational and occupational information area. As part of the counseling and guidance program, the center uses volunteers to assist on tours, to create special programs and arrange contacts, and to identify community resources available to students.

Following the first year of full operation, the center was evaluated, with students, teachers, volunteers, and counselors supplying questionnaire data. In general, it was found that students are using the volunteers and the center materials; they see the volunteers as helpful and the center as necessary and helpful; educational-vocational planning is important to them; and they would like more help in finding jobs. Teacher responses indicated that they consider a career guidance program important; they do not think students get enough help in career exploration; and they like the accessibility of the center and the availability of the volunteers. The responses of the counselors revealed that they regard the center's activities as a useful supplement to their regular program and they see the volunteers as helpful. The members of the volunteer staff stated that they do not always get the satisfaction out of the job they would like; they feel the need for a full-time coordinator; they need differentiated roles and direction; but they feel they are performing a valuable service. The volunteers served about 1200 students and 200 adults who came to the center in the first year of its operation (Hansen, 1971).

Career Development Laboratory. While the Career Resource Center stocks some materials for teacher use, most of the professional materials for teachers and counselors (curriculum guides, research reports, books on career development, conference reports, monographs, etc.) are housed nearby in the College of Education's recently developed Career Development Laboratory. The newness of this facility poses challenges with respect to how it can best be made to serve the curriculum needs of counselor preparation and teacher education, and, further, how its use can be effectively articulated with the aims and activities of the Career Resource Center.

REFERENCES

ACT Research and Development Division. *Handbook for the ACT career planning program* and *Student's booklet, 1971–1972.* Iowa City: American College Testing Program, 1972.

Boocock, S. S. The life career game. *Personnel and Guidance Journal,* 1967, **46,** 328–334.

Borow, H. Conjunction of career development and curriculum. In W. W. Tennyson (Ed.), Final report of the conference on implementing career development theory and research through the curriculum. National Vocational Guidance Association, Washington, D.C., 1966.

Borow, H. Antecedents, concomitants, and consequences of task-oriented behavior in youth. In National Institute of Child Health and Human Development, Perspectives on Human Deprivation, United States Department of Health, Education, and Welfare, 1968.

Borow, H. Guidance and counseling: Overview; Guidance and counseling: History. In *The Encyclopedia of Education.* New York: Macmillan, 1971, Vol. 4, 212–224; 224–233.

Brewer, J. M. The recent progress and problems of vocational guidance. *School and Society,* 1926, **23,** 62–70.

Budke, W. E. *Review and synthesis of information on occupational exploration.* Columbus: Center for Vocational and Technical Education, The Ohio State University, 1971.

Campbell, R. E. The systems approach: An emerging behavioral model for career guidance. An interim report of a procedural monograph. Columbus: Center for Vocational and Technical Education, The Ohio State University, 1971.

Campbell, R. E., Dworkin, E. P., Jackson, D. P., Hoeltzel, K. E., Parsons, G. E., & Lacey, D. W. The systems approach: An emerging behavioral model for career guidance. An interim report of a procedural monograph. Columbus: Center for Vocational and Technical Education, The Ohio State University, April, 1971.

Campbell, R. E., & Vetter, L. *Career guidance: An overview of alternative approaches.* Columbus: Center for Vocational and Technical Education, The Ohio State University, 1971.

Campbell, R. E., Walz, G. R., Miller, J. V., & Kriger, S. F. *Career guidance: A handbook of methods.* Columbus, Ohio, and Ann Arbor,

Michigan: Center for Vocational and Technical Education; Counseling and Personnel Services Information Center, 1972. (Mimeo.)

Crites, J. O. Measurement of vocational maturity in adolescence: Attitude test of the vocational development inventory. *Psychological Monographs*, 1965, **79**(2, Whole No. 595).

Daane, C. J. *Vocational exploration group: Theory and research.* Washington, D.C.: United States Department of Labor, Manpower Administration, 1972.

D'Costa, A. G., Winefordner, D. W., Odgers, J. G., & Koons, P. B. *Ohio vocational interest survey*. New York: Harcourt, Brace & World, 1969.

Departments of Counseling Psychology and Distributive Education. Career development curriculum: Specification of behaviors (performance objectives) which characterize each vocational development task. University of Minnesota, Minneapolis, August, 1971. (Mimeo.)

Dreves, F. J. Implementation of technology for children in New Jersey elementary schools. New Jersey Department of Education, Trenton, March, 1970. (Mimeo.)

Dworkin, E. P., & Walz, G. R. An evaluation model for guidance. In D. Cook (Ed.), *Guidance for education in revolution.* Boston: Allyn & Bacon, 1971.

Gambino, T. W. Career development. Special paper. The Career Development Project, New Jersey Department of Education, Trenton, November, 1970.

Gribbons, W. D., & Lohnes, P. R. *Career development*. New York: Teachers College Press, 1968.

Gysbers, N. C. Elements of a model for promoting career development in elementary and junior high school. National Conference on Exemplary Programs and Projects, Atlanta, Georgia, March 12–14, 1969.

Gysbers, N. C., & Moore, E. J. Career development in the schools. Columbia, Missouri: University of Missouri, 1971. (Mimeo.)

Hansen, L. S. *Career guidance practices in school and community*. ERIC-CAPS Monograph. Washington, D.C.: National Vocational Guidance Association, 1970.

Hansen, L. S. Promoting career development through utilization of volunteers in a career resource center. Project report, volunteers in guidance, Marshall-University High School, University of Minnesota, Minneapolis, August, 1971. (Mimeo.)

Hardwick, A. L. Career education—a model for implementation. *Business Education Forum*, May, 1971, 3–5.

Herr, E. L. *Unifying an entire system of education around a career development theme.* National Conference on Exemplary Programs and Projects, Atlanta, Georgia, March 12–14, 1969.

Herr, E. L. Curriculum considerations in career development programs, K–12. Paper presented at Ohio State Department of Education workshop on guidelines for career development programs, K–12, Columbus, Ohio, June 7, 1971.

Herr, E. L. *Review and synthesis of foundations for career education.* Columbus: Center for Vocational and Technical Education, The Ohio State University, 1972.

Herr, E. L., & Cramer, S. H. *Vocational guidance and career development in the schools: Toward a systems approach.* Boston: Houghton Mifflin, 1972.

Himes, J. S. Some work-related cultural deprivations of lower-class Negro youths. *Journal of Marriage and the Family*, November, 1964, 447–449.

Holland, J. L. *The self-directed search.* Palo Alto, Calif.: Consulting Psychologists Press, 1972.

Holland, J. L., Hollifield, J. H., Nafzieger, D. H., & Helms, S. T. A guide to the self-directed career program: A practical and inexpensive vocational guidance system, Report No. 126, Center for Social Organization of Schools, The Johns Hopkins University, Baltimore, Md., 1972.

Laws, L. *Elementary guide for career development, 1–6.* Austin, Texas: Texas Education Agency, 1970.

Laws, L. The career concept instructional package. Austin, Texas: Education Service Center, Region XIII, 1971. (Mimeo.)

Leonard, G. E. *Developmental career guidance in action.* Detroit: Wayne State University, Plans for Progress, and Detroit Public Schools, 1968.

Leonard, G. E. Career guidance for inner-city youth in action: The Developmental Career Guidance Project. Paper presented at Ohio State

Department of Education Workshop on guidance for career development programs, K-12, Columbus, Ohio, June 7, 1971.

Marland, S. P., Jr. Career education. *Today's Education,* October, 1971, 22–25.

Moss, J. The evaluation of occupational education programs. University of Minnesota Technical Report, Research Coordination Unit, September, 1968.

Muller, P. Progress report. Work Experience/Career Exploration Program. Minneapolis, Minnesota Board of Education, No. 4, March–April, 1971.

Myers, G. E. A critical review of present developments in vocational guidance with special reference to future prospects. In F. J. Allen (Ed.), *Principles and problems in vocational guidance.* New York: McGraw-Hill, 1927.

North Dakota State Board of Education. *Career development.* North Dakota Exemplary World of Work Project, Bismarck, North Dakota, 1970.

Osipow, S. H. What do we really know about career development? In N. C. Gysbers and D. Pritchard (Eds.), *Career guidance, counseling and placement.* Washington, D.C.: United States Office of Education, 1969.

Romberg, T. A. The development and refinement of prototypic instructional systems. Unpublished paper presented at annual meeting of American Educational Research Association, Chicago, Illinois, February, 1968.

Selland, L. A statewide program in developmental vocational guidance (K–12) and occupational preparation for the changing world of work. Proposal for Exemplary Project in Vocational Education, Bismarck, North Dakota, December 29, 1969.

Senesh, L. *Our working world: Cities at work.* Chicago: Science Research Associates, 1967.

Senesh, L. Fulfillment of human aspirations: The strength of a social system. Paper presented at Workshop on Career Development and the Elementary Curriculum, University of Minnesota, Minneapolis, June 30, 1971.

Stiller, A. Beacon lights. Project BEACON Rochester, New York, School District, 1968.

Super, D. E. *The psychology of careers.* New York: Harper, 1957.

Super, D. E. *Manual for the work values inventory.* Boston: Houghton Mifflin, 1970.

Super, D. E., & Forrest, D. J. *Career development inventory, form 1, preliminary manual.* New York: Teachers College, Columbia University, 1972. (Mimeo.)

Super, D. E., & Overstreet, P. *The vocational maturity of ninth grade boys.* New York: Teachers College Press, Columbia University, 1960.

Talagon, D. P. *A comprehensive occupational education program.* Cheyenne, Wyoming: State Department of Education, 1970.

Taylor, J. E., Montague, E. K., & Michaels, E. R. An occupational clustering system and curriculum implications for the comprehensive career education model. Technical Report 72–1, Human Resources Research Organization, Alexandria, Va. Prepared for Center for Vocational and Technical Education, The Ohio State University, January 1972.

Tennyson, W. W. Career development curriculum. Paper presented at workshops in Cochise County, Arizona, January 26–27, 1971.

Tennyson, W. W., & Hansen, L. S. Guidance through the curriculum. In *The Encyclopedia of Education.* New York: Macmillan, 1971, Vol. 4, 248–254.

Tennyson, W. W., & Klaurens, M. Suggested teaching-learning approaches for career development in the curriculum. Departments of Counselor Education and Distributive Education, *Pilot training project focusing on occupational experience and career development.* University of Minnesota, Minneapolis, Summer, 1968. (a)

Tennyson, W. W., & Klaurens, M. Behavioral objectives for career development. Departments of Distributive Education and Counselor Education, University of Minnesota, Minneapolis, 1968. (Mimeo.) (b)

Tennyson, W. W., & Meyer, W. G. *Pilot training project for teachers of distribution and marketing focusing on responsibilities for career development.* College of Education, University of Minnesota, Minneapolis, Summer, 1967. (Mimeo.)

Thoni, R. Career development and the secondary school curriculum. Workshop report, University of Minnesota, Minneapolis, Minnesota, August, 1970. (Mimeo.)

Townsend, L. G. Restructuring of educational practices related to objectives for guidance and placement for career development. In N. C. Gysbers and D. Pritchard (Eds.), *Career guidance, counseling and placement.* Washington, D.C.: United States Office of Education, 1969.

University of Minnesota, EPDA Institute. Career development and the elementary school curriculum, Departments of Counseling Psychology and Distributive Education, College of Education, Minneapolis, Summer, 1971.

Work Adjustment Project Staff. Minnesota Importance Questionnaire. Minneapolis: Industrial Relations Center, University of Minnesota, Revised 1967.

Wysong, E. Evaluation of career guidance programs. Paper presented at Ohio State Department of Education workshop on Guidelines for career development programs, K–12, Columbus, Ohio, June 8, 1971.

7

behavioral counseling for vocational decisions

JOHN D. KRUMBOLTZ
Stanford University

RONALD D. BAKER
Indiana University

Vocational guidance before World War II was of two contrasting types. In the secondary schools, it consisted largely of providing occupational information on the assumption that a direct cognitive emphasis would build the knowledge base that bewildered students needed to choose occupations wisely. In the college counseling centers and nonschool agencies, vocational guidance borrowed heavily from the psychology of individual differences and made prominent use of tests to help clients match personal traits to broad job requirements. The postwar period saw the rapid rise of client-centered approaches in psychotherapy and counseling, a movement which shifted the emphasis in vocational guidance away from diagnosis and prediction and toward acceptance and clarification of the counselee's perceptions and feelings. It is with the logic and methodology of behavioral counseling, a radically different conception of how vocational planning competence may be facilitated, that John Krumboltz and Ronald Baker deal in this chapter.

Far more than any of its predecessors, behavioral counseling is anchored in principles derived from the experimental psychology of learning, particularly those of operant conditioning. It proceeds from the premise that behavior is controlled by its consequences; when the individual's acts lead to rewards, they tend to be strengthened; when they result in threat or punitive experience, outcomes are less certain. In the behavioral approach to career guidance, the client's learning problem must first be clearly delineated and the hoped-for outcomes stated in explicit performance terms. As concerns vocational counseling with students, such outcomes are generally expressed in the form of increases in the amount and appropriateness of the client's decision making and planning behavior. In contrast with insight-oriented approaches, such as client-centered counseling, behavioral counseling stresses the client's relations to his external environment and his style of coping with it.

If counseling is construed and performed as learning activity, then the counselor is to be seen as a teacher who leads the client toward the acquisition and exercise of more productive decision-making skills. How is the behavioral counselor to effect such human changes? Krumboltz and Baker describe and illustrate the techniques of modeling, reinforcement, and work simulation. In the first of these, the client engages in imitative learning by observing personal models who exemplify effective problem-solving methods. Because suitable models for vocational planning are not always available, the counselor may present such models through mechanical means, such as audiotapes and videotapes. When, as a consequence of modeling or otherwise, the client declares his intentions to seek outside information about a field of occupational interest or gives evidence of having carried out appropriate acts of educational and vocational exploration, he is reinforced by verbal approval and other means. Work simulation exercises, like those found in the Job Experience Kits, allow the counselee engaged in vocational planning to encounter lifelike work problems typical of the occupations he is exploring. In helping his client develop a variety of useful information-seeking and decision-making skills, the behavioral counselor may include in his repertoire such additional tools as the Life Career Game and the use of expectancy tables.

Like behavioral engineers in other settings, those who apply their techniques to career guidance have been painstaking both in specifying performance objectives and in putting their practices to the test. Krumboltz and Baker review a number of Stanford University studies designed to gauge the efficacy of behavioral vocational counseling. In general, the results reveal significant increases, as a result of exposure to such methods, in the variety and frequency of overt vocational explorations outside of counseling. These positive research findings, the authors caution, are tempered by such limitations as the use of selected and homogeneous client samples, the restricted geographic regions in which most studies have been conducted, and the absence of data on long-term behavior effects. Nonetheless, it is difficult to avoid the conclusion that behavioral counseling is now exerting a strong influence upon the methodology of guidance, an influence that is very soon likely to be reflected in an appreciable gain in the quality of vocational counseling services.

H. B.

The following excerpt from a counseling dialogue illustrates how vocational planning might begin:

Cl*: I pretty much decided what I'm going to do. I was in radar operations in the Army, and I liked it. I really did. I want a job as an electrical engineer. I get a kick out of working with radios, and around the farm I'm handy with any kind of machinery.

Co*: When were you discharged from the Army?

Cl: Oh, just about two and a half months ago. I've been helping out my brother and father on the farm, and it came to me that I'd rather be working on electronics equipment again than working on the farm. So I wrote and found out about my veteran's benefits, and they sent me here to the counseling service to be sure I was getting into the right thing.

Co: I see. Your records arrived yesterday. We'll review your work and training experiences, but first tell me more of your ideas about engineering. You sound as if you have definitely made up your mind about a career in electrical engineering.

Cl: Yeah, like I said before, I really liked my job in the Army. I didn't lose any sleep about the rest of the Army, but I liked my job.

Co: What did you like best about your work?

Cl: Finding out what was wrong with equipment when it broke down. It was like a puzzle, and you had to get the answer fast. The lieutenant in charge of our outfit always called on me when something went wrong. He even let me teach parts of his classes when it came to maintenance and re-

* Most illustrative counseling dialogues in this chapter were taken from transcripts of actual counseling interviews. Cl = Client; Co = Counselor.

pair. He'd tell 'em about the math and the numbers, and I'd tell 'em how the stuff really worked.

Co: Did you like teaching?

Cl: I sure did. I like to show people how things work.

Co: What about the math and theory parts?

Cl: Mystery hour! I was in the Army four years, and every year we'd get the same lectures. Every year I got more confused. Math and I never got along any too well.

Co: What have you done about your plans for getting into engineering?

Cl: I've applied here at the university. Since I'm a resident of the state it'd be cheaper to go here, and I think I can get in OK.

Co: Your high school transcript shows you graduated in the top half of your class. You're certain to be accepted. How can I help you?

Cl: Well, before I can get my veterans' benefits, I have to show on the forms they sent that my plans are clear and OK. So, I guess that is what I want you to help me with. I'd like to know what kinds of classes I'll be taking and what kinds of jobs I can get later.

Almost everyone in our society must make a series of decisions about his career. Initial decisions about hobbies, courses, and part-time jobs lead to decisions about initial full-time employment. As his career progresses a person must decide from time to time whether to change employers, change localities, accept a new offer, or change his working conditions. Finally, he must decide when and how to retire. Each person wants to make decisions which will lead him not only to economic security but to personal satisfaction.

When a person feels he cannot make a wise vocational decision by himself, he may seek help from a counselor. The client may have a fairly clear goal, but wonders how to get there. Or he may wonder which of two or more alternate occupations is best. Or he may have virtually no idea which occupations might prove appropriate for him. He frequently expects the counselor to give him specific advice—"You ought to become a draftsman." But no counselor knows enough or ever will know enough to give such specific advice. For a behavioral counselor, a major goal of vocational counseling is to help his client learn how to make vocational decisions wisely.

However, the client may not want to learn how to make vocational decisions wisely. Let us assume he wants direct advice on the most suitable occupation for him. Elsewhere Krumboltz (1965) has argued that client wishes provide the basis for evaluating counseling success. But client wishes must be for ends, not means. Suppose a patient asked his physician to give him a pill that would turn him into Superman. The physician would have to say something like this: "I don't have that power, but if you want to learn how to be stronger than you are now, I can help you learn." Similarly a counselor might say: "If I knew what decision you should make, I would tell you. But I don't know. I do know, though, what you will need to do in order to make a decision that you will feel is right for you. You can learn how to make decisions so that whenever you are faced again with a vocational planning problem, you will know how to proceed wisely. Would you like to learn?"

In vocational counseling, especially in educational settings, the counselor is not likely to be present when the individual's problem is finally resolved. The counselor's task is first to identify and explore the pertinent conditions: the individual's skills, interests, and especially his values and wishes. It will be important also to consider societal values, family pressures, and occupational trends. The second task is to assist the individual in learning about and participating in the decision making so that the client's own wise decision-making process provides a model he can use again in the future.

What Does the Behavioral Counselor Do?

The behavioral counselor initially must orient himself to his client's point of view before he can assist him toward a satisfactory decision. He needs information about his client. He needs to know what he wants. Specifically, he needs to know what the client views as critical variables in making the decision. He needs to know what the client has already done to find a solution to the problem.

The steps the behavioral counselor accomplishes with his client can be outlined as the following:

a. Defining the problem and the client's goals.
b. Agreeing mutually to achieve counseling goals.
c. Generating alternative problem solutions.
d. Collecting information about the alternatives.
e. Examining the consequences of the alternatives.
f. Revaluing goals, alternatives, and consequences.
g. Making the decision or tentatively selecting an alternative contingent upon new developments and new opportunities.
h. Generalizing the decision-making process to new problems.

This sequence of steps in behavioral counseling is not a recipe. Rather, the steps are important events in the counseling process. The sequence may vary, but the priorities remain.

Defining the Problem and the Client's Goals

Co: Before we put your plans down on paper, tell me a little more about what you know about electrical engineering. For instance, have you talked to an electrical engineer about his work?

Cl: Ah, yeah—the lieutenant I mentioned. He had a college degree in E.E.

Co: Did you talk to him about his training or what he did on the job?

Cl: Well, not really. We talked about equipment, but I couldn't really say what he did in the Army—he ran our outfit. I do know the kind of equipment these engineers deal with though.

Co: Just suppose you spent a semester or two in electrical engineering and found out that you didn't like it at all. It wasn't what you thought it was. What would you do then?

Cl: I just figured you might ask me something like that. Well . . . I thought about that before, and I can't say right off what else I'd do. I know it's not smart to put all your eggs in one basket, like they say, but I think engineering is just what I want. Hmmm. Well, what else do you think I could do?

Co: That I can't answer, but I can help you look into some other possibilities.

Cl: Yeah. OK, I'd like that. I've farmed a bit and been in the Army, but I don't really know what else I could do.

Co: Think about our discussion so far. You seem not to know too much about engineering or about other possible occupations. When we finish working together on this matter, what will you be doing then that you are not doing now?

Cl: That's hard. What will I be doing?

Co: Yes. What is it you will be doing then that you are not doing now?

Cl: Well, I'll have a job; I'll be working!

Co: Any job? How about farming?

Cl: No, not any job. I mean I'll be working at something I'll like. Of course, I'd like to earn enough to have a little fun now and then. I don't want to have to worry about food and necessities.

Co: What else?

Cl: Before that even, I guess I'll know what some jobs are that I'd like. And then, I'll know how to get 'em.

Co: Let's see. Right now, you seem to have two general goals to work for; one is to work eventually at a satisfying job, and the other is more immediate. That goal is to be able to find out about suitable occupations and how to prepare for them. Am I correct?

Cl: Yeah, two goals—one now, one later . . .

The counselor has begun a systematic and often lengthy process of defining the problem and the client's goals. The client's presenting problem is that he needs help in formulating an educational plan to collect his veterans' benefits. His decision to become an electrical engineer was based on little information or experience other than dissatisfaction with farming. He had no viable alternative to engineering. At this point in the process the counselor is probably more intent on preparing a plan than is the client, who might well be satisfied with any "magic words" that would produce his training money. The counselor, by probing, restating, and conjecturing, assists the client to clarify his situation and objectives.

How will the client's objectives appear when they are finally stated? Let us examine an excerpt from a later interview . . .

Co: All right, Jim. Just to be sure we are clear about what we are going to work on, why don't you repeat the important points we've covered.

Cl: OK. Let's see. For one thing I want to be able to fill out this form for the Veterans outfit, so that means I need a plan for my education and work. I want to be able to tell them at least three occupations I'd like and be suited for. Then I want to make a list of the approved schools to train me for the jobs. I'll write to the schools on the list and find out how long the training programs are, what courses I'll take, and how much it will cost. Then, for each occupation I have in mind I'm going to find answers to this list of questions . . .

The actions the client will perform are explicitly stated. The client will "write," "name," "list," "find answers," etc. The counselor and client have worked together to identify specific observable behaviors in which the client will engage. Because the desired actions are overt and observable, the counselor and client both can assess the progress of the counseling procedures and can decide when the goals have been reached.

Further, the goals were developed for the client as an individual with his full cooperation. Other clients with decision-making problems may have objectives more or less similar to Jim's. However, although the basic steps of wise decision making provide a common framework, the specific actions appropriate for each client may be quite different. Krumboltz (1966a) has described in more detail the criteria for the development of behavioral objectives in counseling. These critera are: (*a*) the goals of counseling should be capable of being stated differently for each individual client, (*b*) the goals of counseling for each client should be compatible with, though not necessarily identical to, the values of his counselor, and (*c*) the degree to which the goals of counseling are attained by each client should be observable.

The statement of the objective, "to name three suitable occupations," appears quite simple, but the means for attaining that objective are not included. Identifying suitable occupations is a complex procedure. Explicitly stating objectives can help to minimize the influence of the counselor's values and biases upon the client (Krumboltz, 1964).

Can the objectives be modified? Definitely, yes. Explicit objectives enhance communication, guide counseling procedures, and provide a basis for evaluation. But the counselor and client may later decide to alter their initial directions and may, therefore, change the original objectives.

Agreeing Mutually to Achieve Counseling Goals

As the counselor proceeds to discover the client's problems, he must also be preparing to make a decision of his own. As Krumboltz (1966a) remarks, the counselor must decide to what extent he is willing to help the client with his problem:

> Each counselor has some responsibility for evaluating the particular goals of his client. This is not to say that he would necessarily attempt to change the goals of his client, but he must make a judgment of whether or not he would be willing to help a client attain his particular goal [p. 154].

Three general issues enter the counselor's decision on whether to accept the client for counseling: his own interests, his competencies, and his ethical standards (Krumboltz, 1964). Counselors may wish to specialize just as many other professionals do. As the client's goals become defined, the counselor can determine to what extent they overlap his own areas of interest. When a counselor's special interests differ from the client's problem, the client's best interests are likely to be served by referring him to another counselor who has particular concerns about that problem area. A marriage counselor might not be interested in vocational counseling. A vocational counselor might not be interested in child behavior problems. The referral should be made just as soon as the counselor is sure he has no interest in the case, sometimes in the first minute, other times only after the goals have been explicitly stated.

Interested or not, however, a counselor may recognize that he does not have the background or skills to assist the client attain his particular objectives. In such an instance the counselor again should refer the client to someone more competent in that problem area.

Given that the counselor has interest and competence in the general area of the client's defined problem, he must further decide whether the client's objectives fall within his professional and personal ethical standards. Possible requests for unethical assistance depend essentially upon the counselor's point of view and, consequently, are hard to enumerate. Examples of unethical objectives for some counselors might include interference in the lives of others aside from the client or use of the counselor's position by the client as a means of evading a personal or social responsibility.

How does the counselor inform the client of his decision? Counselors' personal interviewing styles vary. Jim's counselor might say, "Well, Jim, as we have your ideas and wishes spelled out, I believe I can help you. I've worked with a large number of returning veterans much like you in some ways. I see no difficulty in helping you get what you want." Yet another counselor might have said, "Well, Jim, my background has been mostly working with study problems of college students. I could help you generally with learning to make decisions, but when it comes to specific content about jobs and training programs, there are several other counselors here who are better prepared. If you would like, we can show Dr. McMillen, next door, what we have worked out and see if he could assist you. . . ."

The counselor's commitment to work with the client toward the goals they have mutually defined is highly important. It reflects the behavioral counseling viewpoint that counseling is a planned professional event in which two or more individuals contract to solve a defined problem. It emphasizes the behavioral position that one technique or counseling method is insufficient for all problem solutions. Different clients presenting different problems require a variety of skills and techniques on the part of the counselor (Ullmann & Krasner, 1965; Krumboltz & Thoresen, 1969). Some counselors are likely to be more skilled or experienced at some methods than others. Because each client is different and is likely to seek different objectives, the counselor must be abundantly aware of his own interests, limitations, and values. Failure of the counselor to account for his own skills, beliefs, and competencies is likely to lead to disservice for many of his clients.

In effect, the term client has been misused to this point. The "client" does not become a client until the counselor agrees to accept him in that role. Lawyers, architects, and consultants of all kinds operate in the same way on this matter.

Generating Alternative Problem Solutions

Decision-making models range from complex mathematical statements to broad conceptual plans. Among the latter is an approach described and applied by several behavioral researchers, such as Gelatt (1962) and Yabroff (1969). The plan these and other writers have used emphasizes the following steps in the decision making: (*a*) defining the problem, (*b*) developing alternative problem solutions, (*c*) collecting relevant information on these alternatives, (*d*) examining the consequences of each of the alternatives in relation to desired outcomes, and (*e*) making the decision or selecting a tentative solution among the alternatives.

Producing a variety of alternative courses of action is sometimes difficult for a client who has typically acted on his first impulse. Generating alternatives can be facilitated by starting with a "brainstorming" approach in which no possibilities are excluded or even evaluated.

Co: Jim, what kinds of jobs have you thought about doing in the past?

Cl: Well . . . electrical engineering, as I said.

Co: What else? Have you ever imagined yourself doing other kinds of work? You know, little boys see themselves growing up to be astronauts or cowboys. Even though you are an adult now, there are still some times when you may have thought of yourself in a particular occupation which for some reason appeals to you. What kinds of occupations have you thought about in this way?

Cl: Oh, let's see, uh . . . well, a long time ago, before I went into the Army, I thought I'd like to get into the agriculture extension service. The Ag Extension Agent used to come around to our place—he always knew a lot and visited farms, but didn't really have to work on them. Really he worked with the farmers more than anything. I thought about that kind of work once.

Co: Good. That's the kind of thing we need to work with right now. In fact, while we talk why don't you write down on this paper the job titles that we mention. Now, what other types of work have you thought of for yourself?

Cl: With just a little bit of training I could be a TV repairman right now. You know, after my Army training and all.

Co: Fine, put that down on the list. What else?

Cl: Well, in the Army and on the farm too, I got real interested in the weather. I got pretty good reading the weather on the farm—just by clouds, wind, temperature, and all that. Then working with radar in the service I used to have a little fun now and then betting the meteorologist who was going to be right, me or him. But those fellows have a lot of schooling. I don't know. . . .

Co: Put that on the list, too. Right now it's important to consider each possibility carefully before throwing it out. Try to keep in mind that every career area has all kinds of occupations in it—different ones requiring different amounts or kinds of training. Think, for example, about a career in agriculture. You could be a farmer, an extension agent, a farm manager, a veterinarian, an equipment operator, and so on. Each one of those occupations takes different talents and training, but they are all related to the same field.

Cl: Yeah, I see that. OK, I'll put down weatherman. Well just the other day I was talking to my brother-in-law about . . .

Various aids can help promote the identification of possible options. Interest inventories may serve two purposes at this stage in the process. First, the client's mere responding to inventory items may stimulate discussion about various occupational alternatives. Second, scores from the inventory may indicate a pattern of interests in occupations that neither the client nor counselor would have considered. The age and experiential background of the client as well as published validity studies would influence the extent to which the test results would be viewed as valid indicators of such preferences. However, in the early stages of decision making the client needs some feasible alternatives worthy of further exploration.

Simulation is another aid in the decision-making process. For example, the *Job Experience Kits* (1970) provide short work samples from a variety of different occupations. A client or group of clients can actually experience what it feels like to solve representative occupational problems. Alternatives are too frequently considered or rejected on the basis of popular stereotypes, not actual knowledge or experience. The simulated experience of working on a job for even 50 minutes may give some young people a better idea of jobs they wish to explore more fully. Studies on the effects of the *Job Experience Kits* will be summarized later in this chapter.

How many alternatives should be defined? There is no evidence to suggest an optimal number or range. In most instances three to five can usually be identified as worthy of serious investigation. The counselor can bring to this activity his own perceptions based upon clues to likely possibilities from the client's comments. The counselor may detect references to "working with people" or "liking to see products made by one's own hands," and suggest still other possibilities to the client for his consideration. The counselor need not hesitate to suggest alternatives as long as he does not get personally invested in his own suggestions.

Suppose that the client presents alternatives that seem unrealistic in the counselor's opinion. It is common to have a student who is failing his academic courses still fully intent upon entering medical school, or to have an unskilled construction worker planning a career as a building contractor or architect. At this point should the counselor inject his own perception of reality into the situation? He should not for several reasons. (*a*) The counselor from a behavioral approach seeks to promote the client's thinking and talking about decision alternatives. Discouragement or negative comment at this point is likely to diminish future responses from the client (Krasner, 1965, pp. 214ff.). (*b*) The counselor's rejection of alternatives would override the client's suggestions and perceptions and would falsely imply that the counselor's values were superior. (*c*) The counselor's rejection of alternatives is based upon current information or impressions about the client. In the future, however, the client may acquire the skills necessary to achieve or approximate what previously seemed beyond his reach. (*d*) The counselor's rejection of alternatives at this point in the decision-making process implies that he has already made a decision about the client and, in so doing, has deprived him of the opportunity to learn about his own abilities and aspirations. Equally serious, the counselor has modeled poor decision making by jumping to conclusions before collecting supporting evidence for his decision. He thus fails to teach the client sound decision-making practices. If an alternative is truly "unrealistic," the client will be able to decide that for himself provided he has learned how to make decisions wisely.

Collecting Information about the Alternatives

Co: What does your list of possible occupations have on it now?

Cl: Mmm. I've put down here electrical engineer, farm extension agent, TV repairman, weatherman, farm equipment salesman, electronic equipment serviceman, and wildlife or forestry agent.

Co: As you look over the list can you think of any other possibilities?

Cl: No, not right off. It seemed to take quite a while just to get these few.

Co: You have seven occupations on the list; I'd say that you have done very well. Usually it's hard to think about different kinds of work you could or might like to do, especially when you have thought about only one occupation for yourself for so long. There are enough possibilities on the list to begin another task now. Keep in mind that you may always add other ideas as you go along. Chances are good that you will think of still other possibilities as you look further into the occupations you already have listed. All right, now which of these occupations are you going to choose?

Cl: Choose? Well, I don't think I can choose any one of them yet. I mean, I don't know much about most of them.

Co: You're right, of course, and that is the next task—collect some information about these possibilities in order to help you make a wise choice. Otherwise your decision may be hasty or premature.

Cl: Yeah, I know what you mean; I'm paying for one of those every month right now. When I got out of the Army I just couldn't wait to get a car. I bought the first one I saw mostly because of its looks and the ads—my dream car. Now I wish I had shopped around a little more.

Co: Are there decisions, though, that you think you have made well?

Cl: Umm . . . oh, sure. When I enlisted in the service I really looked around for the right outfit for me. I talked to all the enlistment officers and read their brochures. I talked to buddies of mine who were in the service. After about a month of talking to people and reading things, I got it down to either the Army or the Air Force. There was a better chance of my getting the specialty I wanted in the Army and still get out in time to begin a school term later, if I wanted to. So I took the Army. Things seemed to work out pretty much as I planned. Well, I'm here!

The most time-consuming part in decision making is the information-gathering stage. Although the plans for collecting information about the decision alternatives are developed in the counseling interview, the greater portion of activity will occur outside of the interview setting.

In the interview the counselor will find it useful to review with the client the way in which he has made decisions in the past. In this manner the counselor will be able to understand the client's decision-making style. The client need not, nor will he likely, use the counselor's terminology in relating his decision-making process, but the counselor should be attentive to evidences of wise decision making. In the dialogue above, the client volunteered information about how he chose the Army, a satisfactory decision for him. He also described how he bought a car, an unsatisfactory choice. The counselor could compare and contrast these two instances of decision making to emphasize the need for information and the means of obtaining information in order to make a sound decision.

Suppose the client cannot clearly describe how he makes decisions, or suppose that he describes a careless, haphazard method of arriving at choices which, often as not, leaves him with unsatisfactory outcomes. What may the counselor do to help his client differentiate the elements of wise decision making? How can he teach his client a more fruitful method of decision making? Behavioral counselors and researchers have studied several approaches to encourage information seeking for decision-making purposes: (*a*) modeling, (*b*) reinforcement, and (*c*) simulated work experiences.

Modeling refers to imitative learning. The learner acquires new behaviors by observing a model engage in those behaviors and experience the consequences (Bandura & Walters, 1963; Bandura, 1969). The observer may learn by directly witnessing the model's behaviors or by observing some representation of the model's behaviors, e.g., audio tapes or videotapes, drawings, or written descriptions.

The behavioral counselor might play an audio tape for the client. The tape would be of a counseling interview with a model client or group of clients who reflect many of the characteristics of the present client. In the illustration used here, a model client might be a veteran returning to school or seeking job placement. He could be describing sources of information which he might utilize in his search for desirable alternatives. Each appropriate action and each source of information he described would be positively reinforced by the model counselor who would be free to add other ideas.

Taped model client: I have a friend who works for AGR Data Processing; I could talk to him about his job. He's a computer programmer. He could probably even introduce me to his boss or some other people there.

Taped model counselor: Talking to people who work on the jobs you're interested in is one of the best ways to get information. What are some questions you might ask him?

Taped model client: Well, for sure I'd want to know how he got his job—what training he needed—and what pay and benefits he gets.

Taped model counselor: Those are important questions. What else?

In the actual interview following the playing of the tape, the counselor would ask the client what ideas he had. Some might have been suggested by the model tape, others might be quite original. Each useful suggestion would be positively reinforced, whatever its source.

Cl: When I hear that fellow on the tape talk about his friend, it reminded me that my wife's brother-in-law out on the West Coast just went through his apprenticeship training. I could find out firsthand what he thought of it.

Co: Good! You could write to him?

Cl: Yeah, I could write to him, and I bet I can talk to one of my old shop teachers who's now at the Tech Institute here.

Co: Fine. Who else can you think of to write to or to talk to?

Unfortunately, suitable models for different types of clients are not readily available. A counselor often must prepare his own tapes or find appropriate models for his clients. Some evidence suggests that a given high status model might be equally effective for a wide range of clients (Thoresen & Krumboltz, 1968). However, there is need for a library of models demonstrating a variety of problem-solving and social skills.

Use of the *Job Experience Kits* described earlier may also promote the client's occupational and career information seeking. Performing simulated tasks permits the client to learn firsthand some of the problems to be solved in a given occupation without actual job placement and commitment to employment. The client can experience typical occupational problems and decide whether or not he enjoyed the activities involved sufficiently to warrant further exploration of the field of work he is investigating. The counselor may provide his client with the kinds of kits that have relevance to the occupational alternatives they had previously listed. An illustrative kit and its possible uses are provided by Krumboltz and Sheppard (1969).

Co: One of the possible jobs you have on your list, Jim, is farm equipment salesman. What experience have you had with sales?

Cl: None selling. But I've been on the receiving end—that car salesman was really something. I think he knew I would have bought anything that would roll—his desk, skates, anything. I knew some guys in the Army who could do that, too. I don't really know all that salesmen have to do. I'm not sure at all if I'd like selling.

Co: Well, if you would like to see more clearly what salesmen do in their everyday work, here is a kit you may work with. It will take less than an hour to complete; just start on the first page and follow the instructions. I think you will find it very helpful in deciding whether or not you want to learn more about sales work.

Later:

Cl: Yeah, I can see myself being a salesman. I've got a better idea now about what most salesmen have to do to size up a customer. I could do that, especially if I believed in what I was selling. And that sort of fits in with my liking to show people how things work. That would be important with machinery and farm equipment.

Co: Are you saying that you might like more information about careers in sales?

Cl: Yes, I think so. At least now I know that I don't want to count out selling as a possibility.

The counselor provides opportunities for the client to choose among various exploration possibilities. "Which occupations do you want to look into?" "Which do you want to begin collecting information about first?" "What resources can you use to get useful information?" "What ways can you go about obtaining information—writing, talking, observing, reading?" "What did you gain from the models or the simulation that you can use?" The client is a free agent in determining the nature and extent of his exploration, but the counselor helps him see the possibilities.

Another type of model is a list containing useful sources of information and the kinds of questions to be asked. In the taped model interaction presented above, the counselor inquired about the questions the client would ask his friend. Most clients need assistance in deciding what information would help to make a decision. Vague general plans for seeking information lead to weakly executed inquiries. Magoon (1969) has provided a valuable systematic method for counselors to use in encouraging clients to ask pertinent questions. Magoon's method is called the Effective Problem Solving (EPS) process. It is a structured, self-directed learning program intended to teach the client a sequence of steps in problem solving. The client responds primarily in writing, moving through the program at his own rate and supplying his own problem content which is usually educational-vocational material. The counselor in this process acts largely as a consultant to the client and assists him in transition from step to step in the program.

What information should the client be encouraged to collect? He needs relevant information. Relevance must be considered in relation to several conditions.

1. *Goals.* The goals originally set broadly define the areas of appropriate information. One of the goals Jim established was a list of approved schools or training programs for veterans in order to be able to receive the assistance available to him. Gathering information about unapproved programs is unsuitable in relation to that particular goal. Another of his goals was eventually to find satisfying work. He would have to define what was "satisfying" for him. If a "satisfying" job was

primarily one that enabled Jim to earn $20,000 within, say, ten years, then relevant information for him would be pay or salary rates and income potential in various careers.

2. *Alternatives.* The alternative occupations discussed and listed earlier in the counseling interview define vocational information needs in more detail. For Jim, information about agricultural or electronic technology vocations is appropriate; information about social service vocations is irrelevant as his plan now stands. He may, however, change his plan as he explores further.
3. *Limitations.* The client's personal limitations or occupational requirements guide the search for pertinent information. Information about vocations which demand physical or intellectual skills unattainable by the client is inappropriate. The client may specify other conditions important to him. For example, a client who wishes consistent daytime work minimally influenced by seasonal changes would largely waste his time exploring building or transportation trades.
4. *Trends.* Social and occupational trends influence informational relevance. Jim must be apprised that certain farm-oriented occupations are diminishing, but that service occupations are expanding. Consequently, he must weigh his information about possible agricultural occupations in relation to the likelihood that they may be strongly influenced by continued shifts in agricultural economic conditions.
5. *Timing.* The sequence or priority of decisions to be made is important. Jim identified two general goals, ". . . one now, one later." First his educational objectives, then his work placement. Some data on both of these topics are necessary now for him, but certain priorities exist. The first need is for general information about careers in order to identify suitable options. The second need is for detailed information about training opportunities in line with desired career alternatives. Finally, Jim needs specific detailed information about work opportunities in his selected vocational area. Detailed work information collected at the outset is seldom useful and, if the educational preparation period is lengthy, such details are soon outdated.

Examining the Consequences of the Alternatives

Every act an individual performs has some consequences for him. These consequences may be positive, negative, or neutral in the individual's view. The degree to which the consequences satisfy the person greatly influences his subsequent actions. Many decisions have trivial consequences. If one decides not to carry an umbrella on an overcast day, one may get wet. Other decisions have serious and long-lasting consequences. Vocational decisions affect the activities and satisfactions of a lifetime. Decisions of such caliber require deliberation not only of the choices available but of the probable consequences attending each alternative. Objective empirical data can be useful to counselor and client in their study of outcome probabilities. Such data may be obtained from census reports, labor statistics, reports from universities on characteristics of their student bodies, and predictive studies. Expectancy data, when available to a counselor, are valuable in summarizing the outcome probability of each alternative. Expectancy tables (or experience tables, as some prefer to call them) display the probabilities of specific outcomes in relation to certain information about the client. They are based on the past performance of people with characteristics similar to his. For example, a college freshman wishes to know how well he will do in his studies. If the counselor knows the relationship between academic performance and certain characteristics in a previous class of freshmen, he may be able to make inferences which are useful to his client.

Cl: Do you think I'll be successful in engineering?

Co: Let's take these scores and the high school grades that you have obtained, compare them to last year's freshman class characteristics and see how you might expect to do here. We'll compare you to all of the freshmen last year. Using your total entrance test score and your high school rank, you can see that out of ten students like you last year, nine of them received a "C" average or higher.

Cl: Now you're telling me that last year, out of ten students like me, nine of them got a "C" average or better. Well, then that's pretty good, isn't it?

Co: That's quite good. Nine out of ten received at least a "C" average and four in ten a "B" average or higher. This is compared to the entire freshman class. That wasn't exactly your question, however. You wanted to know how well you would do in engineering.

Cl: That's right.

Co: The best predictor of how well you will do in engineering at this university is your entrance test math score. Of ten students with math scores like yours last year, three of them received "C" averages, one a "C+" average, and none a "B" average or higher.

Cl: Boy, four chances in ten? That's bad!

Co: Your math score is average and in relation to all freshmen your standing is average—certainly adequate. But the students you will be competing with in engineering generally have higher math abilities than the average university freshman. Consequently, your chances of receiving satisfactory grades in that major are lower.

Cl: What you're saying is that I definitely shouldn't go into engineering.

Co: No, what I have said is that students like you have less often been successful in engineering than those with higher math scores.

Cl: There were four out of the ten who made it last year. Well, I might be one of those four. Of course, I could be one of those six! So I kind of need to decide whether I want to take that kind of chance.

Co: That's right. And you may well decide to try a risky alternative. The expectancy tables can give us information also on other majors. Your chances of being successful are greater, for instance, here in agricultural engineering and in farm operations, although you may not want to major in them for other reasons.

Expectancy data neither prescribe for the client what decision he should make nor restrict his judgmental independence. They give only objective information based on past performances of individuals similar to the decision maker. It still remains for the individual to evaluate the probabilities for his success in relation to his abilities, resources, and values. Expectancy tables are useful not only for predicting likely areas of difficulty, but for identifying likely areas of success. They can assist in the generation of additional choice alternatives.

To aid the client to understand the vital importance of delving carefully into the consequences of decision alternatives, the behavioral counselor may apply decision-making games or group problem-solving techniques. Ryan (1968) has described a group counseling approach to learning wise decision making in which a model student is constructed to represent the average student in a given school setting. Students in the group discuss the model student, make decisions about important events in his future, and test the consequences of their choices against expectancies for students in their school. Boocock (1967), Varenhorst (1969), and Yabroff (1969) have provided realistic decision-making games or simulated life experiences which effectively teach the client how to generate decision alternatives, locate relevant informational resources, identify pertinent data, and test expectancies for various decision outcomes. The *Life Career Game* (1969) is designed to show students that the way they use their hours now affects their later satisfactions in life.

Revaluing Goals, Alternatives, and Consequences

The discussions and activities of the counseling process almost invariably lead to the uncovering of new alternatives which in turn require more information. At times the client may discover in the process values, qualities, and misconceptions about himself or the world which lead him to revise his original counseling goals.

Cl: You know, it came to me that all along I've been thinking about a four-year college program I'm not really sure I need. You know? Like if I went into electronic equipment service and repairs or sales, some of those occupations we discussed, I wouldn't need four years of college.

Co: That's true, Jim. You wouldn't need all of that training for those jobs. Is getting a college degree important to you?

Cl: When I think about it now, it isn't at all. It was never what I had in mind. I want a good job, and I don't really care if I have letters after my name. Maybe I should look into the two-year Tech Institute program. It's an approved program and we've already found out that I can get in.

Co: That's right, and if you later decided that you did want a degree, many of the non-laboratory courses would apply to university credit.

Cl: Yeah, that's an idea. Hmmm.

This revaluing process in counseling seldom occurs as a readily identifiable stage. Generally the client develops new or different ideas as he becomes increasingly involved in solving his problem. The behavioral counselor will be alert to these changes and will encourage the reconsideration of their previously defined task. The client has not yet committed himself to a course of action. It costs him less in time, energy, and money to alter his objectives and potential choices now than later. Revisions of goals and alternatives are treated in the same fashion as has been described in the preceding discussion.

Making the Decision or Tentatively Selecting an Alternative Contingent upon New Developments and New Opportunities

Co: In terms of the objectives we originally set, how do things stand now?

Cl: Well, it seems to me that I've gone about as far as I can without deciding just what I'm going to do. I mean laying out a plan of education and work depends on my picking out an occupation that I think I want.

Co: Can you begin to limit the number of occupations you have explored?

Cl: Yeah, I really think that electronics is what I want to get into. Tech Institute training would let me get into servicing or sales. Of course, if I found out that I had some ability I could even go on for a degree.

Co: There's some flexibility for a while if you choose electronics.

Cl: Yes, I'd have a chance to try out the training for awhile and still have some assistance coming, if I changed my mind. You know, the more I think about it, the more I'm sure that's what I want to do.

Co: Tentatively, then, you think you would like to go into electronics technology?

Cl: Yes, that's going to be my first choice.

Co: Now suppose after you enter the electronics technology training program, you find that it is not what you wanted after all . . .

The final decision resides with the client alone and will frequently occur in the absence of the counselor. Jim has developed only a tentative plan for education preparatory to placement. Once embarked upon his plan he will need to make further decisions on his own. He must be open to the possibility that his plans may not work out as he hopes. New opportunities may become available which will need to be compared with his present plan. The client should be encouraged to attend to the feedback from his post-decision experiences to assess the degree to which his choice satisfies his intentions.

Generalizing the Decision-making Process to New Problems

One basic purpose of counseling is that the client learn to make decisions wisely. It is not enough that he make one decision wisely or formulate one wise educational plan. In addition he should be able to describe the process so that in the future he will be more likely to use the same decision-making steps when faced with other important decisions.

Co: You'll be making many more decisions like this in the future, Jim.

Cl: I hope I'll be able to make the right ones.

Co: What have you learned from what we've done together that you might use in making future decisions?

Cl: Decision making is hard work.

Co: It is hard work, and some decisions may not be important enough to you to justify the effort.

Cl: But I'm glad I did the work for this one. I feel it's the best decision I could have made out of all the alternatives I considered.

Co: How would you describe the process you used?

Cl: What do you mean?

Co: Remember when you started work on making this decision. What was the first thing you did?

Cl: At first I didn't realize that I had some decisions to make. I was just putting some words down on paper to collect my veterans' benefits.

Co: So what did you do?

Cl: In talking with you I discovered I had a problem. I saw that first I had to decide on a sensible vocational goal and then consider the educational plans that might help me get there.

Co: Right. You told me exactly what your problem was. We call this "formulating the problem." In the future you could formulate the problem yourself, talk it over with a friend, or consult a counselor. Now that you see how it's done, maybe you won't need a counselor next time.

Cl: I'm not so sure. Let's see, the next thing was I had to think through what I really wanted in life . . .

The counselor is helping Jim learn to use the decision-making steps independently. Ideally counselors should be trying to work themselves out of a job by teaching everyone to make important decisions wisely. Individual counseling is probably not the most efficient way to accomplish the task. Counselors will need to cooperate in large-scale educational programs in addition to continuing individual and small-group counseling. Specialists will certainly be needed in the counseling profession—some to design preventive programs, others interested in group work, and still others preparing to counsel individuals one at a time. The task ahead is to do whatever is necessary to accomplish the goals of counseling as efficiently and effectively as possible.

How Does Behavioral Vocational Counseling Differ from Other Counseling?

The behavioral counselor makes a basic assumption about his client: he is a learner. The implications of this premise are far reaching in the counselor's operations. The behavioral counselor expressly and deliberately applies behavior change methods derived from experimental learning research. He actively uses the most effective educational approaches to bring about the changes desired by his client. The focus of counseling attention is upon the immediate problem with which the client is concerned and for which he has evidently acquired unsatisfactory or ineffective means of coping. In order to assist the client, the counselor must have the learning problem clearly defined and the client's objectives specified in performance terms. Such specification permits both the counselor and client to know when their work is finished and it further acts as an ethical safeguard for them both. For the counselor, it provides a logical basis for forming a judgment about the degree to which he can or may wish to aid the client; for the client, it provides a guideline for the extent to which he wishes to have his behavior influenced.

One nonbehavioral conceptualization of human functioning is what Ullmann and Krasner (1965; 1969) call the medical model. The determinants of observable behavior are assumed to be internal. An individual may act aggressively, for example, because within him is an imbalance of psychic energies, or because he inherently seeks power to compensate for a state of inferiority impressed upon him in his childhood. A variety of specific theories and points of view are incorporated in what we are here calling the medical model. They share in common the premise that the ultimate causes of behavior are internal to the person. The causes may be labeled as instincts, inherited or biological characteristics, needs, traits, or psychic forces. These factors, singly or in combination, are presumed to motivate the individual.

Another nonbehavioral conceptualization is the "understanding" or "insight-oriented" approach. The counselor subscribing to the understanding approach would try to detect the feelings underlying the client's words and communicate his perceptions to the client. The shared perceptions of feelings would facilitate the client's self-exploration and self-insight and would lead to continued client growth, whether the client's problem was vocational indecision or inadequate interpersonal relationships.

In the behavioral model the counselor focuses on the external environment of each client and the interaction of the person with his environment. The individual's behavior is seen as the result of his experiences. He acts in ways that maximize his rewards and minimize threats and punishment. External events, then, are assumed to promote and maintain a person's performances. Once a person acts, certain consequences occur. If these consequences are positive or satisfying to the person, he is likely to repeat such acts in the future. What is rewarding or satisfying for one individual is not necessarily rewarding for another. The counselor who operates according to the behavioral model seeks to bring about those specific changes in performance desired by the client by arranging environmental conditions which increase the opportunity for him to perform and subsequently receive satisfaction from his performance. Michael and Meyerson (1962) explain behavioral counseling:

> The consequences of this orientation should be made explicit: Inherited genetic and constitutional determiners are not under the control of, or subject to, direct experimentation by behavioral scientists. This means that the only channel open to counselors for influencing human behavior is through changes in the environment. Additionally, certain environmental manipulations, such as separating a person from his frontal lobes or administering drugs that have psychopharmacological effects, are not available to psychologists and educators. The phenomenon with which counselors deal, then, is behavior, and the independent variable which controls behavior must be the environment. A behavioral system attempts to specify, without reference to unobservable, hypothetical inner-determining agents, the conditions and the process by which the environment controls human behavior [p. 383].

Each orientation tends to generate different types of research questions for vocational counseling. One criterion for the usefulness of a theory for a vocational counselor is the degree to which research questions meet the "test of relevance" (Krumboltz, Baker, & Johnson, 1968). To what extent would the alternative possible outcomes of a research study influence a vocational counselor's practices?

The behavioral approach tends to generate practical questions, the answers to which might influence counseling practice. For example, how similar should a social model be to the client who is learning how to explore occupations from this model? The answer to this question will influence the types of models counselors will choose to provide to their clients. In contrast, a typical question stemming from a medical model might be the following: did the parents of social workers use child-rearing tactics different from those employed by the parents of engineers? The answer to this question is less likely to influence counseling practices. The vocational counselor cannot control his client's past upbringing, but can at most only help him identify a satisfying pattern of activity for the future.

The study and practice of vocational decision making have been traditionally located within the realm of counseling and guidance. The origins of the counseling movement are to be found in the field of vocational guidance (Walton, 1961; Stephens, 1970). Behavioral counseling draws upon this heritage as do other counseling approaches. Two of Krumboltz's (1966a) three major goals of counseling, improving decision making and preventing problems, have specific relevance to vocational counseling. Borow (1970) notes that the role of the counselor can be conceived as that of a development facilitator—an environmental arranger and social catalyst. This conceptualization Borow poses as an appealing and an emerging direction in career development.

Behavioral counseling requires much planning and deliberate action by the counselor. When possible, he works with his client in the environment in which the client experiences the problem: school, home or work settings (Bijou, 1966). For vocational and educational decision-making problems, the counselor may elect to work with his client in the setting which allows the greatest degree of control over his client's activities in the initial training stages or which has the greatest number of training resources available. Assessing the client's abilities and skills, observing his methods of choosing or problem solving, and engaging in a variety of counseling methods require planning, structure and incremental programing in order to move the client from a level of inadequate skill development to one he desires (Mehrabian, 1970).

The initial goal of the behavioral counselor is to assist the vocationally undecided client to achieve his stated objective of a suitable vocational choice; and, at the same time, to accomplish one of the major aims of counseling, helping the client to become a wise decision maker. A wise decision maker is one who maximizes his chances for making a successful choice by engaging in forethoughtful planning and problem solving. How the client makes a decision is the focal point of the counselor's efforts. What the client decides is his own concern based upon his personal values and goals.

What Evidence Supports the Behavioral Approach to Counseling?

Behavioral counselors and researchers have conducted studies among students of some of the methods that encourage information seeking for decision-making purposes. Studies using reinforcement, modeling, and simulated work experiences have yielded some important findings to support the behavioral approach to counseling.

Studies Using Reinforcement and Modeling

Methods of promoting client information seeking have been the most widely studied topic in preparing students to be wise decision makers. The first studies of this topic were experimental applications of modeling and model reinforcement techniques among secondary school subjects. The objective of these inquiries was to examine the comparative effectiveness of certain methods of increasing the variety and frequency of information-seeking activities among high school students engaged in educational and vocational planning. Early studies shared several important features: (*a*) the subjects were volunteers for counseling about their career or educational planning—none were "abnormal" institutionalized subjects or known to be unusual in any particular characteristic; (*b*) the behavioral outcomes (measures of information seeking) were defined in advance; (*c*) the effectiveness of the experimental treatments was assessed by behaviors or reports of behaviors occurring outside of the counseling setting, not during the counseling session itself; (*d*) the experimental designs involved multiple treatment variables so that it was possible to obtain data on potentially important interactions among treatment, subjects, counselor, and setting characteristics; (*e*) the experimental designs included random assignment of students to treatment groups and replications of treatments; and (*f*) various control treatments were introduced.

The first study to be conducted along these lines was that by Krumboltz and Schroeder (1965). A more elaborate replication with additional treatments and controls was reported by Krumboltz and Thoresen (1964). Both investigations used "reinforcement counseling" and "model reinforcement counseling" methods to promote information seeking. In reinforcement counseling the counselor gave positive verbal reinforcement for any statements by the client which showed his intent to use some source of information relevant to his decision-making goal. Model reinforcement counseling was a procedure in which the client listened to a tape-recorded model being positively reinforced for his reports of having used or intending to use various informational resources. The client subsequently was verbally rewarded for remarks imitative of the model and for innovative statements of his own concerning information seeking. Both experiments found model reinforcement and reinforcement counseling techniques to be superior to the control treatments in increasing information seeking outside the counseling setting. The control treatments included (*a*) no contact (in both studies) and (*b*) counseling interviews lacking any systematic reinforcement of information-seeking intentions (in the Krumboltz and Thoresen study).

Some interesting interactions were found. Krumboltz and Schroeder found that reinforcement counseling was more effective than the control treatment among female clients. Model reinforcement counseling was more effective than the control treatment among males. Similarly, Krumboltz and Thoresen found the model reinforcement treatment more effective than the reinforcement counseling treatment for males. Among females there was no significant difference. The differential effectiveness might well have been due to the fact that male models only were used for both male and female subjects. Krumboltz and Thoresen also found that the effectiveness of these counseling procedures was, on the average, about equal for groups and individual clients, but that some counselors in certain schools were better with groups while others were better with individuals.

Three important findings resulted from these initial studies: (*a*) model reinforcement and reinforcement counseling methods were shown to be effective techniques for the counselor to apply to individual clients or to groups; (*b*) the specific model appeared to influence males and females differently; and (*c*) information seeking outside the counseling setting was directly related to the number of reinforced statements of intent to find information by the client within the counseling session. This latter relationship was examined and substantiated in an additional study by Thoresen and Krumboltz (1967).

What variables influenced males and females differently in the modeling situations? Krumboltz, Varenhorst, and Thoresen (1967) reported that female subjects who observed female models performed more criterion information gathering than did control subjects who received only directions about how and where to get information or who received no attention whatsoever. These results essentially paralleled the results of previous work and showed that females, too, responded to models when they were appropriate. The model counselor's prestige and attentiveness to the model client were also experimentally manipulated but without significant effect. Thoresen, Krumboltz, and Varenhorst (1967) next examined the effect that the sex of model counselors, model clients, and actual counselors had upon male and female subjects. Male students responded best to a combination of male counselor and male model counselor working with a male model client. Female subjects responded best to male counselors in combination with model counselors and clients who were either both male or both female.

Drawing on work by Coleman (1961), Thoresen and Krumboltz (1968) described an experiment in which they varied qualities of the model client, again a secondary school student, along the dimensions of alleged athletic and academic skill. Three categories of athletic and academic accomplishment, high to low, were defined and exemplified in the model students. Similarly, subjects were also identified in these categories and qualities, and paired in all combinations with the various models. All subjects, counselors, and models were male. Athletic models introduced as highly skilled were the most effective in producing information seeking by the subjects. Variations in the academic success model yielded insignificant differences.

Thoresen, Hosford, and Krumboltz (1970) found approximately the same results. In one school, subjects exposed to models portraying high or medium athletic success engaged in more information seeking than subjects exposed to models of low athletic success. Subjects did not imitate the behavior of models similar to themselves any more than the behavior of dissimilar models. Some puzzling interactions appeared. Subjects low in self-concept but aspiring to high success responded more to low- or medium-success models than high, but the low self-concept, self-satisfied subjects responded more to the high- or medium-success models than to the low-success models. Unhypothesized interactions like this need to be confirmed before much weight can be given to them.

Studies Involving Simulation

The *Job Experience Kits* (1970) mentioned earlier were developed from another series of studies on means to promote career exploration and increase involvement in the decision-making process. By providing students with realistic problems faced daily by workers in various occupations, Krumboltz, Sheppard, Jones, Johnson, and Baker (1967) sought to promote educational and occupational exploratory activities. A sample *Job Experience Kit* on the work of the accountant may be seen in

Krumboltz and Sheppard (1969); one on police officer was described by Krumboltz and Bergland (1969); one on appliance serviceman, by Nelson and Krumboltz (1970).

The booklet and film-mediated simulations required active participation by the students in the solution of work-related problems. The simulation materials were entirely self-contained and resembled linear programed texts. Small amounts of explanatory information about some facet of a job were followed by problems in which the information was applied. The problems progressed from simple to complex. Students worked individually on the simulated tasks, recording their responses and continuously receiving feedback about their answers. The difficulty level of the materials, an important factor in the materials, virtually assured problem-solving success. Designed for students in high school, the kits were intended to be enjoyable experiences for the students.

The problem-solving treatments were compared to control treatments in which subjects received either general occupational information, specific information about the same occupations represented in the problem-solving materials, or identical problem-solving materials giving answers without requiring subjects to work the problems. Criterion measures were again the variety and frequency of post-treatment information gathering as well as changes in interest inventory scores and interest questionnaire responses. Although there were some variations in the five studies on vocational simulation, one general result, found also by Krumboltz, Baker, and Johnson (1968), was that the problem-solving materials consistently produced more declared interest and more overt occupational information seeking than did the control treatments. The responses were particularly favorable in those high schools which drew enrollments primarily from lower socioeconomic communities.

Other results from the simulation experiments included the following. (*a*) Students tended to explore not only the occupations for which they solved problems but in addition a greater number of different occupations than did students who experienced the control treatments. (*b*) Girls tended to out-perform boys in information seeking, especially in the lower socioeconomic schools. (*c*) Students in the problem-solving groups exhibited more knowledge of work expectations and estimates of job satisfaction than did control students. (*d*) Students who worked problem-solving kits made more requests to work on additional kits than did control subjects. (*e*) Varying the number of correct answers necessary to have the students' performance labeled "successful" had insignificant effect on the criterion measures. (*f*) Students given their choices of kits to work with were more active information seekers and expressed more positive attitudes toward those occupations than did students who did not receive their choices of materials. (*g*) Students given specific questions to use in their information quests achieved higher scores on occupational information tests than did students who received only general guidelines. (*h*) Students who were notified that they would be asked questions about the information they had gathered achieved higher scores on occupational information tests than did those who were not notified. This effect was especially marked among students who did not receive their choices of kits. (*i*) Added realism in the kits (use of an actual ammeter in the Electronic Technician Kit instead of a diagram) significantly increased several criterion responses (Hamilton & Krumboltz, 1969). (*j*) Eleventh graders tended to seek more information than ninth, tenth, or twelfth graders (Bergland & Krumboltz, 1969).

Simulation permits an individual to have a realistic problem-solving experience without having to endure serious risks or negative, sometimes irreversible, consequences. In the situations described above, each student could work at a variety of jobs vicariously without having to commit himself to employment. Future decisions to explore different occupational areas could then be based on these experiences, not on stereotypes and whims.

Simulation involving problem solving has been used in still other facets of vocational development. Boocock (1967) and Varenhorst (1967, 1969) described the use of a problem-solving program called the *Life Career Game* (1969). The game is designed for secondary school students who make decisions about how a person should spend time to gain "satisfaction." Field tests of the game show that it does arouse interest among the players in the consequences of daily decision making. It communicates the need for factual information as a basis for making sound decisions. Participants are exposed to the consequences of their decisions or the neglect of them. Because the game is designed to offer realistic vicarious experiences in decision making, it presses the student to define many of his values for personal development, income, security, and marriage. Social modeling, discrimination learning, selective reinforcement, and skill building are among the learning principles and procedures included in the game activities. The game is sufficiently new so that long-term effects upon the vocationally relevant behavior of students who have played it cannot yet be known. It trains the individual in a comprehensive decision-making plan, not just parts of it. The primary intent of the program is to provide adolescents with the opportunity to confront decisions of the type they ultimately must make anyway and to simulate the processes and consequences while there is still time to reconsider.

Group Methods

Walker (1969) and Prazak (1969) have reported group problem-solving techniques for resolving unemployment problems. *Pounce* is a method involving confrontation, role playing, and selective reinforcement to assist group members in the solution of their problems. Untreatable problem statements or reasons for unemployment are replaced with achievable behavioral statements of goals. For example, an untreatable problem in employment is age: "I can't get a job because I'm too old (or young)." A treatable problem might be phrased, "At my age, what can I do to make myself employable?" Once the problem is phrased in such terms, skills and talents can be developed to solve the problem.

Ryan (1968) and Stewart and Thoresen (1968) have reported group problem-solving methods which help participants understand the relationship between educational and vocational development, clarify goals, and acquire skill in identifying and utilizing relevant information for their decision-making needs. Cueing participants to appropriate responses and selectively reinforcing goal-relevant statements are important elements in this group method.

The group leader must carefully structure and oversee the group activity to ensure that each group member acquires the skills necessary to resolve his individual educational or vocational problem. Yabroff (1969) and Magoon (1969) each describe systematic group methods for learning decision making and developing skills for solving educational and vocational problems. Both approaches are self-directed learning programs which require the group leader only to introduce various stages of the plan, to monitor the students' progress, and to act as a readily available resource for the participants. Magoon's program assists the student to take detailed account of himself: his values, opinions, skills, and interests. As the student records information about himself and discusses the sequence of topics with the counselor and other group participants, he becomes increasingly aware of the decision-making process and his role in it. Yabroff's approach also requires the student to take stock of himself but in addition includes "experience tables" to help the student estimate his chances of success in various educational institutions. The data are compiled from records of previous students much like the group participants. A student can see the likelihood, for example, of his being accepted by various types of colleges, given his own grade-point average. Both methods help students learn that decision making and problem solving are, or can be, systematic, coherent processes. The intention of these programs is to teach the student how to choose, not what to choose.

Limitations of Research to Date

The evidence cited here on the behavioral approach to vocational counseling is intended to exemplify themes and areas of research. Hosford (1970) has summarized additional research in behavioral counseling. Other excellent summaries are available on operant behavior (Skinner, 1953, 1963), verbal conditioning (Krasner, 1958, 1965), and social learning and modeling (Bandura & Walters, 1963; Bandura, 1969). However, attempts to apply behavioral counseling have not met with universal success. (See, for example, Unick, 1970.)

Current research efforts on behavioral approaches to vocational issues have several limitations: (*a*) Most of the studies have been conducted among volunteer secondary school students. (*b*) Most of the studies have been performed in restricted geographic regions, usually in the immediate vicinity of a major university or college. The generalizability of research results to students and nonstudents of varying ages and in different environments or locations has not been tested. (*c*) No studies have been conducted to assess the long-term effects of the treatments.

These limitations should not discredit the studies. Counselors do most of their work with people who volunteer for counseling at the secondary school level. Moreover, much progress has been made in a few short years. The possibilities for employing different counseling methods for different purposes and different settings have grown. In light of current research directions, there is reason to believe that the array of available methods will continue to expand for a wider range of clients and types of problems. Continuing research is essential for the development of counseling.

What Influences the Vocational Choices People Make?

Central to the analysis of vocational choice and career development is the concept of interest. An interest of any kind, whether it be in work, hobbies, clothing, or members of the opposite sex, is an inferred construct. Like the concept of gravity, it explains certain events or behavior even though it cannot itself be observed directly. Interests are inferred when a person freely chooses an object or activity or approaches a situation in his environment. An individual must act overtly to enable an observer to infer that he "has an interest"; e.g., he must choose, approach, achieve a particular score on an interest inventory, or say "I like . . ." before the observer can ascribe an interest to him. That an individual's interests can be determined only by some overt action on his part is generally agreed to by advocates of both the behavioral and nonbehavioral positions in counseling. There agreement ends.

Roe, Super, Tiedeman, and others have contributed much to the theoretical literature of vocational development (e.g., Roe, 1956; Super, 1957, 1963; Tiedeman & O'Hara, 1963). Collections of writings by Borow (1964) and Zytowski (1968) demonstrate the breadth of viewpoints in the field. Hoppock (1957) cited eighteen noteworthy theories of vocational choice and development. Holland (1964) identified five major research programs concerned with vocational behavior and directed, respectively, by Donald Super at Teachers College, Columbia University, David Tiedeman at Harvard University, Anne Roe at Harvard University, John Holland at the American College Testing Program, and John Flanagan at the American Institutes for Research. More recently, Lofquist and Dawis (1969) have contributed important new work and theory in work adjustment. Gribbons and Lohnes (1969) have posed intriguing Markov chain analyses of career developmental data of adolescents and young adults.

What is important concerning virtually all of the viewpoints is that vocational interests are conceptualized as relatively fixed personality traits. An individual is assumed to choose particular types of work as a result of such fixed traits or of personality characteristics groomed over time in some way by familial or social influences. Evidence for these positions has been based on correlational analysis of data, at times augmented by descriptive survey information. Such research, even though extensive and longitudinal, e.g., Strong (1960), sheds little light on factors which cause interests to develop or change. Cause-effect relationships cannot be assessed on the basis of description and correlation. Little attention has been given to the possibility that specific experiences may cause vocational interests to change.

From the behavioral viewpoint, vocational interests and career development in general are the outgrowth of an individual's experiences. Why does an individual select one alternative over another? The behavioral counselor would answer that he experienced greater satisfaction (received more positive reinforcement) with the chosen alternative, or one similar to it, in the past. Thorndike (1935) proposed that interests were developed and modified by contiguity, suggestion, imitation, and conditioning through rewards and punishment. Interests, then, are assumed to be learned; they are acquired by experience. The more positive the consequences attendant upon a certain experience, the more likely the individual will be to seek it out again or place himself in such a position as to maximize the opportunity for re-experiencing the event. If interests are learned, then it should be possible to alter, shape, promote, or diminish them by means of experimental intervention.

Some evidence that interests are shaped by success experiences has been provided in a series of studies conducted by Krumboltz, Sheppard, Jones, Johnson, and Baker (1967) and Krumboltz, Baker, and Johnson (1968). The investigators wanted to determine the effect that successful experiences with certain occupational tasks had on evidences of interests in those occupations. They hypothesized that students who were given success experiences at certain occupational tasks would subsequently demonstrate more behaviors indicative of interest in occupations than would students not provided such experience.

A study using simulation materials on accounting was performed with 396 eleventh-grade students. Three treatment groups received, respectively, accounting simulation kits, specially prepared accounting information materials, and general career information materials. Criterion measures were inventoried interest changes in accounting, and frequency and variety of information seeking about accounting. Based on an interest survey constructed for the study, interest in accounting was significantly increased by the problem-solving (simulation) treatment but not by the other treatments. Both the accounting problem-solving treatment and accounting information treatment increased the number and variety of information-seeking activities about accounting, as well as other occupations. The investigators had apparently stacked the deck against themselves by making the control materials appealing and personally involving. Nevertheless, the problem-solving treatment had positively influenced expressed interest in accounting more than the control treatments.

Simulation kits were developed for three additional occupations: sales, medical laboratory technology, and medical X-ray technology. In one study involving 561 tenth-grade students, three treatments were applied: (*a*) problem-solving kits (booklets) for the three occupations, (*b*) non-problem-solving kits (booklets identical to the problem-solving booklets except that the problem solutions were given), and (*c*) information about the three occupations drawn from the *Occupational Outlook Handbook*. The problem-solving treatment produced more self-reported interest in the occupations and more information gathering about these occupations than did either of the other treatments. The problem-solving students displayed more knowledge of what would be expected of them on a job and requested the use of more additional kits than did students receiving the other treatments. Reactions to the simulation materials were more positive among students from lower socioeconomic communities than from middle socioeconomic communities.

A second study with 288 ninth- and eleventh-grade boys supported the efficacy of occupational simulation in generating evidences of specific occupational interests. The largest number of information requests about each occupation came from subjects exposed to the corresponding occupational simulation kit.

In a film-mediated simulation study (Jones & Krumboltz, 1970), seven treatments were designated as experimental. Two of the treatments were films which presented problems about banking occupations. In one, subjects actively responded in writing to the questions or problems posed to them; in the other, the subjects simply thought about their answers. The third experimental treatment consisted of a film identical to the other except that the problems were solved for the subjects. The four control treatments consisted of a banking career film lacking problem solving or observer participation, a film on science education also lacking audience participation, printed banking career information booklets, and general career information booklets. Subjects who viewed the experimental films demonstrated more interest, expressed and inventoried, in banking occupations than did the control subjects. Subjects experiencing the problem-solving films expressed higher interest in banking than did the subjects in the non-problem-solving treatment; active respondents also tended to engage in more information seeking than did passive respondents who "thought about" answers to the filmed problem settings. Students from the less economically privileged areas showed more evidences of interest in banking as a result of the experimental treatments than did students of middle socioeconomic backgrounds. Females also tended to outperform males on the criterion measures, a condition noted in the booklet-mediated study as well.

The research described here has limitations as discussed earlier. At the same time, it is important to emphasize that the results obtained were based upon treatments which lasted less than one hour late in the busy spring school term, and criterion data collection occurred a week to a month following treatment applications. Consistent results under these circumstances suggest that successful experiences do cause changes in activities considered to be manifestations of occupational interests. Thus, evidence appears to be building to support a learning basis for occupational interests.

Special Problems in Vocational Counseling: Behavioral Approaches

There are some specific problems related to vocational counseling. (*a*) Occupational titles often convey little meaning to the uninitiated. (*b*) Work experience relevant to vocational aspirations is often unavailable to adolescents. (*c*) The vast amounts of occupational information available to counselors and clients are not being utilized efficiently. (*d*) The time available to counselors and clients for decision making puts limits on the counseling process.

Labels seldom denote the vital qualities or characteristics of things and events. Occupational titles are not exceptions. Car enthusiasts talk at length about the objects of their zeal in words which are foreign to the uninitiated. Their terms often are trade names, abbreviations, and acronyms and may stand for performance characteristics or other functional qualities. To the casual listener, however, the words are meaningless. Similarly, job titles which have meaning and utility for job analysis and other occupational specialists may prove befuddling to the inexperienced adolescent. Some titles, like astronaut and special investigator, convey excitement and adventure which mask vast amounts of routine activity. Other titles are out-of-date, like teamster which no longer refers to mule drovers. Still others, like steamfitter, convey no immediate image of plausible activity.

Job titles have indexing value and have meaning once the operations of the jobs are understood. Of the hundreds of students who worked with the job experience kit on medical X-ray technician, only a very few knew in advance what the job of an X-ray technician entailed. When asked, "Would you like to be a medical X-ray technician?" on a survey form, audible responses ranged from indifference, "Beats me!" and "How should I know?" to acceptance, "Yes, I've always wanted to be a doctor," and rejection, "Ugh, I can't stand blood." Classroom observers of the simulation sessions noted that pre-simulation acceptance and rejection of the medically oriented kits were based on misconceptions of the work content conveyed by the words "medical" and "technician." Upon finding that X-ray technicians are much like photographers in their day-to-day work activity, students expressed different reactions to the job.

Counselors need to be able to provide students with a realistic view of job functions and the varieties of problems workers at diverse jobs must solve. Titles tend to obscure commonalities among jobs and level off critical differences among them. Observing workers in action may help youngsters evaluate certain occupations. Simulation of occupational experiences may be a more feasible method of conveying meaning to many other job titles.

Although *work experience* is considered to be valuable both by educators and parents (Wrenn, 1962), schools provide systematic work experiences for only a minority of their pupils. Adolescent work experience relevant to vocational aspirations and abilities is often denied by law or lack of opportunity. Yet, pertinent experience is essential for sound decision making. Because the social structure tends to minimize avenues for direct work experience, simulated work experiences acquire an important function.

The flood of *occupational information* grows; its crest is not in sight. The amount of information available to counselors exceeds their capacity for collection and retention. Retrieval of information and maintenance of current files are two pressing problems for the vocational counselor. Computerized retrieval systems are developing and may eventually provide the optimum solution (see Super, Chapter 8).

In the vocational simulation studies by Krumboltz, Sheppard, Jones, Johnson, and Baker (1967) and Krumboltz, Baker, and Johnson (1968), one criterion measure, use of the occupational library, consistently produced the same results. So few students used the library stores of occupational information that statistical analyses could not be applied. However, students did seek information outside of the library in significant amounts. Perhaps the students did not know how to use the library, did not know what to look for among the occupational titles, or found the information to be irrelevant to their needs. Whatever the reasons, these vast collections of information were used only sparingly.

Printed media are difficult to use. Some suggestions for counselors: (*a*) Discover the client's interests and inclinations before referring him to more detailed occupational information. If it has not been first established that the client has the ability to perform factory work and that it appeals to him, furnishing him with a paper pulp industry brochure containing details about mill work is likely to be a waste of time. (*b*) Give the client specific guidelines for locating and using informational resources. Show him the occupational information file and review with him the alternatives to be explored. Where feasible, use taped models who have information needs similar to his. Help him develop specific questions preferably in written form, for which he seeks answers. (*c*) Let him seek out his own information. The counselor can have some general resources available, but the studies in information seeking indicate that the clients can and do generate many informational resources once their alternatives are clear and they know what questions they want answered.

Coleman (1969) noted that colleges have access to much more critical decision-making information about applicants than applicants have about the prospective colleges. A comparable condition exists for the client who has narrowed his job choices to certain companies or agencies and is ready to make applications. The companies can exact from the applicant the kinds of information they need to arrive at a hiring decision. The applicant, on the other hand, seldom has information about the people he will work with, the morale of the organization, or layoff and hiring practices.

Time available for decision making is always limited. The amount of time available to the counselor and client before a decision is to be concluded puts limits on their mutual tasks. How many alternatives can be generated? How much information can be collected? What informational resources may be available?

Decision making is a painful process for many clients. A client may well wish to limit the time he invests in decision making even though additional time is available. The counselor should respect the client's decision to limit problem-solving time and help him to learn wise decision making as well as possible within the allotted time.

REFERENCES

Bandura, A. *Principles of Behavior Modification.* New York: Holt, Rinehart and Winston, 1969.

Bandura, A., & Walters, R. H. *Social learning and personality development.* New York: Holt, Rinehart and Winston, 1963.

Bergland, B. W., & Krumboltz, J. D. An optimal grade level for career exploration. *Vocational Guidance Quarterly*, 1969, **18,** 29–33.

Bijou, S. W. Implications of behavioral science for education and counseling. In J. D. Krumboltz (Ed.), *Revolution in counseling.* Boston: Houghton Mifflin, 1966.

Boocock, S. S. The life career game. *Personnel and Guidance Journal*, 1967, **46,** 328–334.

Borow, H. *Man in a world at work.* Boston: Houghton Mifflin, 1964.

Borow, H. Career development: A future for counseling. In W. H. Van Hoose and J. J. Pietrofesa (Eds.), *Counseling and guidance in the twentieth century: Reflections and reformulations.* Boston: Houghton Mifflin, 1970.

Coleman, J. S. *The adolescent society.* New York: The Free Press of Glencoe, 1961.

Coleman, J. S. Proposals to the commission on tests: The symmetry principle in college choice. *College Board Review*, Fall, 1969, **73,** 5–10.

Gelatt, H. B. Decision making: A conceptual frame of reference for counseling. *Journal of Counseling Psychology*, 1962, **9,** 240–245.

Gribbons, W. D., & Lohnes, P. R. Career development from age 13 to age 25. Final Report, Office of Education Grant 1-7-062151-0471. Weston, Mass.: Regis College, 1969.

Hamilton, J. A., & Krumboltz, J. D. Simulated work experience: How realistic should it be? *Personnel and Guidance Journal*, 1969, **48,** 39–44.

Holland, J. L. Major programs of research on vocational behavior. In H. Borow (Ed.), *Man in a world at work.* Boston: Houghton Mifflin, 1964.

Hoppock, R. *Occupational information.* New York: McGraw-Hill, 1957.

Hosford, R. E. Behavioral counseling—A contemporary overview. *The Counseling Psychologist*, 1970, **1**(4), 1–33.

Job Experience Kits, Chicago: Science Research Associates, 1970.

Jones, G. B., & Krumboltz, J. D. Stimulating vocational exploration through film-mediated problems. *Journal of Counseling Psychology*, 1970, **17,** 107–114.

Krasner, L. Studies of the conditioning of verbal behavior. *Psychological Bulletin,* 1958, **55,** 148–170.

Krasner, L. Verbal conditioning and psychotherapy. In L. Krasner & L. P. Ullmann (Eds.), *Research in Behavior Modification.* New York: Holt, Rinehart and Winston, 1965.

Krumboltz, J. D. Parable of the good counselor. *Personnel and Guidance Journal,* 1964, **43,** 118–124.

Krumboltz, J. D. Behavioral counseling: Rationale and research. *Personnel and Guidance Journal,* 1965, **44,** 383–387.

Krumboltz, J. D. Behavioral goals for counseling. *Journal of Counseling Psychology,* 1966, **13,** 153–159. (a)

Krumboltz, J. D., Baker, R. D., & Johnson, R. G. Vocational problem-solving experiences for stimulating career exploration and interest: Phase II. Final Report, Office of Education Grant 4-7-070111-2890. School of Education, Stanford University, 1968.

Krumboltz, J. D., & Bergland, B. W. Experiencing work almost like it is. *Educational Technology*, 1969, **9** (3), 47–49.

Krumboltz, J. D., & Schroeder, W. W. Promoting career exploration through reinforcement. *Personnel and Guidance Journal,* 1965, **44,** 19–26.

Krumboltz, J. D., & Sheppard, L. E. Vocational problem-solving experiences. In J. D. Krumboltz & C. E. Thoresen (Eds.), *Behavioral counseling: Cases and techniques.* New York: Holt, Rinehart and Winston, 1969.

Krumboltz, J. D., Sheppard, L. E., Jones, G. B., Johnson, R. G., & Baker, R. D. Vocational problem-solving experiences for stimulating career exploration and interest. Final Report, Office of Education Grant 5-8-5059. School of Education, Stanford University, 1967.

Krumboltz, J. D., & Thoresen, C. E. The effect of behavioral counseling in group and individual settings on information seeking behavior. *Journal of Counseling Psychology,* 1964, **11,** 324–333.

Krumboltz, J. D., & Thoresen, C. E. *Behavioral counseling: Cases and techniques.* New York: Holt, Rinehart and Winston, 1969.

Krumboltz, J. D., Varenhorst, B., & Thoresen, C. E. Non-verbal factors in effectiveness of models in counseling. *Journal of Counseling Psychology,* 1967, **14,** 412–418.

Life Career Game. Palo Alto, California: Instructional Materials Center, Palo Alto Unified School District, 1969.

Lofquist, L. H., & Dawis, R. V. *Adjustment to work.* New York: Appleton-Century-Crofts, 1969.

Magoon, T. M. Developing skills for solving educational and vocational problems. In J. D. Krumboltz & C. E. Thoresen (Eds.), *Behavioral counseling: Cases and techniques.* New York: Holt, Rinehart and Winston, 1969.

Mehrabian, A. *Tactics of social influence.* Englewood Cliffs, N.J.: Prentice-Hall, 1970.

Michael, J., & Meyerson, L. A behavioral approach to counseling. *Harvard Educational Review*, 1962, **32,** 382–402.

Nelson, D. E., & Krumboltz, J. D. Encouraging career exploration through "simulated work" and "vocational detective" experiences. *Journal of Employment Counseling*, 1970, **7,** 58–65.

Prazak, J. A. Learning job-seeking interview skills. In J. D. Krumboltz & C. E. Thoresen (Eds.), *Behavioral counseling: Cases and techniques.* New York: Holt, Rinehart and Winston, 1969.

Roe, A. *The psychology of occupations.* New York: John Wiley, 1956.

Ryan, T. A. Effect of an integrated instructional counseling program to improve vocational decision making of community college youth. Cooperative Research Project HRD 413-655-0154, Corvallis: Oregon State University, 1968.

Skinner, B. F. *Science and human behavior.* New York: Macmillan, 1953.

Skinner, B. F. Operant behavior. *American Psychologist,* 1963, **18,** 503–515.

Stephens, W. R. *Social reform and the origins of vocational guidance.* Washington, D.C.: National Vocational Guidance Association, 1970.

Stewart, N. R., & Thoresen, C. E. Behavioral group counseling for career development. Symposium presented at the Annual Meeting of the American Personnel and Guidance Association, Detroit, 1968.

Strong, E. K., Jr. An 18-year longitudinal report on interests. In W. L. Layton (Ed.), *The strong vocational interest blank: Research and uses.* Minneapolis: University of Minnesota Press, 1960.

Super, D. E. *The psychology of careers.* New York: Harper, 1957.

Super, D. E., Starishevsky, R., Matlin, N., & Jordaan, J. P. *Career development: Self-concept theory.* Princeton, N. J.: College Entrance Examination Board, 1963.

Thoresen, C. E., Hosford, R. E., & Krumboltz, J. D. Determining effective models for counseling clients of varying competencies. *Journal of Counseling Psychology,* 1970, **17,** 369–375.

Thoresen, C. E., & Krumboltz, J. D. Relationship of counselor reinforcement of selected responses to external behavior. *Journal of Counseling Psychology,* 1967, **14,** 140–144.

Thoresen, C. E., & Krumboltz, J. D. Similarity of social models and clients in behavioral counseling. *Journal of Counseling Psychology,* 1968, **15,** 393–401.

Thoresen, C. E., Krumboltz, J. D., & Varenhorst, B. Sex of counselors and models: Effect on client career exploration. *Journal of Counseling Psychology,* 1967, **14,** 503–508.

Thorndike, E. L. *Adult interests.* New York: Macmillan, 1935.

Tiedeman, D. V., & O'Hara, R. P. *Career development: Choice and adjustment.* New York: College Entrance Examination Board, 1963.

Ullmann, L. P., & Krasner, L. *Case studies in behavior modification.* New York: Holt, Rinehart and Winston, 1965.

Ullmann, L. P., & Krasner, L. *A psychological approach to abnormal behavior.* Englewood Cliffs, N. J.: Prentice-Hall, 1969.

Unick, S. P. Reducing sexual desire. *Personnel and Guidance Journal,* 1970, **48,** 851–852.

Varenhorst, B. Information regarding the use of the life career game in the Palo Alto Unified School District guidance program. Unpublished manuscript. Palo Alto, California: Palo Alto Unified High School District, 1967.

Varenhorst, B. Learning the consequences of life's decisions. In J. D. Krumboltz & C. E. Thoresen (Eds.), *Behavioral counseling: Cases and techniques.* New York: Holt, Rinehart and Winston, 1969.

Walker, R. A. "Pounce": Learning responsibility for one's own employment problems. In J. D. Krumboltz & C. E. Thoresen (Eds.), *Behavioral counseling: Cases and techniques.* New York: Holt, Rinehart and Winston, 1969.

Walton, L. E. The scope and function of vocational guidance. In H. B. McDaniel, J. E. Lallas, J. A. Saum, & J. L. Gilmore (Eds.), *Readings in guidance.* New York: Holt, Rinehart, and Winston, 1961.

Wrenn, C. G. *The counselor in a changing world.* Washington, D.C.: American Personnel and Guidance Association, 1962.

Yabroff, W. Learning decision making. In J. D. Krumboltz & C. E. Thoresen (Eds.), *Behavioral counseling: Cases and techniques.* New York: Holt, Rinehart and Winston, 1969.

Zytowski, D. G. *Vocational behavior: Readings in theory and research.* New York: Holt, Rinehart and Winston, 1968.

8

computers in support of vocational development and counseling

DONALD E. SUPER
Teachers College, Columbia University

The late 1950s witnessed the beginnings of widespread interest in computer-assisted instruction. A few years later, John Cogswell and others undertook to investigate the technical possibilities of computerized vocational guidance, and he, John Loughary, and others generated experimental computer models to simulate the function of the counselor in automated vocational counseling systems. In this chapter, Donald Super presents a balance sheet on the state of the technology—major types of application to manpower decisions and career guidance, current systems which exemplify these applications, the strengths and limitations of such systems, and an analysis of problems to be circumvented in bringing operational computer-supported guidance to reality.

Computers can be used for *(a)* educational and manpower planning, *(b)* broadening the range of client exposure to data which are relevant to counseling, *(c)* simulating counselor functions, and *(d)* training staff members in counseling, personnel management, and administration. Because computers can potentially handle several information media simultaneously, such as hard-copy print material, screen-projected messages, graphic and pictorial material (slides and filmstrips), and sound stimuli, they can be used to deal with the information needs of counselees who are indifferent readers or poorly motivated or to whom certain types of relevant data are not readily accessible in conventional guidance. Adaptability and versatility are special computer virtues.

Much current attention centers on the promise of the computer to take over and augment certain of the services commonly provided in face-to-face counseling, and it is this subject that Super treats in some detail. The computer can be programmed to supply answers to a broad range of questions about personal attributes and opportunities to which typical counselees are likely to seek answers. Beyond that, it can be programmed to ask its own questions relevant to life planning, it can store and analyze the client's responses, and it can summarize and interpret the responses for him. In this interactive process, a sophisticated computer-assisted counseling system can direct the client's attention to disparities between his self-estimates of abilities and interests and the objective record of these traits, and it may suggest strategies for resolution.

The process by which the computer analyzes and interprets counselee responses is called monitoring. Client information may be gathered and treated by the batch-processing method (indirect inquiry) or by the individual's use of a computer terminal (direct inquiry). Super cites examples of both types. He reminds us that computerized vocational guidance systems are merely simulators and counseling aids; they do not replace counselors. In the handling and dissemination of information, they are probably superior to the personal counselor. But the humaneness of automated counseling, he contends, ultimately depends on a program which is directed to say, when it is wise to do so, "You may want to discuss this with your counselor or with some other informed and understanding adult."

What are the roadblocks to progress in the adoption of computer-assisted career guidance? Perhaps surprisingly, Super does not cite equipment purchase and maintenance costs as major obstacles. Resistances are of a more personal nature and relate to counselors' perceptions of threat in the machine's allegedly superior accuracy, in its potential for wresting from him part of his control over his own work, and in its reliance upon assumptions of determinism in dealing with human behavior. Super addresses each of these fears and suggests how at least some of them have been dealt with where computer-based systems have been successfully installed. He turns finally to the insistent problem of evaluation and specifies a variety of performance criteria, many drawn from the theoretical literature on career development and vocational maturity, on which the use of such systems must be justified. Will computer-supported vocational counseling vindicate itself? Super supplies a ringing affirmative response. Its many strengths, he feels, make a compelling case for its incorporation into counselor training programs and into standard guidance practice. One readily senses that the author believes these changes will occur sooner than many anticipate.

H. B.

It has often been pointed out that careers unfold in a series of decisions. Life is clearly one decision after another. Careers are too. Understanding decision making is therefore essential to understanding career development and to the practice of vocational guidance and counseling. This principle has been recognized in career development studies (Super & Overstreet, 1960), in the application of decision theory to vocational development and counseling (Gelatt, 1962), and in exploration and development work with computer systems for guidance (Super et al., 1970).

Developments in the application of decision theory and of computer systems to vocational guidance have all taken place since 1960. The years 1969 to 1971 witnessed installation of computer-assisted guidance systems in schools for regular student use; the decade of the 1970s will see them operating not merely experimentally, but routinely, in the service of high school and junior college students, as aids to counselors, and as important components in school and college guidance systems.

It will be helpful to begin the examination of this important new technology with a brief discussion of decision making, next to deal with the principal types and current examples of computer-assisted guidance systems, then to review the advantages and disadvantages of using such systems, and finally to consider problems which are encountered in the use of computer support in guidance and some of the ways in which these problems may be minimized.

Decision Making

Decision making is essentially problem solving. The steps taken in making a personal decision therefore resemble the steps which philosophers and psychologists have identified in thinking and in problem solving. In the guidance applications five major steps emerge: (*a*) anticipation, (*b*) crystallization, (*c*) clarification, (*d*) specification, and (*e*) implementation.

The term *anticipation,* used in one well-known paradigm of vocational decision making (Tiedeman & O'Hara, 1963), connotes several processes which are not identical with those represented here. But some steps in the Tiedeman-O'Hara model are listed above on the bases of empirical analyses of vocational maturity, e.g., readiness for vocational decision making and planning (Super & Overstreet, 1960; Gribbons & Lohnes, 1968). Not only is it axiomatic that one must be aware of the need to make a decision before one consciously makes it, but career interviews, carefully analyzed, scored, and factor analyzed, support the existence of such a behavior tendency. This is true also of attitudes such as the acceptance of responsibility for choice and planning, awareness of factors which should be considered in making decisions, and knowledge of sources of information and of resources which may be helpful. In several studies this anticipating attitude emerged as *planfulness* or a planning orientation toward life.

The *crystallization* of a vocational preference results from the process of exploration, a term which has often been used (Super, 1957; Jordaan, 1963) to connote the major constellation of behaviors in adolescence. These are the attitudes and behaviors underlying the seeking of information about the roles one might enact and the trying out of activities in which key adult and peer figures engage and which symbolize their roles. Taking part in activities, reading, watching motion pictures, and working during vacations or after school are exploratory behaviors which often have vocational implications and help to crystallize vocational preferences and aversions.

The *clarification* process takes place as the result of thinking and talking about information which has been acquired. The consequences of decisions become clearer, and the relative desirability of each consequence is better seen. Decisions are thus confirmed or contraindicated, a condition which leads one to proceed with confidence or to begin the cycle of decision making over again.

The *specification* of a choice is the result of confirmatory experiences. Information is synthesized in a process leading to a definite but not always definitive choice. The Project Talent *Career Development Tree* (Cooley & Lohnes, 1968) shows how plans and decisions change during the high school and college years. Inspection of Figure 1 discloses that 249 high school seniors planned to be scientists, only 137 were in that same category one year later, and only 117 were pursuing scientific careers one year after college graduation. But specification is definite and can serve as a basis for action whether it is a preference leading to little action or an implemented choice which can be easily changed because acting on it has involved little commitment.

The *implementation* of a decision turns a preference into a choice; it is the action that counts. Some implementing acts are tentative and far from definitive, as for example, when a high school student chooses the college preparatory course. Others involve a greater commitment of oneself, as when a high school graduate enters engineering school or an economics major begins graduate study in anthropology.

Computer Systems for Counseling

There are various ways in which present approaches to the use of computers as aids to counseling can be classified. The system used here is a synthesis of Myers' (1970) and Miller's (1970) general classifications, the Harris (in press) Commission's more refined categorization, and some distinctions which exposure to the forenamed methods has suggested may be useful.

Four major categories of computer assistance to vocational guidance are identifiable, serving four different functions:

a. Educational and Manpower Development and Planning;
b. Extension of Counseling by Client Access to Data;
c. Simulation, Supplementation, or Supplanting of Counselors by Programming Counselor Functions with Data Access;
d. Staff Training and Development.

Inherent in each of these types of computer assistance are the peculiar computer capabilities of data storage and retrieval (a computer is a library with a card catalog and index), data proc-

Figure 1
Project TALENT
Career Development Tree

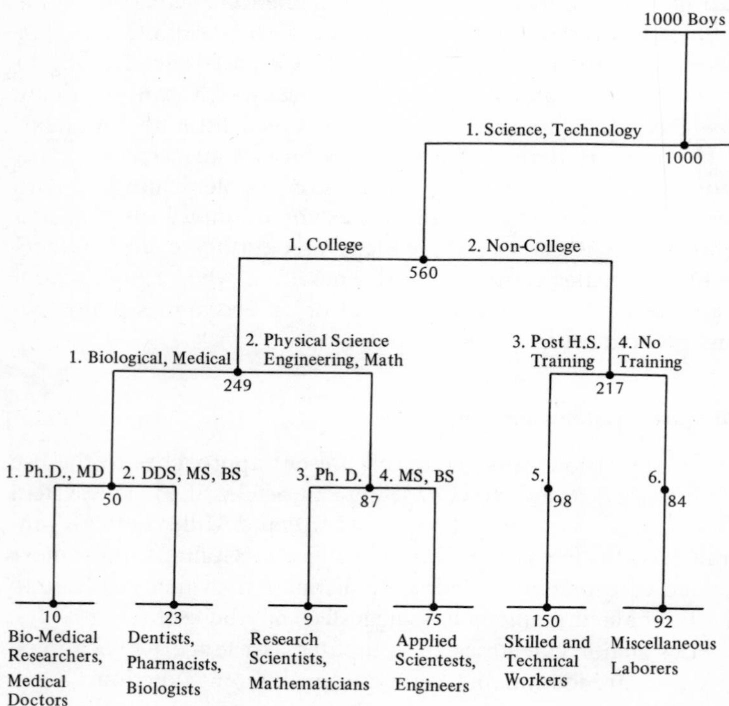

This diagram has been reproduced with the permission of William W. Cooley (Cooley and Lohnes, 1968, p. 4-57).

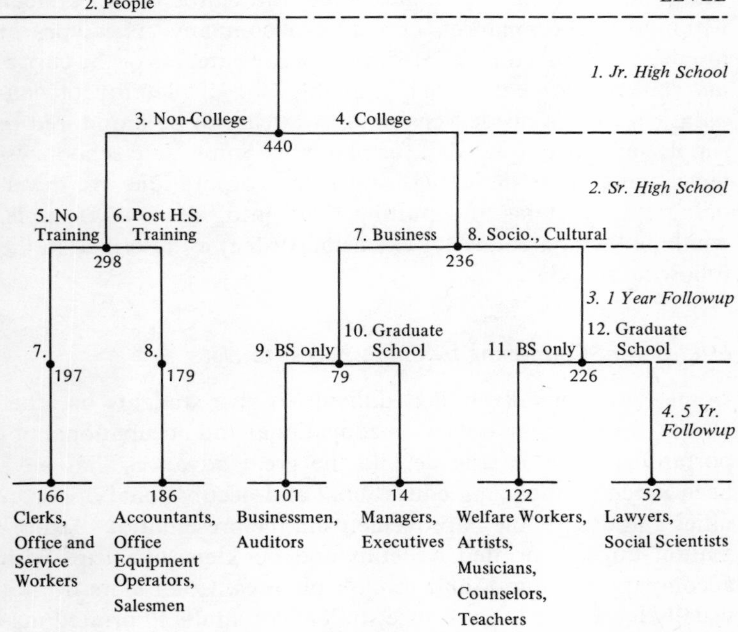

LEVEL
2. People
1. Jr. High School
3. Non-College
4. College
440
2. Sr. High School
5. No Training
6. Post H.S. Training
7. Business
8. Socio., Cultural
298
236
3. 1 Year Followup
7.
8.
197
179
9. BS only
10. Graduate School
79
11. BS only
12. Graduate School
226
4. 5 Yr. Followup
166
Clerks, Office and Service Workers
186
Accountants, Office Equipment Operators, Salesmen
101
Businessmen, Auditors
14
Managers, Executives
122
Welfare Workers, Artists, Musicians, Counselors, Teachers
52
Lawyers, Social Scientists

essing (a computer is a calculating machine), reporting (a computer has a printer and a typewriter), and, in some instances, even data generating (a computer may have a program which enables it to synthesize what it has in storage in order to report new data).

Educational and Manpower Development and Planning

In systems designed to serve these purposes, student, employment applicant, or employee data are stored in the computer. The progress of individuals and of types of individuals can then be followed as the individuals move through a school system, within the labor market, or within a company. The types or numbers to be accommodated, the appropriateness of the curricular or employment outlets available, the availability of candidates with the needed characteristics can all be monitored to supply information needed for planning. Some state school systems, some labor ministries, and some corporations are developing such systems and putting them into use. One example, combined with a counselor extension system, is described in the following section.

Extension of Counseling by Client Access to Data

Counselors generally find it difficult to give students or other clients direct access to data on educational and occupational opportunities. This is true despite the great advances that have been made in analyzing educational and occupational opportunities and despite the improvements in the presentation of information through printed bulletins and booklets, filmstrips with accompanying sound, and motion pictures. Counselors do not usually have time to introduce students or adults to printed materials in ways which challenge their interest. They do not have time to give students guided tours of college catalogs or to discuss their reading in detail. Most high school students and adults are not in the habit of reading serious career information material, and filmstrips and motion pictures tend of necessity (until new individually controlled audiovisual aids become common) to be used on a somewhat indiscriminate basis. The information dissemination process is thus typically an unsatisfactory one because it is not tailored to the readiness, interests, values, and abilities of the individual.

Computers, with their programmed command of a variety of media, and with their programmed methods of facilitating inquiry by the user, make possible the individualization of the information dissemination process as only an unusually leisurely, dedicated, and informed counselor can handle it. The computer can inform the inquirer of its capacities for supplying information, and it can, within those clearly stated limits, supply the information requested—all of the information requested, and only the information requested.

It can do this on an *indirect inquiry* basis if it is a batch-processing system in which the inquirer fills out questionnaires that are turned over to the computer center. These forms are then processed along with batches of other such forms, and the result is a printout which gives the inquirer both his answers and the opportunity to ask further questions. An educational example of this system is Project PLAN in which the American Institutes for Research (Palo Alto, California) batch-processes material for high school students. An industrial example is ECHRIS, the Educational Career and Human Resources Information System being developed by IBM-Germany (Frank Minor in consultation with Donald E. Super) for employee orientation and career development as well as for manpower development and planning. For reasons of economy the employee or manager using ECHRIS makes inquiries by means of forms which are machine processed overnight, gets replies the next day by means of a printout, and uses additional forms in the same way for further communication with the computer.

The computer can also supply information on a *direct inquiry* basis. In its simplest form the inquirer, whether student, job seeker, or employee, asks the computer a question (which must be within its repertoire) by pressing keys on a terminal (typewriter or cathode ray tube with keys or light-pen to close circuits); the computer responds either by typing out answers on hard copy which the inquirer can remove and keep or by flashing messages on the tube (screen). An example of such a system is that of Interactive Learning Systems. The inquirer can, in this system, specify the characteristics which he desires in a college (from the list of college characteristics supplied by the computer), and the computer types out a list of appropriate colleges for him. Then another question can be asked, perhaps for a somewhat different list of colleges, perhaps about college majors, or perhaps about vocational schools which are nearby.

Simulation of Counselor Functions

When the inquiry system, whether indirect (batch-processing) or direct (via a terminal), is so programmed that the computer stores and analyzes the responses of the inquirer, summarizes them for him, or interprets them, thus making the inquirer a counselee, the process is called monitoring. Monitoring is possible in both indirect and direct inquiry systems: PLAN and ECHRIS are pioneering in the former. CVIS, the Computerized Vocational Information System developed at Willowbrook High School (JoAnn Harris) in Villa Park, Illinois; ECES, the Educational and Career Exploration System developed by IBM (Frank Minor, with Roger Myers and Donald E. Super); and SIGI, the System of Interactive Guidance and Information of the Educational Testing Service (Martin Katz) are experimental-operational systems which provide for direct inquiry with system monitoring.

In these systems, the computer is programmed not only to supply information about education, occupations, and the inquirer's scholastic or work record, but also about his test scores, his aspirations, and his self-estimates of ability and interest. The student or employee can modify his self-ratings if he so desires. In monitoring the inquirer's questions and responses, the computer can point out discrepancies between self-ratings and the record of experience in school, on tests, or at work. It can comment on apparent inconsistencies, ask about their meaning, suggest possible lines of inquiry, and recommend a conference with the counselor. It can point out types of education or work which the inquirer may not have thought about but which are in line with his interests, abilities, or aspirations. It can, in other words, simulate what a counselor does. The computer can do this rather well (Loughary, Friesen, & Hurst, 1966). It can do this in ways that high school students, their parents, and their counselors like, and in doing so it encourages discussions of school and occupational plans and experiences between students and parents who have not done much in the way of such discussion (Bohn, 1970).

It is also possible to program the computer in such a way that the student or employee does his own monitoring. ECES and SIGI achieve this in a small way by making it possible for the student to change his self-estimates when he sees fit. But the prime example to date is ISVD, the Information System for Vocational Decisions, developed at Harvard University (David V. Tiedeman with Allen Ellis and Robert P. O'Hara). This system pioneered with a rationale and with methods which proved beyond present financing capacities, but which were implemented to a point which made it clear that both the rationale and its associated methods will, in a few years, become practical. Using natural English, rather than the multiple-choice dialogue plus page-turning methods of CVIS or the multiple-choice plus brief paragraph dialogue methods of ECES, ISVD sought to give the student-inquirer a very strong sense of agency through freedom of expression and naturalness of response. It did not always achieve this, chiefly because sufficient time for editing, debugging, and elaboration was not available.

The simpler direct-inquiry systems use a cathode ray tube, a kind of television screen on which letters and other symbols, but not pictures, can be quickly produced in light blue on black by the computer. The messages are transmitted more rapidly than by a teletypewriter. The type, however, flickers slightly, and its size and style soon seem unnatural and monotonous. Interested students and employees have no difficulty following it and do not tire unduly, but the system does little, aside from the magic of quick "printing" on the screen, to challenge and to hold interest, little to turn the viewer into an inquirer. CVIS is a system which was quickly and economically developed both because it relies solely on the tube and teletypewriter for communication and because it disseminates information in blocks of 50 or 300 words like the pages of a book; it has the consequent limitations of dependence on reading with minimal interaction and minimal monitoring.

The more complex direct-inquiry systems make use of some combination of slides or filmstrips with the teletypewriter and, in some instances, the cathode ray tube. ECES (Model I) economized by dispensing with the tube, depending on a film-image (filmstrip) projector to display standard material, both verbal and pictorial, and on the teletypewriter for personalized messages. ECES (Model II) added the cathode ray tube with the light-pen for responding. It thus does more to challenge and to hold interest. ISVD assembled a variety of components to use the cathode ray tube for speedy transient messages, the teletypewriter for hard copy messages, and slides for standard and pictorial material. ISVD, like ECES, tried sound in its early stages, but abandoned it for practical and financial reasons; computer-controlled sound and motion will no doubt become practical in due course as technology improves and as production costs go down with volume usage.

Staff Training and Development

In the development of programs to teach the use of computer-assisted guidance systems such as CVIS, ECES, and ECHRIS, it quickly becomes clear that these systems are not only helpful counseling aids for students, job seekers, and employees, but are also important orientation and training devices for staff members such as counselors, personnel managers, and administrators. The motion pictures and slides developed for these purposes have proved useful in clarifying the nature of the educational and vocational guidance process, giving new meaning to the Parsonian model of counseling (analysis of the assets of the individual, analysis of occupations, and counseling of the individual by relating the former to the latter) and to the decision models described in the first part of this chapter.

The steps through which the inquirer goes in using the computer system, the questions asked and answered, the types of data encountered, and the uses made of the data, all provide the counselor with a model of counseling behavior. For some counselors, especially those who have not had much exposure to vocational counseling, who have never had the opportunity to observe an experienced counselor at work or to tape-record and analyze their own preparation for counseling and their own interviewing, a computer system provides new insights into the nature and use of educational, occupational, and client information in career orientation and guidance. The development of a computer-assisted guidance system requires the detailed analysis of information and counseling processes. In becoming oriented to the system, in the demonstration and training use of the system, and in working with students or employees who use it, the counselor, like the student inquirer, gains new insights into the processes.

As systems are refined it will become possible to provide opportunity for the counselor to practice counseling with data stored in the computer and to get feedback as to how his handling compares with that of the program (the programmed handling of data is the result of the pooled judgment of experts). Thus, counseling practice with supervision will be possible without the demands on supervisory time which now constitute the main bottleneck of counselor training. Such training use of the computer will also make it possible to eliminate or reduce the demands on student time which videotaping requires. Simulated counseling will become a training method intermediate between the case conference and the handling of real cases.

Simulation Systems in Guidance

Adoption and Installation

New methods of meeting familiar needs, new devices for performing services which have been rendered by established instruments, new types of staff members for the performance of standard functions—all of these tend to arouse fears and suspicions in those who have not yet become accustomed to innovation. Horsemen must have terrified nomadic men used to moving their flocks and their families by foot. Carts must have been frightening to horsemen used to managing with what a pack animal could carry. Steam locomotives stampeded horses whether ridden by mounted men or driven by carters. Pictographs on rocks must have looked like black magic when first read to an illiterate primitive man by one who had become "picturate." Books must have been very threatening to a priest who had learned all of the accumulated wisdom of man by rote memory, only to find that another man could get it all from a book which he had never seen before!

Computers, with their vast storage capacity, their rapid and accurate retrieval power, and their programs which make possible selective retrieval with personalized interpretation and summaries, could therefore easily be threatening to counselors, to teachers, and to other dispensers and interpreters of knowledge. They could be equally threatening to administrators faced with planning for changing methods and systems, and to the public asked to support practices which they themselves have never experienced.

How is the unknown to become known, the strange to become familiar, the threat to be made reassuring? At an elementary level, by contact and experience; at a higher level, by involvement and responsibility. The new father is less fearful of the infant once he has held it in his arms, and he begins to feel that it is really his once he has changed a diaper for it.

Familiarity with and confidence in an instrument, a method, or a system come with opportunities to observe its use, to take part in demonstrations, to use it oneself, and to work with others who are using it. To become familiar, computer-support systems for vocational guidance need to be demonstrated at professional meetings and in workshops and courses. They need to be available for observation at appropriate times in schools in which they are being used. Training sessions in their use need to be organized for counselors. IBM's ECES, which is now in use in Flint, Michigan, was the subject of training for two hours each day, for one week, for local counselors. Willowbrook High School, constantly improving its CVIS, but alert to the fact that counselors might come to take its presence and functions for granted, planned a program of continuing exposure to the system, focusing on innovations, for local counselors.

Involvement and responsibility are essential if those using a good device are to develop more than mild interest in it. Having a part in its development or refinement is more likely to result in support. What "I helped to make" is more likely to be used, and used well, than what "they imported." In this way CVIS, developed and used at Willowbrook High School by local staff members, may get a more intensive trial and more intelligent use by counselors in that school than by counselors in some other schools to which it is being adapted for use. One way of minimizing the chances of apathy and resistance in new situations is to involve counselors in identifying the changes that need to be made in the system as it is being adapted and to get their help in preparing the data or the program to implement these changes. ECES now operates in this manner in some of the schools of the Flint complex. Counselors should also help plan and carry out programs of explanation and demonstration for students, teachers, and parents. They may also accept responsibility for preparing local manuals and other supporting or explanatory material.

Obstacles to the acceptance of computer-assisted vocational guidance systems, other than that of unfamiliarity, are of four kinds. These are: (*a*) the person orientation of counselors, as contrasted with their technology orientation; (*b*) the accuracy of the machine compared to the fallibility of the human counselor; (*c*) the threat to the counselor of loss of control of his schedule and method of work with the introduction of a machine which may set his work pace and direct problems to him; (*d*) the apparent deterministic nature of computer-support systems which simulate counseling and the consequent fear of the mechanization of life.

The counselor's orientation is often an obstacle to effective computer use, for men and women who become counselors have typically done so because of an interest in working with people. Few of them were trained in science or technology, and those who were shifted to guidance from those fields because they found themselves more interested in students than in academic subject matter. Teachers entering counselor training programs see themselves more as counselors than as teachers, more as helpers of students solving personal problems than as instructors in subject matter (Bingham, 1966). This means that computers, whose very name spells arithmetic and algebra, are somewhat frightening to those who have limited quantitative skills. It means, too, that computer systems, which are based on a rigorous type of logic more familiar to scientists than to humanists, are strange and threatening to many counselors. That they need not be is shown by the fact that English teachers often make good programmers (it does help to be able to write a clear sentence).

The counselor newly exposed to computer systems thus needs help in learning a new thought process, a new way of ordering ideas and data, a new way of solving problems. Once oriented, he is likely to be intrigued and impressed by the regularity and manageability of the world of science and by the discovery of the clear logic of systems.

Accuracy and fallibility are relevant concerns when computers and counselors are compared. Computers can and do make errors. But they generally do so because a clerk has misread a number or punched the wrong key, a card has been misplaced by an operator, telephone lines have been overloaded, or a program has been badly written—in short, because of some human error which is not inherent in the computer itself. Such errors can generally be avoided by careful planning, by debugging before the system goes into regular use, or by verification procedures.

There is, thus, a major difference between computers and people. Once the computer installation, data base, and programs have been made operational, errors are not likely to occur; but human error and human forgetting occur at unforeseeable times and with erratic frequency. The counselor knows that he cannot remember all of the occupations in the *Dictionary of Occupational Titles* nor all of the trends reported in the *Occupational Outlook Handbook,* and he knows, too, that the computer can. The counselor can know the entrance requirements of a number of colleges to which many of his students go, but he cannot remember those for all of the four-year colleges in the country nor what the various curricular offerings of each of those colleges are. When the counselor is viewed (by himself or by others) primarily as a source of information, the computer becomes something of a threat to him, for the computer can do that kind of counselor's job better than he can.

Behavior control possibilities, in the work of elementary and secondary school counselors are sometimes the object of some jealousy on the part of classroom teachers. Counselors do not have to face a classroom full of pupils all day long; they do not have to stop one class at the sound of a bell and begin the next at the sound of another bell five minutes later. Their students do not take examinations which show how well they have done as a result of working with the counselor. Counselors plan their activities to meet the needs of the students with whom they work, but to a degree they make their own judgments as to these needs and they plan their own work. It is true, of course, that the needs which counselors must move to meet are generated by many circumstances—the developmental experiences of students, the program of the school, the personalities of students, teachers, and parents, the admission requirements of colleges, and the employment procedures of the community. But the computer is one more determinant of the work of the counselor, and a rather obviously demanding determinant. The computer supplies information to the pupil, which stimulates many pupils to make demands on the counselor; the computer has information which the counselor can get but does not have; the computer raises issues and refers the student to the counselor for help in resolving them. The computer in effect makes demands on the counselor, demands of a kind and frequency that did not prevail before computer-assisted guidance became a reality. Some counselors resent these demands, although others welcome them.

Determinism is another common issue in programmed learning and exploration. When a person sees a causal connection, as when the counselor's knowledge of human abilities and human behavior leads him to believe that a student's choice of a certain course will lead to failure, this is likely to be viewed as insight or understanding. When a statistical formula is applied to the same data and goes through the same logical processes, this is likely to be called determinism. And when computers are programmed to use these data and to go through these processes, the cry of mechanization and dehumanization is likely to be raised.

It is helpful, in this context, to remember that it is people's use of ideas and of facts which is deterministic. It is people who function as counselors, as authors of books, as planners of systems, and as writers of programs for computers. Counselors may be highly directive or very nondirective, authoritarian or permissive, in seeking to produce behavioral outcomes in their students or clients. Books and kits on the choice of an occupation or on the development of a career plan may outline steps to be taken, data to be analyzed, decisions to be made, in a directive or in a nondirective manner. The computerized guidance systems which counselors help to develop will, obviously, reflect any of the approaches to guidance and counseling which the authors wish to incorporate in them.

The guidance machine, it must be remembered, is a simulator. It does what counselors do, the counselors on whose work and processes the program is modeled and whose best data are stored in the data bank. The machine does what people tell it to do; the system is as good as the men who make it. Machine and system, however, are still not as human as the men who make them, for the machine can do only what the makers tell it to do in writing the program; it depends for its final humaneness on a program which is directed to say, when it needs to: "You may want to discuss this with your counselor or with some other informed and understanding adult."

In Montclair, New Jersey, and in Illinois' Willowbrook School Districts, no counselors, no parents, and no pupils criticized ECES or CVIS for determinism or for dehumanization. In Flint, Michigan, the issue was raised in inquiry but not in accusation. If anything, the reactions to the machine are quite the opposite: one can ask it good questions and get good answers; it is unbiased; it tells one what it knows when asked; it does not beat about the bush when it does not know something; talking with the computer before deciding next year's courses is helpful; it tells one a lot but does not tell one what one should do.

The obstacles to the acceptance by counselors of computers as counseling aids, though real, do not seem insurmountable. They can be handled by good orientation and training activities for counselors and by good programming of the computer. Counselor orientation and training can diminish the perceived threats of technology, of exposed fallibility, and of behavior control. The computer simulation of counseling as done by competent counselors can remove the fear of determinism and of dehumanization. Counselors who are comfortable with computer assistance can help students make effective use of that assistance.

The problems which counselors have in considering and in using computer-supported guidance systems are of course faced by school administrators, teachers, parents, taxpayers, and others contemplating their use. But these latter groups often have some additional problems, those of fear of the invasion of privacy and of high cost.

Invasion of privacy through the storage and retrieval capacity of computers has for some years been a much discussed danger. The idea that a person's cumulative record in school, his record of traffic violations, his health record, his credit history, and now his occupational qualifications, career aspirations, and work history might all be permanently stored and easily retrieved for a variety of purposes, however legitimate, evokes pictures of Orwell's *1984* and of a police state. Non-computerized records have occasionally been abused. But computerized records lend themselves to larger scale abuse.

Again, however, it must be pointed out that systems such as books, automobiles, and guidance, are as good as the men who make them and use them. Despite newspaper publicity, talks to interested groups, and open house for parents of users, or perhaps because of them, no voices were raised in protest in Montclair, in Villa Park, or in Flint when computers were made available experimentally to assist in the guidance programs. No one in those towns appeared to fear that the users of the systems would invade privacy, and no user of the programs has shown any feeling that his privacy was being invaded. The system is evidently what its makers make it.

Cost is frequently questioned and is another problem in public acceptance of computer-supported guidance systems. No truly interactive computer-assisted guidance system is on the market at the time of this writing, although CVIS is being made available to some schools and other systems may soon reach the market. CVIS has no price tag, the data base and programs being in the public domain, and adaptation and installation being the responsibility of the user-school. When, as in CVIS, the computer is used simultaneously for administrative purposes such as accounting, scheduling, and keeping pupil records, the cost is minimized. ECES should cost more than CVIS because it is a more complex conversational and pictorial, as well as verbal, system. Perhaps only one generalization concerning costs is possible at this time: multiple sessions at a computer terminal to carry on a personalized dialogue concerning educational and occupational decisions will in due course cost little if any more per pupil than the price of a good book.

The question then arises as to how many "books" a school or college can afford to buy for each of its students. If a computer system were to cost about what three counselors cost, should the school acquire the computer system for guidance or should it add the counselors to its staff? The question is not easily answered, for it depends on what the student-counselor ratio is at the time, how well prepared the counselors are for the task of counseling, and how they are using their time in the school. One does not ask whether it would be better to have a school library or three more teachers, for libraries (available books) are thought of not as teacher-substitutes, but as teaching aids. The same point can be made about laboratories and shops. In the same way, computer-support systems for guidance are not counselor-substitutes (simulation to the contrary notwithstanding), but counseling aids, as has been shown by the increased and more effective use of counselor time reported by a number of counselors after the introduction of ECES into the Flint school systems. The real question is how good a support system can the community give to its students and to its counselors?

The Evaluation of Computer-assisted Guidance

From the inception of work on the development of computer-assisted educational and vocational guidance, attention has been paid to the problem of evaluation. Questions have been asked about its effects on students, on counselors, and on programs of guidance services. The first projects sought to identify criteria appropriate for assessing the value of the systems and to devise methods for collecting relevant data. The criteria chosen and the methods devised have differed somewhat according to the stage at which the work was done and according to the duration of the project. Some important types of effects have yet to be studied, and some of those investigated have been chosen more for convenience than for importance. In the following section a number of the possible evaluation criteria and methods are identified and briefly discussed together with the conclusions drawn from their use.

Counselor Simulation

One way of judging the efficacy of a computer-assisted counseling system is to compare the judgments and predictions made by the computer with those made by a human counselor; another is to compare the decisions which students make with the aid of the computer with the decisions which they make alone or with the aid of a counselor. These methods are especially appropriate since current systems are modeled on the work of counselors or upon a logical analysis of what counselors do in working with students and clients.

These are the methods used by Loughary and associates (1966) in developing and testing the Systems Development Corporation computer approach in Palo Alto. The SDC machine system agreed with the human counselor in about 75 percent of the appraisal statements, but it predicted higher GPA's and more potential dropouts, and, in addition, it encouraged more exploration of academic fields than did the human counselor. The decisions made by students concerning courses in 10th, 11th, and 12th grades differed somewhat from computer-assisted to counselor-assisted decisions, but the differences were not great in number or in content. More students indicated having problems with courses when dealing with the computer than when dealing with the counselor.

Student Usage

The fact that a computer can be programmed to keep records of how it is used, and that computer terminals are used by students according to some sort of schedule, makes easy the analysis of what kinds of students use the system and of how often and for what purpose they use it.

Thus, students completed a brief Student Reaction Form at the end of each session at the terminals in Montclair High School (Bohn, 1970), and the records of student use were analyzed by grade, sex, race, and college vs. noncollege aspiration. The typical student used the system seven times, each session lasting 40 minutes. Grade, sex, race, and aspiration differences were not significant, except that black females who did not plan to go to college made less use of the system than did other categories of students. Harris (personal communication, 1971) has used similar methods and obtained similar findings with CVIS at Willowbrook High School.

Student Interaction with Others

The impact of computer-assisted guidance can be assessed through the interaction of students with their counselors, teachers, parents, employers, and workers. Comparisons can be made between students who are using a system and students who do not have access to the system. Student self-reports, school records, and recorded interviews are helpful in assessing student interaction.

Students can, in completing questionnaires before, during, or after a period of computer use, report on their discussions of educational and vocational plans and experiences with their parents, teachers, and counselors, and on their exploration of occupations with people at work. In the Montclair experiment, students in the experimental (user) and control (nonuser) groups did this both before and after using ECES. Boys and girls of lower socioeconomic status who used the computer system showed a significant increase in parent interaction.

In the current Genesee County (Flint) study, Student Weekly Activity Reports by a sample of students permit the analysis of the effects on interaction with key people as these interactions take place, thereby minimizing the distorting effects of retrospective reporting.

When accurate records of student contacts with counselors are kept, either in the form of appointment books or counseling logs, an objective analysis can be made of student interaction and of counselor functioning as a result of the use of the computer system. Simple though this sounds, it is difficult to achieve. In the pressure of work counselors generally find the keeping of detailed notes on each contact difficult, and even simple records of appointments must be kept for long periods if the chance effects of routine scheduling are to be controlled (as when all students are being called in to plan next year's programs). One objective of evaluation, however, should be to ascertain not only the frequency with which experimental and control students see their counselors, but also the content of their contact with counselors and the ways in which they make use of the counselors' time and skills. A frequently expressed hope or expectation is that, having presumably become better informed as a result of using the computer system, the student will use the counselor as a counselor, not as an information source, reviewing alternatives and weighing values, considering probable outcomes and choosing means of attaining them. Many counselors in Genesee County have volunteered that this does happen. The obvious way to find out if this is, indeed, the effect of a computer system is to keep and analyze records of student interaction with counselors.

Although counselors find it difficult to keep running notes on the content and processes of interviews, many do find it possible and rewarding to tape-record interviews. Recording can be planned to cover samples of students having and not having access to a computer system. The taped records can later be analyzed for content and process to reveal the impact of the experience with the computer system on interaction with the counselor. This method is being tried on a small scale in the Genesee County evaluation of ECES.

Student Use of Resources

The resources used by students in educational and vocational exploration include more than counselors, teachers, parents, and employed adults who know about education and work. Some of the most important resources are impersonal, and include books, pamphlets, films and filmstrips, and places of employment such as factories, laboratories, stores, hotels, restaurants, and offices.

The use of such resources by students before and after experiencing a computer-support system, and their use by experimental and control groups, can be analyzed by means of self-report questionnaires. The Student Questionnaire used in the Montclair ECES study is a typical before-and-after self-report instrument; the Student Weekly Activities Report of the Genesee County ECES study is an example of an instrument used for concurrent reporting. The data on effects are still not sufficient to permit dependable judgment to be made as to their importance; longer term use of a system may be needed to study its impact.

Several types of observable behaviors and observational records have been proposed for the evaluation of computer-assisted guidance and counseling systems. The use of educational and occupational information materials, whether books, pamphlets, filmstrips, catalogs, or directories, can be recorded by librarians, clerks, or receptionists who are in charge of such materials or who are stationed at desks which make observation possible. In the Genesee County field trial, consideration was given to the possibility of having students observed while awaiting turns at the computer terminals or, in the case of control students, while in a study hall similar in all respects save for the waiting room function. When library materials are withdrawn by means of call slips, these latter can be analyzed for differences between system-users and control nonusers, but this method has the defect of not including the record of browsing which an observer can keep. The ECES experiment was unable to include a resource room in its design because of space and scheduling problems, but waiting-and-resource room observation reports will undoubtedly be used in field trials which can supply the observer in a resource room set up as a study hall.

Attitudes of Students, Counselors, and Parents

The attitudes of persons using computers as aids to guidance, whether as students, as parents of users, or as counselors, have frequently served as criteria of the value of the systems. The value criterion is justified on the ground that if the systems are not valued they will not be used, and that if they are valued they must be having some worthwhile effect despite the possibilities of Hawthorne effects and fadism.

Rating scales and questionnaires have been the standard attitude assessment devices, some of them completed before and after use, some by experimentals and controls, and some by experimentals after each session or only after final use of a system. In Palo Alto (Loughary et al., 1966), in Montclair (Bohn, 1970), in Willowbrook High School (Harris, 1968), and in other experimental programs, combinations of such criteria and methods have been used with consistently favorable results. Students like using the computer in educational, vocational, and self-exploration, and they value the help it gives them. Parents, too, like what it does for their children, especially those children who were previously unmotivated. Finally, counselors, a significant percentage of whom are skeptical at the outset, come to recognize that the computer-support system can help some students whom they do not reach, while facilitating counseling with others with whom they do work effectively.

Vocational Maturity

Suggested as the fundamental personal variable to be studied in vocational development many years ago (Super, 1955), vocational maturity has since become widely accepted as a criterion of the effectiveness of vocational development and vocational guidance programs. This has been true despite the fact that measures employed in the assessment of vocational maturity have been difficult to use and are still in the early stages of development (Super & Overstreet, 1960; Crites, 1965; Gribbons & Lohnes, 1968; Westbrook & Cunningham, 1970; Jordaan, 1971).

The basic work of the Career Pattern Study (Super & Overstreet, 1960) paved the way for the development of an instrument for use in the evaluation of IBM's Educational and Career Exploration System in Montclair (Thompson, Lindeman, Clack, & Bohn, 1970) and later, of a new format for use in Genesee County (Forrest, 1971). The initial trials of the Career Questionnaire, put into multiple-choice form and factor analyzed, led to the identification of six factors constituting vocational maturity (not all of them highly enough developed to be observable at every age level). These were:

a. Resources and Information
b. Trait Maturity
c. Planning and Information
d. Acceptance of Responsibility for Choice
e. Occupational Orientation
f. Planfulness

A subsequent revision of the questionnaire (Forrest, 1971) was organized around the three factors which were most clearly identified. These were:

a. Planning Orientation
b. Resources for Exploration
c. Decision Making and Information

In the Montclair field trial of ECES one measure of information was affected by the use of the computer system. That others were not affected may be due to the brief three-month duration of the field trial and to the relatively small size of the sample (156 students). In Genesee County large numbers of students have access to the system over a longer period of time in a field trial which, when completed, should make possible more definitive conclusions. The availability of the revised Career Questionnaire for research use, with supporting reliability, normative, and construct-validity data should make possible more adequate evaluations of the effects of computer-assisted and other guidance methods and programs on the various dimensions of vocational maturity.

Vocational Aspirations

Vocational aspirations may be examined for their breadth or specificity and for their degree of realism. Two of the vocational maturity factors identified in the Career Pattern Study and in the ECES evaluations are of the latter type, for the agreement of vocational preferences or aspirations with abilities and interests can be viewed as evidence of realism. This type of agreement was shown to be meaningless in ninth grade boys, but it increases with age and is a meaningful index in twelfth graders (Heyde & Jordaan, in preparation). Agreement between vocational aspirations and labor market conditions can also be viewed as evidence of realism, although in the use of all of these presumed measures of realism it is important to bear in mind that there are occasions when it may be proper for a student or a worker to fight rather than to accept the odds against his chosen career plan.

Breadth and specificity of vocational aspirations have also been shown to be associated with age and grade in junior and senior high school in the Career Pattern Study (Heyde & Jordaan, in preparation). During the early exploratory period, wide-ranging exploration, evidenced by a variety of inconsistent vocational preferences, is often desirable. But by the final year in high school some specificity and consistency of preferences is more common. More importantly, specificity and consistency of preferences are predictive of later occupational and career success and satisfaction; clarity of goals facilitates both progress toward them and their earlier attainment. These are, therefore, suitable criteria for measuring the effects of computer-assisted guidance. The evaluations in Montclair High School and Willowbrook High School show that increased breadth of vocational aspirations in the lower high school results from use of the system, and that increased specificity is a result in the last years of high school.

Occupational and Career Success and Satisfaction

In the long run, it is the success and satisfaction of individuals in their occupations and in their careers which should be the criteria of the effectiveness of vocational guidance systems, whether computerized or conventional. Occupational criteria are those which apply to the occupation engaged in by the individual at a given point in time; career criteria are longitudinal in that they take into account both movement from one position to another and the character of this sequence of moves. The nature and measurement of these different types of criteria have been explored (Super, 1963) and tested (Super, Kowalski, & Gotkin, 1967; Super & Bohn, in preparation), but the criteria have not yet been used in evaluation studies. Such studies have so far covered time spans of only a few months, but this will undoubtedly change as computer-assisted guidance systems gain wider use.

Impact on the Work of Counselors

It has frequently been suggested that the availability of a good interactive information system should save counselors time and effort in collecting, organizing, and disseminating educational and occupational information. Counselors should have more time for counseling. Counseling time should be used more consistently for considering the import of data, for planning exploratory activities, for evaluating the outcomes of exploration, for formulating plans, and for decision making.

The use of criteria of this type, i.e., effects on counselors' activities, requires detailed data on the number, frequency, duration, and content of counselor-client interviews; it requires logs which show how counselors use their time (seeing students, collecting data, organizing files, etc.). Such records are difficult to obtain from busy people. The ECES evaluation in Genesee County is exploring the use of several data collection methods, including tape recordings of counselor-student interviews, interaction reports, and counselor attitude questionnaires, for such analyses. However, this is only a small part of the data needed for the study of the impact of a computer system on human and social systems. To get such data is a challenge to counselors and to researchers.

The great storage capacity of the computer, its rapid and accurate retrieval of information, its programming power for the multimedia use of information, its use of a dynamic conversational mode—all these capabilities make computer technology the new counseling technology. It is one which counselor education programs will soon find essential to include in their instructional and practicum programs, which schools, colleges, employment services, counseling centers, and even public libraries, will consider important aids. As one employment service expert said, after spending a day observing the use of one computer-assisted guidance system, talking with students who used it, and trying it out himself: "It's too important to put in schools; it ought to be in telephone booths on every street corner." Many experts believe that, in due course, computer-assisted vocational guidance systems will be as readily available as that, through telephones and the television set in one's living room.

REFERENCES

Bingham, W. C. Change of occupation as a function of the regnancy of occupational self-concepts. Unpublished doctoral dissertation, Teachers College, Columbia University, 1966.

Bohn, M. J., Jr. Field trial and evaluation of a system. In D. E. Super et al., *Computer-assisted counseling.* New York: Teachers College Press, 1970.

Cooley, W. W., & Lohnes, P. R. *Predicting development of young adults.* Palo Alto: Project TALENT Office, American Institutes for Research and University of Pittsburgh, 1968.

I am indebted to my colleagues, Roger A. Myers of Teachers College, Columbia University, and David Forrest, now at Drew University, for their helpful criticisms and suggestions in the preparation of this chapter.—D.E.S.

Crites, J. O. Measurement of vocational maturity in adolescence: I. attitude test of the Vocational Development Inventory. *Psychological Monographs*, 1965, **79** (2, Whole No. 595).

Forrest, D. J. The construction and validation of an objective measure of vocational maturity for adolescents. Unpublished doctoral dissertation, Teachers College, Columbia University, 1971.

Gelatt, A. B. Decision-making: A conceptual frame of reference for counseling. *Journal of Counseling Psychology*, 1962, **9,** 240–245.

Gribbons, W. D., & Lohnes, P. R. *Emerging careers.* New York: Teachers College Press, 1968.

Harris, J. The computerization of vocational information. *Vocational Guidance Quarterly*, 1968, **17,** 12–20; also in Super, D. E. et al., *Computer-assisted counseling.* New York: Teachers College Press, 1970.

Harris, J. *Toward guidelines for computer involvement in guidance.* Report of the Commission on Computer-assisted Guidance Systems, National Vocational Guidance Association, in press.

Heyde, M. B., & Jordaan, J. P. *Vocational development in the high school years.* Career Pattern Study Monograph No. 3. New York: Teachers College Press, in preparation.

Jordaan, J. P. Exploratory behavior: The formation of self and occupational concepts. In D. E. Super, R. Starishevsky, N. Matlin, & J. P. Jordaan. *Career development: Self-concept theory.* New York: College Entrance Examination Board, 1963.

Jordaan, J. P. Vocational maturity: The construct, its measurement, and its validity. Paper presented at the XVIIth International Congress of the International Association of Applied Psychology, Liège, Belgium, July, 1971.

Loughary, J. W., Friesen, D., & Hurst, R. Autocoun: A computer-based automated counseling simulation system. *Personnel and Guidance Journal*, 1966, **45,** 5–15; also in D. E. Super et al., *Computer-assisted counseling.* New York: Teachers College Press, 1970.

Miller, J. Information retrieval systems in guidance. *Personnel and Guidance Journal*, 1970, **49,** 212–218.

Myers, R. A. Computer-aided counseling: Some issues of adoption and use. In Super, D. E. et al., *Computer-assisted counseling.* New York: Teachers College Press, 1970.

Super, D. E. Dimensions and measurement of vocational maturity. *Teachers College Record*, 1955, **57**, 151–163.

Super, D. E. The *psychology of careers.* New York: Harper, 1957.

Super D. E. The definition and measurement of early career behavior: A first formulation. *Personnel and Guidance Journal*, 1963, **41**, 775–780.

Super, D. E., & Bohn, M. J., Jr. *Floundering and stabilizing: Vocational development at age 25.* Career Pattern Study Monograph No. 4. New York: Teachers College Press, in preparation.

Super, D. E., Kowalski, R. S., & Gotkin, E. H. *Floundering and trial after high school.* Cooperative Research Project No. 1392. New York: Teachers College, Columbia University, 1967.

Super, D. E., & Overstreet, P. L. *The vocational maturity of ninth grade boys.* Career Pattern Study Monograph No. 2. New York: Teachers College Press, 1960.

Super, D. E. et al. *Computer-assisted counseling.* New York: Teachers College Press, 1970.

Thompson, A. S., Lindeman, R. H., Clack, S., & Bohn, M. J., Jr. *The Educational and Career Exploration System: Field trial and evaluation in Montclair high school.* New York: Teachers College, Columbia University, 1970.

Tiedeman, D. V., & O'Hara, R. P. *Career development: Choice and adjustment.* New York: College Entrance Examination Board, 1963.

Westbrook, B. W., & Cunningham, J. W. The development and application of vocational maturity measures. *Vocational Guidance Quarterly*, 1970, **18**, 171–175.

9

epilogue: a sense of vocation

C. GILBERT WRENN
Arizona State University

In his epilogue, Gilbert Wrenn sets down his observations on some of the salient issues introduced in the preceding chapters and contributes his own perspectives on a society in flux and the future of career guidance. It is not fruitful, Wrenn counsels, to compare the social and economic forces which marked the beginnings of systematic vocational guidance with those that now prevail as a means to charting the future of the field. Better to comprehend today's circumstances and today's human needs and then to construct something suitable to the times. What may emerge may or may not conform to our past conceptions of vocational guidance.

The guidance of the future may be profiled in terms of certain pervasive characteristics of today's changing society. Among these, Wrenn identifies a "post-industrial" climate in which concerns must be brought to focus more sharply on human development than upon the controlling forces of technology, an economy of abundance in which few men and women labor as a means to sheer biological survival, a fluid occupational universe where a quickened exchange of new occupations for old occurs and where the job mobility of workers is commonplace, a society of shifting values in which the life meanings traditionally attached to work may be waning, and a social order in which family and school are acquiring less prominent functions in the occupational socialization of American youth. What is needed, Wrenn argues, is a social ethic which honors our capacity to care for one another and which establishes safeguards against a spreading technology's interference with that capacity. It would be an ethic in which the motive to work does not spring mainly from the specious threat of economic scarcity or from an obsession with material comforts. If, in fact, that is all work implies, then it may be better to seek life's meaning and purpose through leisure, as one segment of today's youth culture appears to be saying. Wrenn's assessment of the future meaning of work seems here to be starkly counterpoised against that offered by Levenstein (see Chapter 4).

Formal education has long been uncritically regarded as the crucible in which callow youth is best tempered for his ensuing career as worker. Wrenn vigorously challenges this conventional wisdom. Our academically oriented schools, he feels, fail to provide young people with realistic preparation for the occupational world. On the contrary, school is society's instrument for prolonging the dependency of adolescents and delaying their entrance into a tight labor market. Wrenn recommends a plan of "staggered education," periods of formal schooling meshed with intervals of occupational experience extending through the later adult years. If we find the concept of continuous education to be too resistant to change, our strategy should then be to expand cooperative vocational education and to infuse school and college curricula with community-based programs and unpaid occupational apprenticeships.

What of the future? Wrenn foresees the need for bold new directions and methods if practitioners are to serve the life planning needs of their clients. Tomorrow's career guidance procedures, he believes, will incorporate Blocher's intervention strategies (Chapter 2), the systems approaches to curriculum described by Hansen and Borow (Chapter 6), the behavioral counseling of Krumboltz and Baker (Chapter 7), and the computer-supported vocational guidance espoused by Super (Chapter 8). But there will be more to the new career guidance. It will embrace eclecticism in preference to dogmatic theory with its confining assumptions about personality; it will reflect the accelerating thrust of humanistic counseling; and it will engage the practitioner's skills as a facilitator of group counseling. Finally, in accepting under the rubric of work "any activity in which one engage[s], whether for pay or not, and which one [sees] as contributing to a sense of personal significance or the enhancement of the welfare of others," guidance will ultimately come to be as concerned with assisting people to prepare for personally satisfying and socially responsible leisure activities as for paid employment. We can only speculate whether Wrenn's imaginative prescription is more than an ardent advocacy for what he believes is required, whether it is, in fact, an accurate portent of the future of career guidance.

H. B.

This collection of essays bears a two-factor title, "Career Guidance" and "A New Age." The logic of the situation is such that the "new age" must be understood before the "career guidance" or vocational guidance that is appropriate to it can be proposed. That sequence is precisely the basis of Blocher's development (Chapter 2) with the two factors receiving approximately equal emphasis. Building upon an historical perspective, Miller (Chapter 1) has also identified and interpreted contemporary social conditions that affect vocational choice and career patterns. Levenstein (Chapter 4) and Murphy (Chapter 5) have provided penetrating analyses of one significant dimension of the new age—the meaning of work and, in particular, its contemporary psychological meaning. Katz's (Chapter 3) delineation of vocational guidance is best understood against a background of shifting social conditions, with the expanded meanings of guidance brought into sharper focus through a description of far-reaching societal changes. The presentations by Hansen and Borow (Chapter 6), Krumboltz and Baker (Chapter 7), and Super (Chapter 8) accept the reality of "the new age" and take it for granted. These authors offer several emerging approaches to the practice of vocational guidance that require a clear understanding of contemporary developments in curriculum design, the psychology of learning, and communication technology.

So both "Career Guidance" and the "New Age" factors have been accorded a balanced treatment, sometimes separately, sometimes as a blend, sometimes with one of the two implicit rather than explicit yet never neglected. A good ending to the book should also build upon these dual factors. In what follows here, the reader will inevitably find some duplication of what he has already read. No attempt will be made to introduce original concepts. But what is said may cast new light on familiar ideas.

Yesterday and Today?

The urgent social needs of an earlier day (see Miller, Chapter 1) brought about the organized attention to vocational guidance that is now recognizable history. Are there novel elements in today's social picture that demand different emphases in today's—and tomorrow's—vocational guidance? If the social conditions described by Stephens (1970)—urbanization and poverty, a changing morality, the loss of individuality in large organizational structures, and the decline of apprenticeship—were instrumental in the establishment of formal vocational guidance programs during the first decades of this century, do these same conditions or do different conditions now prevail in the establishment of vocational guidance programs?

Certainly, the concentration of people in urban centers is as evident as ever; so, too, are poverty, impersonality, and a changing morality. But today's cities are more structured with the inner city, a decaying perimeter, a network of suburbs, and satellite towns—together comprising a metropolitan area or megalopolis that spills across county or even state lines. Not only do people cluster in cities, but the cities themselves cluster together. In 1970 there were 16 urban regions (clusters of cities or metropolitan areas), the populations of which exceeded one million. These high-density areas accounted for 69 percent of the population of the United States. Ghettos are still present, but their inhabitants are not primarily immigrants; they are chiefly our native unfortunates with a legacy of several generations of unhappy citizenship.

Morality *is* changing, not as "a decline from puritan morality," but rather as a sober questioning of all values as absolute or universal. Organizational influence is greater than ever. Now, however, scientists and professionals of all kinds are affected as much as "the working man" was formerly, and they are affected not by industry alone but by government and professional organizations which often exhibit highly dogmatic, bureaucratic, and self-serving practices. Labor unions for both blue- and white-collar workers frequently seem to push men around today more than do "greedy employers." Apprenticeship may not be as potent a training force as formerly, but under conditions of rapid economic and occupational change perhaps it should not be, unless preparation for flexibility and change are built into the apprentice experience.

No, I do not think that we gain much by comparing the social conditions of 50 years ago with those of today in order to get our bearings on needed change in vocational guidance. Today—and the immediate tomorrow—are best seen as a completely new ball game. We may be held back rather than benefited by dwelling upon anything that vocational guidance was. Progress cannot be made by a strategy which attempts to adapt the old vocational guidance to today's information systems, computer and communications technology, and the best of today's counseling. It would be better to start with today's needs and create something to meet them. The result may be an entirely new use of the term vocational guidance.

Today—Perhaps Tomorrow

Several conditions of today's society seem critical to our "new age" considerations.

Post-industrial

In this post-industrial age in which we live, individuals and human relationships have begun to take precedence over things and organization. It follows that education should be focused more on the growth of humans and less on technology. We have advanced technology to the point where its ability to affect people is critical. The United States grew great in conquering first a geographical frontier and then a frontier of technology and industry. Our new frontier is human relations, our responsibility to and for each other. It is a climate which calls for a new ethic, an ethic which controls the impact of technology upon the human qualities of love and of concern one for another, our capacity to care.

Abundance

While it can hardly be said that we have managed an equitable distribution of our material resources, we live nonetheless in an era of an abundance of goods, not in our prolonged former state of scarcity. In *The World of Contemporary Counselor* (Wrenn, 1973.) I have written about what this may signify with regard to changing social assumptions and human goals.

> The history of our country is based upon an assumption that "the world's goods" such as land, minerals, food, things, are in relatively scarce supply. This meant that each man (or woman) was in competition with every other person to get his share. At first the "share" meant enough food and other necessities for any man and his family to live; later it meant that he wanted his "share" to be more than the other person's share whether he needed it or not. Those who take the largest share of the world's resources are even today said to be the most successful. Those assumptions of scarcity and competition are part of a culture which tends to give preference to property rights over person rights (witness the man who, in defending the National Guard action taken at Kent State University, said—"those kids had to be kept in control by some means, they have just destroyed some very valuable property!"). Such a culture also gives preference to technological requirements over human necessities, concentration and control over distribution, the producer over the consumer, etc.
>
> This assumption of scarcity is no longer valid for a large segment of our population. It is maintained as a kind of myth widely believed but without basis in fact. It is, indeed, a spurious scarcity. Philip Slater writes that this spurious scarcity is ". . . man-made in the case of bodily gratification and man-allowed or man-maintained in the case of material goods." As spurious scarcity it "now exists only for the purpose of maintaining itself." This maintenance of spurious scarcity is perpetuated via the components of Lewis Mumford's (1970) mega-machine, his Pentagon of Power: progress, profit, productivity, property, and publicity. . . .
>
> Some see this as a movement into an Aquarian Age of Abundance. But perhaps the young who are moving us in new directions are operating on a scarcity-based assumption also, but a

new type of scarcity. What the young perceive as scarce in our society are the things they are pleading for: *congruence within the individual, mankind in harmony with nature, men at peace with each other.* This counter culture is based on assumptions of abundance of goods rather than scarcity. It asserts that the resources for satisfying human needs are plentiful, that competition is unnecessary, and that the most serious danger to humans is human aggression.

Vocational Instability

Today's economic order is marked by vocational instability. One contributing factor is the oft-cited wholesale appearance and disappearance of occupations as the result of rapid shifts in our technology. The concept of the one-job-for-life career is no longer viable.

Another factor in the existing vocational instability is the presence of a huge military-industrial complex and its impact upon the economy. There is more to this than the deeply rooted resentment against the unpopular Vietnam war and a resulting distaste for all that is military. Whether or not we like it, maintaining even a modest military establishment calls for increasing technological support and, consequently, for constant changes in strategy and equipment. All of this affects defense industries and defense jobs. Witness the heavy unemployment beginning about 1970 of engineers, particularly aerospace and astrospace engineers. This labor force trend was the direct result of decisions which were political rather than the result of normal fluctuations in the economy. Every person employed in a defense industry doubtless wonders, and should wonder, to what he should be prepared to shift in the event his firm fails to obtain one of the next wave of government contracts. But political decisions also affect the employment stability of large numbers of workers who occupy non-military-related positions. Increasing numbers of both professional and clerical people are employed by federal and state governments. Each employing bureau is subject to quick cutbacks as a result of legislative or Congressional action.

Work and Other Values

The attitudes of our youth toward work, leisure, social responsibility, authority, and the value of past experience are in a rapid state of transition. Several of the authors in this volume have dealt with the phenomenon of attitude change and have pointed up significant implications for the altered meanings of work. What is not always readily apparent is that the shift in work values is part of a larger pattern of value changes. The necessity of working is being questioned by many youth as part of their challenging of a broader set of assumptions which they ascribe to their parents and to the adult social order in general. Perhaps most of all, youth is questioning the goals and outcomes of work—"What are you working for? More money in the bank, more things in the house? Is that kind of security in today's society an adequate reason for working?"

Changes in the valuing of work constitute only one segment of the far-reaching ideological reassessment that is shaping youth's emerging conceptions of the purposes and meaning of life, of one's reason for being. Hard work, dependability, compliance, respect for authority, "Hey, listen to what I have learned in my long years of experience"—these are all part of the package of previously held convictions that is being questioned. Youth, and some adults as well, are asking rhetorically, "What's wrong with leisure and enjoyment? Who gave another an inalienable right to *authority over me?* And *whose experience* in what world is relevant to me?" Katz (Chapter 3) has written that the vocational guidance movement has been "fathered by economics, mothered by ideologies, housed by education, and befriended by psychology." I doubt that the complex of influences on the vocational guidance of the future will be anywhere near that simple.

Family and School

Family and school are no longer the only resources of wisdom for the youth of today, and a question might well be raised as to whether they are, indeed, any longer the major sources contributing to the decisions that must be made by youth. Blocher (Chapter 2) asserts that the influence of the relatively recent "conjugal family" (a small nuclear unit composed only of parents and children) lies mainly in the important area of human relations training, that is, in the development of children's interpersonal skills. Little is done by the family in the way of furnishing direct vocational experience or guiding choice. As important as is the influence of the conjugal family, that influence is likely to be seen principally in middle-class society. Less economically favored families ("working class" families) are likely to have less verbal communication, more pressure from close relatives, and fewer general satisfactions for husband and wife from the marriage relationship itself. However, in both types of families few resources exist to aid directly in the formation of mature work values, realistic plans, and appropriate career choices.

Schools, on the other hand, are academically focused. When educational information and educational choices are at issue, schools have much to offer. Counselors and teachers know schools and colleges—they have experienced them, in fact their life has often been confined to them. Yet, when it is a matter of vocations other than those in the educational world, what school personnel know is secondhand, information gained from courses and books. I do not say this in criticism but as a reminder. Blocher's vivid statement is all too true that "In simpler societies, biological clocks and cultural clocks keep the same time," but that in our society discontinuity between developmental stages is the rule (Chapter 2). The break can be quite traumatic between the relatively casual life in school (you can "con" many teachers into lenience; failure to get something in on time doesn't mean flunking the course) and the tight time and production requirements of the first full-time job.

Many teachers and counselors have no experiential understanding of this break: they have always been in school. If they are lucky enough to have had summer jobs that were demanding or a year or two out of school "to make money" so that they could complete school, their contribution to the vocational realities of their students may be greater. It is not important that their jobs or duties be similar to those of their students; of importance is their attitude toward time-clock demands, "unreasonable" employers, competition and throat-cutting among fellow workers, and pay check satisfaction from a job having tangible outcomes. All of these firsthand experiences will make them more vocationally understanding. Will this help as they work with students? I am not sure at all; I am guessing. But where does the student get exposed to this kind of realism before he applies for a job? Will the less accurate but more vivid representations by television characters impress them more than teachers and counselors? Or the emotion-laden stories told within the family? The secondhand stories told by peers?

Family and school are important and meaningful influences in the vocational plans and decisions of some students. For many students, however, both in suburb and inner city, they are peripheral influences, some unconcerned, some unrealistic, some ineffective, and some all of these.

More Schooling?

The pressure to get more and more education is an American phenomenon, but the reasoning back of it is beginning to wear thin. Americans have an abiding faith in the merit of education. "You can't get too much of it." But indeed you can! The sheltered life within a school or college with teachers who are sympathetic and understanding in comparison with most job colleagues and work supervisors can lull one into an interpretation of life that is shockingly unrealistic. To "leave school" is a stigma; everyone urges against it. Yet some combination over the years of job experience and school experience would probably result in more maturity and greater realism. After all, school is society's institutional prolongation of child and adolescent dependency. Eventually the student gets the idea. He is a "kept" child and so why not maintain it as long as possible?

Does this sound like a hard-bitten father from the blue-collar world or a "hard hat" striking out at these undisciplined college kids? There are some serious scholars who question the wisdom of our expectations of indefinite extension of schooling. Of course, in a society which possesses more people than jobs, to delay entry into the vocational world is an economic advantage, but it may be unfair to the individual. We are just entering an era in which universal education is being extended beyond the eighteenth birthday to the twentieth year of life. "College is good for everyone" and if not all can get to a "regular" college or university, then we will provide junior college for almost everyone. Between 1967 and 1970 the number of junior colleges doubled, and the establishment of another 50 percent is being projected for 1975, bringing the total to over 1,500 institutions (Jennings, 1970). By 1970, total enrollments in American colleges and universities had reached 8.5 million.

Many rejoice at this wealth of education but I have a caveat. Education throughout life, yes, but 14 years at a continuous stretch for all, no. I have no doubt that each succeeding generation will get more schooling or at least more education from various sources. This will not be a luxury but a necessity in a world of rapidly expanding knowledge and increasing social complexity. However, I plead for staggered education, short periods of it at intervals throughout 60 or 70 years of life. We have not really become accustomed to the continued schooling of adults, but we will. Adults have been "educating" themselves for a long time, but I speak here of planned, formal periods of education, often in a school or college, perhaps soon by television and other decentralized means. EVR (Electronic Video Recording) involving the playback of cartridges through an ordinary TV set is not "just around the corner"—it is here.

For both adequate motivation and a sense of realism in life I propose alternating periods of educational and occupational experience. I would wish that millions of those entering junior college immediately after high school would taste the occupational world instead. One to five years of experience in an occupation would diversify and broaden personality development much more than would continued education. When the student returned to school his motivation would be stronger; he would want to acquire knowledge in certain areas. To the argument, "He might not return to school after holding a job—that's why we want to keep him in school," my reply would be that if he did not want to return to school, the choice should be his. It is his life. He would be more likely to return if dropping out were not portrayed to him as a disgrace. There is a strong *Zeitgeist* in America for schooling and, in a curious way, it is even stronger than the cultural imperative for getting and holding a job! The opportunities for continuous education will be present in many forms, university sponsored evening programs, TV courses (the other end of "Sesame Street"), and nearby junior colleges which have become community colleges serving all segments of the community.

Failing to stem the drive "to stay in school as long as you can," I would hope for a healthy improvement in cooperative vocational education and in other work-study opportunities. Any school or junior college could build such community-centered programs into its curricula if it took the initiative to get in touch with the local occupational world. If there were too few paid jobs for youth, then non-paid apprenticeships or internships in occupational experience could be developed. I have a feeling that many employers in the community would be flattered to find that experience in their occupations or businesses was considered an essential part of a young person's education.

This may be a dream, I know, because education for education's sake still holds a favored spot in the value structure of many in our society. But I can dream that some day a better bridge will be built between education and occupation to support the personal development and career adjustment of individuals. The "Career Education" concept which has recently been promulgated by Sidney Marland, Commissioner of the United States Office of Education, appears to be an important stride in this direction (Marland, 1971).

The Vocational Guidance of the Future

At least four of the preceding chapters have contributed specific vocational guidance methods or approaches that will be incorporated into the future. Blocher's proposals (Chapter 2) of both direct and indirect intervention procedures based upon his concept of life stages and resulting discontinuities are so psychologically relevant that they are certain to be part of the future of vocational guidance. Hansen and Borow's (Chapter 6) description of systems approaches to the cultivation of career development through a K-to-12 or K-to-14 curriculum points to the broader base which vocational guidance services are likely to enjoy in schools of the future; such a theory emphasizes the shift away from the older prediction-of-choice strategy in vocational guidance and toward the nascent goals of occupational socialization. Likewise Krumboltz and Baker's (Chapter 7) behavioral counseling concepts and Super's (Chapter 8) analyses of computer-assisted vocational guidance are based upon such solid evidence that they are likely to have a prominent influence upon the work of tomorrow's practitioners. However rapidly new concepts may be developed within psychology during the next half decade, or whatever new technological developments take place within that period, I believe that the approaches set forth in these chapters are close enough to the "growing edge" to be still part of the expanding picture five or ten years from now.

Another approach in the contemporary mood is counseling variously known as phenomenological, humanistic, or existential. Few who read *Career Guidance for a New Age* seeking to understand the forward thrusts of vocational guidance will think of phenomenology or existential counseling. They will have been brought up in a different school. There is no chapter on it in this volume. In fact, only small attention is given by the various authors in this book to the psychology of affect in general or to the role of self-perception in particular. Much attention is given to cognition, to behavior directed by cognition, and to decision making which is rooted in cognition. Yet I believe that attitudes and self-perception, highly important factors in vocational choice, can be greatly aided by client-centered counseling.

Those who practice career guidance, or in particular the vocational counseling aspects of career guidance, cannot afford the luxury of being insular or single-minded in their work. Leave the dogmatism to the theorists. The practitioner who is open to a wide variety of clients would profit from an eclectic attitude. I do not think that the old adage, "Jack of all trades and master of none," applies here. The mastery demanded in counseling is not one of method but of a keen awareness of the individuality of each client. This great variance of individuals, both the basic differences between individuals and the variance of mood from time to time within one person, calls for an ideographic approach to the study of the counselee and for variance in method. The counselor who utilizes the concepts of developmental stages, behavior reinforcement, and computer assistance could also benefit by being able to counsel *some* clients (or a given client at a *given* time) within the existential framework. He should also be able to function as a facilitator of group counseling which involves both the affective and cognitive dimensions of experience.

The future of vocational guidance depends upon much more, of course, than the restrictive personality assumptions and methods generally used in formal vocational counseling. As Miller (Chapter 1) has pointed out, economic and industrial shifts may drastically shift occupational opportunities and will greatly increase the range of age levels at which vocational choices must be made and remade.

The vocational incentives of the past may not prove effective for the future. For a large portion of our population, monetary earning as the sole or principal incentive to work will be less effective than in the past. As Ginzberg (1971) puts it in his comprehensive and realistic *Career Guidance*, even young people at the lower end of the economic scale know that if they do not work they will still eat. "Survival without working for pay is a new phenomenon [p. 315]." Levenstein believes that the new incentive to work will be a sense of contributing to others, to society. I cannot object to this, certainly, but I do not think it can be made effective for any large proportion of our population. Perhaps no one incentive can be expected to cover all people. For some the incentive will be money and, through it, the purchasing of power and greater security than they would know otherwise; for these people vocational guidance will focus on training programs at the technical school and community college level. For others the incentive will be a sense of service, of seeking significance through being of worth to others as well as to oneself.

I do not think that either the practitioners of vocational guidance or the clients for which it is designed will be happy with progress during the next few years. Professionals will still be trying to adapt old approaches; vocational information as such is constantly shifting; youth will be unsure of the relation of their employment to their vaguely formed goals and aspirations. Ginzberg points out that once the extrinsic rewards for work such as income and security begin to lose their influence, people will be uncertain about other rewards and job discontent will increase.

Katz (Chapter 3) writes about "vocation," "career," "occupation," and "employment." These terms are often used interchangeably by others, but this is an unhappy practice. Employment or "a job" is a world away from vocation. I define vocation, as does Katz, as a calling, a sense of commitment. In the earlier commemorative volume of the National Vocational Guidance Association (Wrenn, 1964), I argued for "work" to mean more than paid employment. Work I interpreted to mean any activity in which one engaged, whether for pay or not, and which one saw as contributing to a sense of personal significance or the enhancement of the welfare of others. I wanted to get away from the sharp distinction between work and leisure. There could be a blending of employed and non-employed work into "a committed or responsible whole in which one works for both self-fulfillment and for the fulfillment of others [p. 38]."

So I should like to add the development of "a sense of vocation," of commitment to being and to Life, as a reasonably encompassing goal for career guidance. Employed or not, one *can* have a vocation, one can feel significant. The adults of our generation are employed-work oriented. Many of our youth are not —they are by intent leisure oriented and not ashamed of it. Acceptance of this reality is difficult for many adults. However, we must become as knowledgeable about leisure as we are about employment. Vocation encompasses both. For millions who work at mechanized jobs or thankless service and maintenance jobs, leisure means more to them than their jobs. It is from their non-employed hours that they get any sense of significance and worth. Can we help our youth to plan for non-employed activity? This may be the next big step forward in the new career guidance.

REFERENCES

Ginzberg, E. *Career guidance.* New York: McGraw-Hill, 1971.

Jennings, F. G. The two-year stretch: Junior colleges in America. *Change*, 1970, **2**, 15–25.

Marland, S. P., Jr. Career education. *Today's Education*, October 1971, 22–25.

Mumford, L. *The myth of the machine: The pentagon of power.* New York: Harcourt Brace Jovanovich, 1970.

Stephens, W. R. *Social reform and the origins of vocational guidance.* Washington, D.C.: National Vocational Guidance Association, Division of the American Personnel and Guidance Association, 1970.

Wrenn, C. G. Human values and work in American life. In H. Borow (Ed.), *Man in a world at work.* Boston: Houghton Mifflin, 1964.

Wrenn, C. G. *The world of the contemporary counselor.* Boston: Houghton Mifflin, 1973.

about the authors

Ronald D. Baker is currently a faculty member in the Department of Counselor Education at Indiana University. His earlier work included assignments as instructor at Stanford University's Counseling and Testing Center, independent contractor for the development of reading programs and courses for a number of industrial firms and school systems in California, senior staff counselor at Iowa State University, and faculty member in the Psychology Department of that institution. He has held consultantships with the Scientific Manpower Commission, the Des Moines Veterans Administration Hospital, and the Adult Correction Unit of the Iowa Department of Social Services. His research at Stanford with John Krumboltz dealt with the facilitation of students' vocational problem-solving behavior and decision-making ability. Under support from the United States Office of Education, he collaborated in the conduct of regional post-doctoral workshops in counselor supervision. Dr. Baker has been active on committees of the American Educational Research Association and the Association for Counselor Education and Supervision, and he has delivered papers at conferences of the American Personnel and Guidance Association, the American Educational Research Association, the American Psychological Association, and the College Entrance Examination Board.

Donald H. Blocher is a professor in the Department of Counseling and Student Personnel Psychology at the University of Minnesota where he has been a faculty member since 1960. His earlier positions included secondary school teaching in Indiana and Minnesota and counseling in the Minneapolis Veterans Administration Hospital. Dr. Blocher's major research interests have centered on counseling theory, analysis of counseling process, the role of counselors as consultant and change agent in schools, and occupational psychology. Support for his study of the analysis of counselor behavior was furnished by the United States Office of Education. He has been active as a consultant to the Veterans Administration Counseling Psychology Training Program and to a number of schools on the evaluation and improvement of guidance systems. He has lectured widely at schools and colleges and spent a year as Fulbright Professor at the University of Keele in Great Britain. Dr. Blocher's writings include books titled *Developmental Counseling* and *Guidance Systems* (with E. R. Dustin and W. E. Dugan), chapters on guidance and counseling in several books, including *The Encyclopedia of Education*, and numerous journal articles on counseling research and theory. He has served on the Executive Council of the Association for Counselor Education and Supervision and on the Executive Committee of the American Psychological Association's Division of Counseling Psychology.

Henry Borow has been on the faculty of the University of Minnesota since 1946 where he is professor of psychological studies in the General College. He formerly held positions at The Pennsylvania State University as a personnel research technician and Department of Psychology faculty member. He has served as Consultant to the Social Security Administration, Veterans Administration, and United States Office of Education, and has lectured under the auspices of The Asia Foundation in Japan, South Korea, Singapore, and the Philippines. His work in Japan has also included experience with the Japanese Universities Institutes on Guidance and Counseling and the Asian Student Counseling Seminar. Editorial assignments have included service as consulting editor, *Journal of Counseling Psychology*, and coeditor of the *Research Frontier Department* of that journal, and as a member of the editorial boards of the *Personnel and Guidance Journal* and *The Encyclopedia of Education.* Currently, he serves on the National Advisory Board of the Center for Vocational and Technical Education. Dr. Borow's publications include *Vocational Planning for College Students* (with Robert Lindsey) and *Man in a World at Work* (editor), as well as chapters in several other books. He has chaired the International Relations Committee of the American Personnel and Guidance Association and has served as trustee and president of the National Vocational Guidance Association.

Lorraine S. Hansen is professor of education and counseling psychologist at the University of Minnesota. She was associated with the Laboratory School at the University of Chicago, conducted studies in comparative education in Norway on two occasions, and taught high school English and journalism in Minnesota. Later, she served as a counselor at the University of Minnesota High School and as coordinator of counseling and guidance in an experimental school where she developed a training program for community volunteers in career guidance. One of her major interests is the improvement of career development through school curriculum, and she has been involved in the development of curriculum materials and instructional strategies, as well as with a number of sponsored career development workshops for teachers, counselors, and administrators. Dr. Hansen has been a consultant on guidance and career development to several school systems. Under sponsorship of the ERIC Center on Counseling and Personnel Services, she published *Career Guidance Practices in School and Community* for the National Vocational Guidance Association. She was a consultant to the Ohio State University and University of Michigan ERIC Centers on the *Handbook of Vocational Guidance Methods.* She is a former editor of *The School Counselor.*

Martin R. Katz has been at the Educational Testing Service since 1956 where he is senior research psychologist and chairman of the Guidance Group in the Developmental Research Division. He had worked earlier in Connecticut as a high school teacher, guidance counselor, and director of guidance. Previous positions at ETS included service as principal investigator of that organization's Guidance Inquiry and assistant director of the Evaluation and Advisory Service. One of his major current responsibilities involves the development of a computer-assisted System of Interactive Guidance and Information (SIGI) for junior college students. Among Dr. Katz's many publications are *Decisions and Values, You: Today and Tomorrow*, and an article on secondary school guidance in the *Encyclopedia of Educational Research.* He served as editor of the *Yearbook of the National Council on Measurement in Education* and as a member of the Editorial Board of the *Vocational Guidance Quarterly.* His consultantships have included assignments with the Russell Sage Foundation, the United States Office of Education, and the Conservation of Human Resources program at Columbia University, as well as projects in a number of state, county, and local school systems. He has been a visiting lecturer at the University of Wisconsin and the University of Pennsylvania.

John D. Krumboltz is professor of education and psychology at Stanford University where he has been a faculty member since 1961. Former positions include high school counseling and teaching in Iowa, teaching at the University of Minnesota, psychological research with the United States Air Force, and an associate professorship in educational psychology at Michigan State University. Much of his recent research and writings have focused on the application of principles of operant learning and behavior modification to counseling practice. He has been principal investigator of a number of research projects funded by the United States Office of Education. Among his books are *Changing Children's Behavior* (with Helen Krumboltz), *Learning and the Educational Process* (editor), *Revolution in Counseling* (editor), and *Behavioral Counseling: Cases and Techniques* (coeditor with Carl E. Thoresen). He has been active on the editorial boards of the *Journal of Counseling Psychology* and the *Journal of College Student Personnel.* Dr. Krumboltz has conducted workshops and lectured widely in the United States, Canada, and Japan. He has held leadership positions in a number of professional societies, including the chairmanship of the Education and Training Committee of the American Psychological Association's Division of Counseling Psychology and service on that organization's Executive Committee. He was awarded a Guggenheim Fellowship in 1967–68 and three times was a recipient of the Outstanding Research Award of the American Personnel and Guidance Association.

Aaron Levenstein is currently professor of management at the Bernard M. Baruch College of the City University of New York. He was directing editor of the Research Institute of America from 1940 to 1960. He is a member of the New York bar and has specialized in labor law. Dr. Levenstein is a consultant to many organizations, especially in the health care field, and has directed training programs for many hospitals, such as Mt. Sinai in New York and the City of Hope Medical Center in Duarte, California. He has done research in many parts of the world, including Southeast Asia, Africa, and the Middle East. During the summer of 1971, he served as director of the International Rescue Committee's program in India, setting up emergency hospital facilities for Bangladesh refugees. Among his publications is *Labor Today and Tomorrow*, which has been quoted frequently in United States Supreme Court decisions. His books also include a popular work on problem solving, *Use Your Head*, which has been translated into many languages; the highly commended *Why People Work*; and *Freedom's Advocate* (with William Agar). Dr. Levenstein is editor of *Interaction*, the management psychology publication of the Organizational Behavior Institute. He is heard frequently on radio and television panels on current issues.

Carroll H. Miller retired in June 1972 as Professor Emeritus of Education at Northern Illinois University where he had been a faculty member for ten years. He had formerly been a high school teacher and principal, a personnel technician with the Kansas State Civil Service, and a specialist in the preparation of personnel workers with the United States Office of Education. Previous academic assignments included teaching at Wittenberg University and at Colorado State University, where he also served as head of the Department of Psychology and Education and Assistant Dean in the College of Science and Arts. His off-campus activities have included leading behavioral science workshops for personnel in American Dependent Schools in Japan and serving as a consultant for the Illinois State Department of Education. Dr. Miller's books include *Foundations of Guidance* and *Guidance Services: An Introduction.* He has also written chapters for several other counseling and guidance volumes. For two years he held the chairmanship of the Board of Editors of the *Vocational Guidance Quarterly.* In 1972, he received a Merit Award from the National Vocational Guidance Association in recognition of his noteworthy contributions to career guidance.

Gardner Murphy was for many years director of research with the Menninger Foundation. Before his retirement, he was a professor of psychology at George Washington University. Earlier in his career he had been a faculty member in psychology at Columbia University and the City College of New York. He has done research and has written and edited books on a wide variety of human behavior topics, such as social psychology, personality, psychological factors in conflict and peace, and Asian psychology. Among his earlier influential books are *An Historical Introduction to Modern Psychology*, *Experimental Social Psychology* (with Lois Barclay Murphy and Theodore Newcomb), and *Human Nature and Enduring Peace* (editor). His more recent volumes include *In the Minds of Men*, *Human Potentialities*, *Development of the Perceptual World* (with C. M. Solley), *Encounter with Reality* (with H. E. Spohn), and *Psychological Thought from Pythagoras to Freud.* Dr. Murphy has held high offices in the American Psychological Association, president and member of the governing Council, and in 1972 received the American Psychological Foundation's Gold Medal Award. Among his overseas assignments was that of UNESCO Consultant to the Indian Ministry of Education in New Delhi.

Harold J. Reed holds the position of Assistant Division Chief for Counseling in the United States Employment Service. In his previous work, he served as a training supervisor, director of a school guidance system, lieutenant colonel in the United States Air Force Reserves, Veterans Administration psychologist, coordinator of vocational guidance and work experience education in the Los Angeles County Schools, chief of the Occupational and Career Guidance Section of the United States Office of Education, and associate project director for the National Planning Association. Dr. Reed has been a lecturer and visiting professor at a number of universities, including the University of Southern California, Stanford University, the University of Florida, and Michigan State University. His publications include numerous journal articles and a chapter in *Administration and Organization of Guidance Services.* He is past president of the National Vocational Guidance Association and the California Personnel and Guidance Association and was the recipient of merit awards from both these organizations and also from the California Association of Work Experience Coordinators.

Donald E. Super has been associated since 1945 with Teachers College, Columbia University, where he is currently professor and director of the Division of Psychology and Education. His earlier positions include the directorship of the Cleveland Guidance Service, teaching at Clark University, and psychological research in the United States Air Force. Among his consultantships have been assignments with the American Institutes for Research, the United States Office of Education, the United States Civil Service Commission, and the Veterans Administration. He has been a Fulbright Lecturer at the University of Paris, a Ford Fellow in Poland, and a consultant for the United States Department of State and The Asia Foundation in Japan, Korea, Burma, and Ceylon. Dr. Super has been continuously involved since 1951 in longitudinal research on vocational behavior as director of the Career Pattern Study. In collaboration with

Frank Minor and Roger Myers, he has in the past several years been active in the development and testing of the Educational and Career Exploration System (ECES), a computer-assisted approach to vocational guidance. He has been an associate editor or consulting editor of the *Journal of Counseling Psychology*, *Journal of Educational Psychology*, *Personnel and Guidance Journal*, *Journal of Human Resources*, and the *International Review of Applied Psychology*. Among his books are *The Psychology of Careers* and *Appraising Vocational Fitness* (with John Crites). Dr. Super is a past president of the American Personnel and Guidance Association, the National Vocational Guidance Association, and the Divisions of Consulting Psychology and Counseling Psychology of the American Psychological Association; and he is a former member of the Board of Directors of the International Association for Applied Psychology. He now serves as a vice-president of the International Association for Educational and Vocational Guidance. In 1972 he received the Eminent Career Award of the National Vocational Guidance Association.

C. Gilbert Wrenn has been affiliated with Arizona State University since 1964. He held earlier positions as a high school director of guidance, college counselor, United States Navy personnel officer, faculty member at Stanford University and the University of Minnesota, and as a distinguished professor at Macalester College. Among the national agencies he has served as consultant are the United States Department of Labor, United States Office of Education, Department of State, Veterans Administration, and American Council on Education. In the 1960s, he successively directed the project of the American Personnel and Guidance Association's Commission on Guidance in American Schools, led a seminar in Taiwan, spent a year at the University of Keele in Great Britain on a Fulbright Award, and visited the University of Hawaii as Scholar-in-Residence. Dr. Wrenn has published well over 350 books, chapters in books, articles, and monographs. Among his books are *Student Personnel Work in College* and *The Counselor in a Changing World.* He was for many years editor of the Houghton Mifflin publication series in counseling and student personnel work, and for ten years he edited the *Journal of Counseling Psychology* which he had been instrumental in founding. Currently, he serves on the Editorial Board of the *Personnel and Guidance Journal.* He has held the presidencies of the National Vocational Guidance Association, American College Personnel Association, and the American Psychological Association's Division of Counseling Psychology; and he has served on the APA Council of Representatives. For several years, he sat as a board member both on the American Board of Examiners in Professional Psychology and the American Board for Psychological Services. In 1964, Dr. Wrenn received the Nancy Wimmer Award, the highest award conferred by the American Personnel and Guidance Association.

Photo Credits:

Chapter 1 Arthur Furst
Chapter 2 Ulrike Welsch
Chapter 3 Murray McGuirk
Chapter 4 Frank Siteman
Chapter 5 Daniel S. Brody/Stock, Boston
Chapter 6 Frank Siteman
Chapter 7 Mark L. Rosenberg/Stock, Boston
Chapter 8 Frank Siteman
Chapter 9 Arthur Furst

index